Engaging the Age of JANE AUSTEN

HUMANITIES AND PUBLIC LIFE

A collaboration with the

University of Iowa Obermann Center

for Advanced Studies

Teresa Mangum and Anne Valk,

series editors

ENGAGING THE AGE OF

Jane Austen

Public Humanities in Practice

by BRIDGET DRAXLER and DANIELLE SPRATT

UNIVERSITY OF IOWA PRESS, IOWA CITY

University of Iowa Press, Iowa City 52242
Copyright © 2018 by the University of Iowa Press
www.uipress.uiowa.edu
Printed in the United States of America

Design by Rich Hendel

The University of Iowa Press is a member of Green Press Initiative
and is committed to preserving natural resources.

Printed on acid-free paper

ISBN 978-1-60938-614-6 (pbk)
ISBN 978-1-60938-615-3 (ebk)
Cataloging-in-Publication data is on file with the Library of Congress.

A previous version of chapter 1 and brief portions of chapter 2
were included in *Persuasions On-Line* 34, no. 2 (Spring 2014) and are used
here with the generous permission of the journal's editors.

To Frank Boyle, Eve Keller, Moshe Gold,

Susan Greenfield, Devoney Looser, Teresa Mangum,

Katie Moermond, Hannah Schell, Susan Twomey,

and the other mentors in our lives who helped us

create lasting connections between our academic work

and our communities.

CONTENTS

ACKNOWLEDGMENTS

Robert Darnton has long reminded us that no book is produced in isolation: there is a vast network of agents, forming what he calls a "communications circuit," who play a role in turning the idea of a book into the object that you hold, or see, before you.

We are exceptionally grateful that our communications circuit includes the vibrant and diverse voices that punctuate the pages of this book. The inspirational work of our partners continues to transform how we work as teachers, scholars, colleagues, readers, and most fundamentally, as people. Chawton House, the National Endowment for the Humanities (NEH), the California State University, Northridge (CSUN) College of Humanities, the Society for the History of Authorship, Reading and Publishing (SHARP) funding for the California Rare Book School, the Old Capitol Museum, the Monmouth College Summer Opportunities for Intellectual Activity (SOFIA) program, the St. Olaf College Collaborative Undergraduate Research and Inquiry (CURI) program, and Digital Humanities on the Hill (an initiative made possible by a grant from the Andrew W. Mellon Foundation) all provided financial support, and an ever-expanding network of partners and colleagues allowed us to research and complete this project.

Teresa Mangum, Anne Valk, Ranjit Arab, Meredith Stabel, Anna Polonyi, Catherine Cocks, and the anonymous reviewers at the University of Iowa Press provided exceptional rigor and support to transform this book from a set of ideas and practices into a coherent work. Michael Taber indexed this book with clarity and precision, and Breanna Draxler gave polish to our final edits.

Finally, as we continue to look outward to the public-facing possibilities of the humanities, we find ourselves returning again and again to our formative and foundational relationships. We thank our families for their love and unending support for our love of reading, writing, and community work. We could not have started or completed this project without them.

Bridget Draxler and Danielle Spratt

FOREWORD
☙❧

Teresa Mangum in Collaboration with Anne Valk

As a scholar of the British Victorian novel, I am often disheartened that so many of my colleagues teaching earlier literatures see their work as distant from publicly engaged teaching and scholarship. True, we study long dead worlds. True, our tools are words and sentences flattened onto printed pages. Yet most of us were drawn to those earlier literatures by the storms of emotions, the scintillatingly subtle sexual stratagems, and the rousing struggles for social justice that grab us by the throat and hold our imaginations hostage (the first few pages of *Wuthering Heights* or *Bleak House*, among so many other novels, have just that effect on innumerable readers, including me). In a twenty-first-century context where the academic humanities are misunderstood, dismissed, and even derided, teachers of literature can hardly afford to confine their teaching to their classrooms. How, then, do we connect our immediate public—our students—and communities beyond our classrooms with the power that past literatures hold between their covers?

In this important new book, Bridget Draxler and Danielle Spratt address this question—Why revisit past literatures?—with refreshing frankness. Though they ask that question of potential nonspecialist readers in their introduction, their responses are also a warm invitation to literary scholars contemplating new approaches to teaching or sharing the literature they love. Draxler and Spratt argue that their own field of study, eighteenth-century British literature, could hardly be more relevant to audiences today. Writers and philosophers of the period argued for political freedoms and for the need for public institutions like libraries and museums to serve as sites of democracy in action. Advances in printing technology spawned newspapers and magazines in what must have felt like a version of the social media explosion we have experienced in our own time, complete with radical screeds and fake news. I also appreciate Draxler and Spratt's honest admission that they understand one of the goals of literary study to be the teaching of empathy. Literature offers us the opportunity to occupy diverse points of view and to contemplate the consequences of ill-intended but also ill-judged actions from the safe distance of print and the past.

This book enriches the Humanities and Public Life series because the coauthors, along with the students, faculty, and public humanities experts who contributed to this volume, offer such concrete, imaginative ways to engage diverse audiences in reading and interacting with earlier literatures. Moreover, they contextualize their applied approach to the humanities in theoretical explorations of those problematic categories "public" and "community." Drawing deeply from the work of theorists, literary historians, and public humanities experts, Draxler and Spratt thoughtfully reflect on their experiments. Throughout their chapters, they seek ways to enliven, expand, and challenge long-held assumptions about the value of literature, and they consider how and why our pedagogical practices may need to change if we want these literatures to survive.

The range of projects captured in this book demonstrates the co-authors' willingness to experiment, to seek out partners with complementary expertise, to reflect, regroup, and reinvent their approaches to teaching literature in the broadest sense. Draxler and Spratt open with two chapters that consider the public contexts of Jane Austen's novels. Austen scholars (and fans) will find much to admire in Spratt's triangulation of a creative writing nonprofit, an undergraduate classroom, and Austen's work. Spratt offers a fascinating study of a service-learning class she developed with diverse communities in and around the Echo Park and Mar Vista neighborhoods of Los Angeles. As the students contemplated their service project, they considered Austen's wry representation of the "savior complex" when the title character of *Emma* is tempted to play Lady Bountiful. Austen also plays an important role in the library reading groups Draxler designed both on her own and with her undergraduate students. While Austen's reputation as a novelist interested in manners and morals drew a group of elderly community members to the public library, the novel's tough backbone of social issues from women's economic needs to slavery produced intergenerational discussions that transformed younger and older readers, leading Draxler to theorize the value of silence and listening.

Draxler then considers her early attempts at collaboration with a campus museum during her years as a graduate student at the University of Iowa. Working with curators and public education experts at a museum trained her to consider the multimedia potential for teaching novels by eighteenth-century women writers. How, she found herself asking, do you responsibly weave together color, images, biography, and books to welcome nonexperts into a multisensory, multidimensional experience of literature? How do you make a scholarly argument through the design of space as well as the choice of words? The project also opened the door to thinking of women writers in relation to one another and to the field of publishing rather than focusing solely on canonical writers like Jane Austen.

The rich potential of archives, both physical and virtual, is another topic that threads throughout projects described in this book. Draxler, Spratt, and the scholars whose voices they include share creative ways that they motivate students and other readers by introducing them to archives and archival research skills. One outstanding model is a seminar, designed by Draxler with a colleague in Religious Studies, at the Newberry Library in Chicago. In addition to learning to use archives themselves, the undergraduates interviewed people across Chicago about their experiences in neighborhood libraries and archives.

Draxler and Spratt also explore the many ways digital tools can power interactive literary projects. Spratt argues that framing digital projects as a form of service — acknowledging the complexities of that term — helps students grasp the impact of information explosions then and now. However, she makes clear that the intensely detailed work of transcription and optical character recognition (ocr) correction teaches "networked" close reading skills, foundational for the humanities. Through digital work, students become rigorous readers, careful social critics, and cultural conduits, bringing largely inaccessible texts back into the reach of readers. Here, as throughout this inspiring book, Spratt thinks with leading scholars of digital humanities about the public potential of collaboration, cross-sectoral research, and humanities practices. At the same time, she asks tough questions about who has access to education, literature, and virtual commons.

One of the most moving questions George Eliot asks in her many novels focuses on vocation. In *Middlemarch*, the passionate young Doctor Lydgate fights to bring new ideas about medicine to the unyieldingly conservative town of Middlemarch even as the beautiful Rosamund Vincy tempts him into a conventional marriage. Why, laments the narrator, cannot the romance of vocation compel us as thoroughly as the work of romance? The book that Bridget Draxler and Danielle Spratt have written responds to Eliot's call. It is not possible in this short foreword to anticipate the pedagogical storms, stratagems, and struggles you will encounter as you share their fascinating experiments, Dear Reader. But we promise you will emerge — as one so often does from a good book — with a grander vision of learning, a greater sense of purpose, and myriad ways to convince your students, your future collaborators, and your communities that literature is life.

PREFACE

You have likely opened this book because you are a scholar, teacher, or student of historical literature (or perhaps you identify as all three simultaneously, as we do). When you tell people your area of interest or expertise, your friends and family might look at you quizzically or dismiss you as a lover of all things esoteric. But as you read and write about history and literature, you find yourself interacting with ideas, topics, and issues that resonate equally with your current cultural and geographic moment: as you read Mary Astell, Mary Wollstonecraft, or Laurence Sterne, you might start thinking about how your love of their writings relates to the news you read about earlier in the day on the internet. As you discuss concepts of happiness and liberty that were galvanized intellectually and politically in the Enlightenment, you instantly connect these developments with incidents from our own current political moment.

Or, as a teacher at the secondary level, you might consider how historical debates about literacy rates and educational access — the public school, after all, is a product of the eighteenth century — resonate with questions of equal education today. You might be a librarian or archivist who wonders how you can publicize the fascinating holdings in your institution in a way that engages your community in meaningful ways, but you're not quite sure where to get started. Perhaps you are a nonprofit coordinator who wonders how you can take better advantage of the literary, historical, educational, and cultural institutions in your community: how do you make, and organize, the potential connections? How do you navigate the complicated maze of insurance and liability forms, permissions rights, and publicity — let alone the daunting task of making connections with people who seem to exist on another planet entirely, tucked away in an ivory tower or behind a wall of membership fees and marble foyers? Or, you might simply be a card-carrying fan of Jane Austen, a member of your local chapter of JASNA (the Jane Austen Society of North America) who wonders how your love of *Emma* might link your son's college campus with libraries, senior centers, or after-school agencies. You have great ideas, but you're not sure where to start or which parties might be interested.

[xv]

Although we write from one particular perspective—we are both academics with PhDs who teach at the college level—we also have experience working with community institutions and people from all of the categories noted. This work and these connections have deeply informed the trajectories of our intellectual, professional, and personal lives. We take as a founding principle of this book the idea that reading—and loving books—is itself a practice that makes us better thinkers and more engaged, empathetic individuals. We also believe that there is something distinctive about historical literature, and eighteenth-century works in particular, that makes it worthy of visiting, or revisiting, in our own time. As we outline in the introduction and describe throughout the chapters of this book, the cultural moment of the eighteenth century reverberates in manifold ways in our own time. The era that we refer to as the "long eighteenth century" was fundamentally shaped by the English Civil War and the Restoration of King Charles II (1641-1660) and by the American and French Revolutions (1776-1790s). These events were punctuated by colonial rebellions throughout the Caribbean, including the First and Second Carib Wars in St. Vincent (1769-1773 and 1795-1797) and the Haitian Revolution (1791-1804), and came to a close when Napoleon's wars of empire ended at the Battle of Waterloo in 1815. This period was one of dramatic political, economic, intellectual, and social change. These rapid changes overlap with our own cultural moment in the early twenty-first century, when issues of basic civil rights have returned to the fore in dramatic ways. We hold that grassroots movements that have reshaped the landscape of our political and personal conversations—from #blacklivesmatter and #invisibleillness to #disabilitysowhite, #metoo, and #timesup—find their ideological origins in the eighteenth century, a time when an expansion of rights for many started being codified in law and represented in literature and popular culture in new and unprecedented ways.

As we hope the ensuing pages will show, there are many innovative, generative, and exciting ways for you to connect a historical period like the eighteenth century to a wide range of people today. And although the book is organized around our own narratives, practices, and experiences, the voices that punctuate this book—from colleagues in academia to students, community organizers, and community members—are those that have deeply and importantly informed our own understanding of how to go about doing public humanities work. Our chapter narratives are simply the platforms and contexts that allow these voices to guide us, together, as we embark on future engaged humanities work. We look forward to offering some ideas and advice to help inspire your own community work, and we are excited to make this process about not only what happened in the eighteenth century, but also the vibrant and important place of historical literature in the present and future.

Engaging the Age of JANE AUSTEN

INTRODUCTION

The introduction that we thought you would be reading was a sweeping survey of debates about the public value of the humanities since the eighteenth century, tracing conversations about its utilitarian versus its intrinsic value through the writings of John Locke, Adam Smith, Jean-Jacques Rousseau, and other Enlightenment-era political theorists. We talked about the radical decline of violence and the radical rise of social justice in the eighteenth century, developments that were often reflected in the emergence of the novel.[1] Witch-burning, torture, slavery, despotic governance, child labor, the oppression of women, and other social ills were not cured in the eighteenth century, but "it was in the eighteenth century that the arguments were generated that made these inhumanities both visible and, in the end, insupportable. Yes, Jefferson had slaves. But he knew that he *shouldn't* have slaves."[2] How can books, you might ask, have this kind of social impact? Because language—and more importantly, stories—profoundly shape our perception of reality. We went on some fascinating tangents on the invention of copyright and intellectual property, digitization as a flexible yet fragile form of preservation, the neuroscience of reading on pages versus screens, Neil Postman's reclusive philosopher versus the change-making eighteenth-century philosophe, and the differences between civic and merely civil dialogue. We talked about the value of the humanities for a thriving democracy, a need that feels sharper by the day. But at its heart, the introduction you aren't reading was about how those of us who love old books can use that love to forge more meaningful connections with our contemporary surroundings. Of course, we said it in a much more eloquent way with an assembly of scholars behind us.

But we lost that introduction in a strange twist of digital fate. And although we will return to what was lost a bit later in this introduction, we realize now that this loss affords us the opportunity to consider a different question altogether. Does the mention of *Pride and Prejudice and Zombies* make you laugh with joy or bristle with rage? While the 2009 Seth Grahame-Smith literary adaptation of Austen's most famous novel incited equal parts excitement and outrage among her various twenty-first-century fans, its reception nearly a decade on seems to have become, in general, positive. If we take as a baseline register the website Goodreads.com, for instance, Grahame-Smith's adaptation receives an average of 3.3 out of 5 stars from 115,772 ratings and 12,439 written reviews.[3] By contrast, according to film review aggregator Rottentomatoes.com, the reception of the 2016 film adaptation, starring Lily James as Elizabeth Bennet, Lena Headey as Lady Catherine de Bourgh, and Sam Riley as Mr. Darcy, fares far worse, receiving positive criticism in only 43 percent of 167 reviews.[4] While a variety of issues might influence this difference, considering the cultural and literary contexts of the eighteenth and twenty-first centuries enables us to highlight one possible explanation.

Both versions may seem, at least superficially, to be opportunistic mashups of two wildly (and thus effectively memorable) disparate popular genres. Yet if we ask ourselves three questions about some of the more subtle or subversive elements of Austen's novel—1) why does it feature a standing army?; 2) how do the novel's class politics inform its marriage plot?; and 3) how do these elements combine in the novel?—then Grahame-Smith's amalgamation starts to brim with potentially brilliant insights about Austen's work and time as well as our own. Protagonist Elizabeth Bennet's training in Shaolin kungfu signifies her lower-class status, since it is less prestigious than the martial arts training of the Darcy and Bingley families. Her low rank is further complicated (as in the original novel) by the fact that her father's estate is entailed and will pass to a distant cousin. The law of primogeniture barred any of the five Bennet daughters from inheriting property, thus promising a future of dispossession and relative poverty for any who remained unmarried after their father's death.

Both the original novel and its adaptation confront this class structure in the verbal battle between Lady Catherine de Bourgh and Elizabeth, when the wealthy widow questions Elizabeth about her plans to marry Darcy, who (in an unlucky twist of fate for the Bennets) is related by marriage to the de Bourghs. Elizabeth famously rejects Lady Catherine's haughty request that Elizabeth promise not to defy decorum and class by considering such a match, declaring, "I am only resolved to act in that manner, which will, in my own opinion, constitute my happiness, without reference to *you*, or to any person so wholly unconnected with me. . . . Neither duty, nor honour, nor gratitude have any possible claim on me, in the present instance."[5] In this moment, Elizabeth proclaims her own happiness to be as valuable as the tyrannical, old-fashioned concerns of Lady Catherine, who hoped to match Darcy with her daughter to combine their fortunes and family power. In Austen's time, Elizabeth's words had revolutionary undertones because they echoed the famous phrase guaranteeing "life, liberty, and the pursuit of happiness" in the Declaration of Independence. Grahame-Smith resituates this revolutionary retort into a physical and verbal battle in the Bennet family's dojo. After a tense struggle, Elizabeth triumphs over Lady Catherine, who in this version of the story is herself a world-renowned martial artist. The contemporary adaptation tips this class tension toward overt class violence and, through the threat of a zombie apocalypse, further raises the possibility of a radical overthrow of entrenched hierarchies.

The zombie as a symbol of class warfare is well known in contemporary American culture, starting perhaps with George Romero's satire of mindless consumer culture in *Dawn of the Dead* (1978). Yet the film adaptation of *Pride and Prejudice and Zombies* loses nearly all of the novel's satirical energies by rewriting the climactic scene — the battle between Elizabeth and Lady Catherine — such that Lady Catherine doesn't fight at all. Instead, she outsources the battle to her henchman and looks on as an eager observer. When Elizabeth finally defeats the henchman, Lady Catherine commends her, proclaiming, "I do not know which I admire more, Elizabeth Bennet, your skill as a warrior or your resolve as a woman." Reframed in this way, the film effectively sidesteps the class tensions that both print versions uphold. By minimizing issues of class and rank from the conflict at the core of the plot, the film defuses the radical potential of the original novel and a key component of its continued relevance for contemporary audiences. These alterations may help explain the higher approval rating for Grahame-Smith's mashup.

The cultural charge of the zombie also has the potential to tease out other contentious elements of contemporary society. Austen of course could not have foreseen how Romero's first zombie film, *Night of the Living Dead* (1968), would register concerns about veterans returning from Vietnam, or the film's ability to allegorize the struggle between civil rights activists and beneficiaries of America's racist Jim Crow laws and legacies. Yet the zombie — this ghastly figure who seems to register distinctive postmodern anxieties — emerged in seventeenth- and eighteenth-century Haiti (then called Saint-Domingue) to represent the barbaric conditions experienced by its enslaved peoples.⁶ Even in Austen's own time, then, the zombie articulated cultural violence and oppression. Grahame-Smith's seemingly random (and perhaps even seemingly absurd) choice to situate zombies in Austen's tranquil, domestic England quite appropriately connotes the harsh realities of the British Empire. Eighteenth-century imperial England's increasing militarization compelled the expansion of a standing army that worked, in various ways, to support colonial practices that brutalized generations of people of African descent in the nation's American and Caribbean colonies. Other film adaptations of Austen's work also render overt what was latent or understated in the novels; we need only think of Patricia Rozema's adaptation of *Mansfield Park* (1999), which emphasizes the novel's potential anticolonial impulses via the film's overt depiction of the violence of slavery.

Austen's awareness of the British Empire did not only track west toward the Caribbean and the Americas; it also looked anxiously to the east. In *Mansfield Park*, for instance, Fanny Price attempts to distract herself from the sensational prospect of performing *Lovers' Vows* by reading a volume about Lord George Macartney's failed attempt to create a British embassy in China in 1793.⁷ Significantly, it was Macartney who was credited with proclaiming the ever-expanding dominance of the British Empire after the Seven Years' War (1756–1763), when he described it as "this vast empire on which the sun never sets, and whose bounds nature has not yet ascertained."⁸ Likewise, in her personal life Austen was all too aware of the ties between Britain and the East: her aunt, Philadelphia Austen Hancock, moved to India at age twenty-one to find an eligible husband, and Hancock's daughter (one of Austen's most sensational cousins), Eliza Hancock de Feuillide, was born in Calcutta in 1761.⁹

These examples of confrontation between past and present, as well as those between East and West, appear in innovative ways when we pair Austen (or other authors of the increasingly distant past) with an unexpected topic or symbol from a chronologically distinct era (or one that, in the case of the zombie, actually has its origins in an equally distant past). In this way, Grahame-Smith's *Pride and Prejudice and Zombies* illustrates a core proposition of this book: that an engagement with myriad forms of contemporary culture helps us become more nuanced readers of historical literature. Likewise, we posit, works from the eighteenth century help clarify how we understand our own moment, allowing us to rethink the value of narrative, perhaps especially the narratives of personal experience that are often cited as originating in the eighteenth-century novel. *Pride and Prejudice and Zombies*, with its potential to raise issues of race, class, gender, and other marginalized identities that remain precarious in today's fraught political landscape, can spark multiple levels of dialogue from many community members across a variety of venues. Many of us already know the creative possibilities forged in online fan fiction forums and similar digital spaces. Imagine this energy transposed to reading groups or film screenings held in classrooms after-hours, in library community rooms on weekends, or in retirement homes during Halloween; or consider how middle-school children participating in an after-school creative writing workshop would respond to creating their own zombie mashups of books they have been assigned in class.

Peter Brooks reminds us that "in claiming a place for the humanities in public life, we are arguing that fictions are not distractions from reality but a central means to an understanding of where and how we live in reality."[10] We are lucky that of late there are truly extraordinary examples of public and digital humanities projects grounded in the eighteenth century: Janine Barchas's What Jane Saw (a website that allows viewers to experience two exhibits that Austen saw in 1796 and 1813), and Laura Mandell's 18thConnect (an online eighteenth-century text digitization project about which we will hear more later).[11]

In addition to offering models of the public humanities focused on eighteenth-century materials, these projects also suggest the breadth and scope of the most exciting collaborations between cultural organizations, community participants, and institutions of higher education. If the analysis of *Pride and Prejudice and Zombies* shows us the potential value of cross-cultural, transhistorical communication and affords the potential for meaningful discourse between academia and popular culture, the public digital humanities projects by Barchas and Mandell remind us that claiming a place for the humanities in public life is an act of community. These kinds of generative acts of collaboration create and renew our collective sense of community, demonstrating how the humanities truly magnify some of the best qualities of being human.

But if collaborative work can highlight human possibility, it also invites human error. Our lost introduction exemplifies an important lesson about any collaborative project. On the first day of every class, Bridget always writes "something will go wrong" in big letters on the board. She tells her students that when we embark on the kind of collaborative, project-based learning that her classes include—relying on the stars to align so that schedules, transportation, events, community partners, and not least of all group dynamics all coordinate seamlessly—it is simply inevitable that at some point in the term a crisis will occur. Then Bridget tells them, when that crisis does happen, don't panic. We've anticipated the fact that something will go wrong. We'll figure it out together. These crisis moments become a mystery to be solved, rather than an insurmountable barrier. And learning to manage a crisis in a productive, calm, collaborative way is part of what we want to equip our students to do in their future lives, so that when a community partner catches the flu, when funding gets delayed to the following year, or when Bridget deletes the introduction to a coauthored book, we can respond with patience, dignity, and empathy.

In many ways, the creation of this book has modeled the simultaneously messy and rewarding nature of collaborative work. As coauthors, we offer perspectives from a large state university and a small liberal arts college; from an urban and a rural community; from within the English major and the general education curriculum; from a traditional tenure track job and a less traditional alt-ac position. We also offer the perspectives of multiple academic and community partners and audiences: students at both undergraduate and graduate stages of their academic careers, faculty and administrators, and community agencies and partners.

But for all these differences between us, we both went into the field of literary studies because we believe that reading has the potential to make us better people: more discerning in our thinking, more deliberate in our values, more conscious that these values are partially constructed by our cultural context, more open-minded in our perspectives, more intentional in our appreciation of beauty, more comfortable holding multiple truths at once, more articulate in our own speaking and writing, more careful in our listening and reading, more driven by curiosity and an intrinsic motivation to learn, more committed to living a life of meaning and purpose. But most of all, we believe that reading facilitates the growth of human empathy. Publicly engaged scholarship has not been so much a shift in our approach to the humanities as a return to what drew us to them in the first place. When we can take what we've learned in books and apply those same principles to the people in our lives, taking principled action,[12] that is humanities in practice—that is the public humanities.

What Is a Public Intellectual? And Who Cares, Anyway?

In an essay that considers Jonathan Swift as a model for today's public intellectual, Carole Fabricant writes that "Swift's texts abundantly testify to the absurd sterility of theories spun out of the brain with no consideration given to their practical application or their consequences for daily existence. . . . We must instead [embody] some form of what we might call 'theoretical practice,' a position fusing general principles, critical analysis of specific situations, and empirical action."[13] In other words, Swift's notion of the public intellectual is driven by a deep intertwining of theory and practice, of thinking and action, of broad principles and their specific implementation. She points out Swift's interest in local concerns, "never actually relinquishing his role as a 'bearer of universal values,' but devoting much of his career to involvement in local insurgencies and acts of resistance."[14] Swift, in Fabricant's argument, engages with big ideas and theories, but is concerned with their local application.

Speaking to other literary scholars, Fabricant says that our work in and of itself has no direct political consequences. She writes, "My own feeling is that as long as we view ourselves simply as academics, rather than as intellectuals in a broader (and less institutionally defined) context, most of what we say or do can have little political import beyond narrow professional (re)alignments and careerist maneuvers."[15] It's a somber and familiar critique of higher education, one that feels urgent but also wellworn. But our work in eighteenth-century studies — informed equally by canonical (often male) figures like Swift and also members of the Bluestockings like Elizabeth Montagu and later Hannah More — offer us examples of engaged scholars and public intellectuals in Enlightenment-era writers and thinkers. Studying the eighteenth century can be a sterile process of system-building divorced from reality, or it can teach us how to engage with reality as public humanists.

When we were graduate students and early professionals, some of our colleagues and mentors framed the kinds of projects described in the following chapters as distractions — research on the side, as opposed to our "real" research; pedagogy that took too much time; service that didn't count as scholarly service in making our cases for tenure. But far from being a distraction that blew us off course, the public humanities became our rudder, our anchor, our compass. We suspect that the same held true for many of our collaborators, who range from our students and professors to librarians, community activists, archivists, editors, and teachers. And we also suspect that these experiences hold true for you, our reader.

As teachers, archivists, librarians, or community leaders, we help run cultural institutions and design syllabi that determine what counts: what's worth preserving, what's worth paying attention to, what's worth passing on to future generations. We sometimes forget that the books we read shape the work we do in the world. We sometimes forget that our reading and our community action go hand in hand. We hope to speak to book lovers of all kinds in this volume, but in particular, to book lovers who teach historical literature, or to book lovers who work in cultural institutions that can work collaboratively with institutions of higher education. We imagine this book as modeling the kind of community projects and literary interpretation that combine the best of academic and public humanities.

But engaging with the community in our study of literature is also risky business. Most colleges and universities encourage classroom-based community work that falls under the general rubric of service learning; but, as many scholars have rightly pointed out, "by focusing attention on the nobility of self-sacrifice and away from the republican spirit of reciprocal civic needs and benefits, service learning may, in fact, teach students to accept poverty and inequality as permanent conditions."[16] Historical literature, we want to acknowledge, is particularly fraught in this sense, suggesting to students that societal problems have long histories and are deeply ingrained in our culture. At its worst, historical literature may reinforce helplessness in the face of ongoing injustice, the sense that things have always been this way and therefore can't be changed, or the often hasty, self-congratulatory conclusion that recognizing a social problem amounts to eradicating it.

At the same time, however, the larger goal of a meaningful humanities education, which scholars of historical literature are in a particularly good position to advance, is "to have students see themselves as part of a human story that is larger geographically and more enduring in time than the contingencies of their homework assignments and job prospects."[17] We see historical literature (and the humanities in general) as playing a crucial and unique role in the lives of our students, our communities, and ourselves. In the face of an expert-scoffing, diversity-averse, post-truth society that rejects care for language as mere political correctness, it has never been more critical to teach the past with a public purpose.

To see the world from the perspective of someone else—to face systematic oppression, violence, or invisibility through another person's eyes; to read works from two hundred years ago and see how much the world both has and hasn't changed—is to find a civic purpose in and for literary studies. When we perform public humanities work through the study of eighteenth-century literature, we develop a whole host of intellectual possibilities at the same time that we foster open-mindedness and empathy; these texts from the distant past allow us to grapple with the injustices that permeate eighteenth-century literature and that may remain today.

Fundamentally, this book argues that critical public spaces can help forge a strong connection between the study of eighteenth-century literature and culture and twenty-first-century issues. In these spaces, people from within and beyond the university gates can engage with important intellectual traditions and ethical questions that are grounded in the humanities. This book series's choice of the term "public" is a resonant one for us. It avoids the political charge and potential exclusiveness of terms like "citizen," "civic," or "democracy," and it equally resists the civilizing and unifying connotations of the word "society." As Raymond Williams's seminal *Keywords* observes, although "society" often refers to general and abstract relationships among large groups of people (an abstraction that Williams notes begins to occur in the eighteenth century), the term's "primary meaning . . . was companionship or fellowship."[18] While public humanities work aims to create such a sense of fellowship between different community agents, it nevertheless must always recognize the systemic barriers and ongoing injustices inherent to our contemporary moment. We also value the term "public humanities" because it evades hierarchical or even patronizing alternatives like "service," "outreach," and "volunteerism," encouraging participants to confront and ultimately avoid what Laurie Grobman has called the "savior complex" that many university participants experience at the start of their public work.[19]

Most importantly, though, the value-neutral connotations of the term "public" harken to its roots in eighteenth-century culture. The *Oxford English Dictionary*'s definition of the word calls attention to the idea of being open. In particular, we value how the concept of the public helps readers (both academic and not) reconceive and reconsider the Habermasian binary of public versus private and the implied spatial conceptualization of both terms. The opposite of private, the term instead signals devotion to "the promotion of the general welfare" and a commitment "to the best interests of the community."[20] Also of interest for this study: the *Oxford English Dictionary* lists "public" as not only a noun but also a verb, linked to the term "to publish." The intersection between these terms is significant for our discussions of scholarship in public life, as we think about the value of literary research more broadly as serving a public good in our communities.[21]

The notion of a public good combines "public" with yet another fraught and overgeneralized term. We see the public "good" as rooted in attitudes that inspire intellectual shifts and prompt action. Before we can close the wage gap between men and women, we need to tackle systemic prejudice against women in the workplace. Before we can promise equal access to education, we need to think through institutionalized racism in our communities. Literature is a medium uniquely positioned to work on the deep beliefs we hold about ourselves and other people, and reconsidering those beliefs is the first step toward creating sustainable, actionable change in our communities and our nation. Literature gets to the heart of these problems, creating a potential for public good by changing and challenging the ways we think.

Describing our work in terms of public humanities does not exclude digital humanities, public scholarship, service learning, or engaged learning, but rather signals a careful amalgam of elements from all these. We see the public humanities as variations on a theme rather than a single tune; as Caryn McTighe Musil does in her concept of the faces/phases of citizenship, we understand public humanities on a spectrum that privileges long-term, reciprocal, generative engagement but acknowledges the range and incremental development of ways of making the humanities publicly viable.[22] For us, the public humanities are a mode of engaging with ideas that are relevant in a form that is accessible to a wider community. The public digital humanities, by taking advantage of technologies that are increasingly accessible and available, are an exciting part of the future of the public humanities because digital media offer access to new content, new forms of communication, and new communities (while simultaneously complicating and sometimes fracturing our understanding of all three). Indeed, just as this book hopes to demonstrate how the spaces of the university are a fundamental part of the public, we also hope to reconsider what publicly engaged humanities work means: digital public work can create and develop connections in ways that complement in-person public humanities work.

But Why the Eighteenth Century?

If at this point we can agree that the public humanities are valuable, you may still have some doubts about our particular argument: that the public stakes of historical literature, and eighteenth-century British literature specifically, remain relevant in twenty-first-century contexts. We respond to this important concern in three main ways here, and we believe that our ensuing chapters bear out this three-pronged framework. First, and perhaps most obviously, we revisit the eighteenth century every time we consider our political freedoms; public spaces like the museum — places where people could exist as public entities — emerged as institutions in the eighteenth century. These spaces were the sites of democracy in action. We thus find it significant that the literature of the eighteenth century documents the origin story of modern democratic institutions across English-speaking countries; when Jefferson invoked the American people's right to "life, liberty, and the pursuit of happiness," he articulated a guarantee of political freedom (one that was, of course, not extended to those who were unable to own land: people of color, women, and the poor) at the same time that he referenced Laurence Sterne's writing.[23] Our civil and political rights, the foundation of our legal system, all derive from ideas that were articulated and interrogated almost incessantly in the eighteenth century. At a moment when the basic civil liberties of many groups of people are being threatened across the United States and in other countries, we must rigorously question the philosophical and legal origins of basic human rights and the deployment of these rights in modern contexts. In so doing, we recognize their progressive and egalitarian nature as well as the fundamental limits of these historically based values. We find the literature of the eighteenth century to be particularly salient in this regard; the spaces of fiction and imaginative production in this period are telling in the ways that they constitute what it means to be human.

In the eighteenth century, literary marketplaces made possible the debates about legal and political agency; advances in printing technology allowed for daily newspapers to be circulated for the first time.[24] This shift in media technologies leads us to our second point: there is something structurally relevant—and, we think, intellectually fascinating—about the significant parallel between the explosion of information and media technologies in the long eighteenth century and in the twenty-first. In 1641, on the eve of the English Civil War, the first weekly "newsbook" was published; by 1770 there were seventeen daily newspapers published in London, and by 1790 that number had expanded to twenty-three.[25] This explosion of media provided audiences with a wealth of new information, ranging from reports on Parliament to publications that documented a variety of voices, events, and perspectives. Thanks to developments in infrastructure and the postal system, correspondence written at the front lines brought news of war to audiences in much closer to real time than ever before, while reviews of plays and books mixed with advertisements. The creation, consumption, and sharing of information was radically democratized, giving the masses access to massive quantities (and various qualities) of information and open platforms for publishing.

At the same time, plagiarized and pirated works abounded, making the authenticity and truthfulness of a given text unstable. Such a seeming inundation of information resonates with our own moment, when technological developments, particularly with regard to social media outlets, have enabled the proliferation of information (and often misinformation) in real time with the potential to go viral. Whether inspired by hand-press sheets of the eighteenth century or a modern politician's tweets, this anxiety over the quality of printed information makes an exploration of eighteenth-century fiction all the more relevant. This literature often self-consciously seeks to negotiate the blurry lines between fact and fiction, private and public life.

Our third reason for presenting eighteenth-century literature and culture as particularly relevant for twenty-first-century public humanities projects is a pragmatic one. It is perhaps worth noting that major open-access projects, such as the Digital Public Library of America and the WhatEvery1Says (WE1S) Project, and online academic communities, such as the Humanities, Arts, Science, and Technology Alliance and Collaboratory (better known as HASTAC), were founded (at least in part) by eighteenth centuryists[26]—and that the term "luddite" is a neologism of the long eighteenth century. As a result, the plethora of copyright-free material now available online makes accessible texts that were once squirreled away in archives where they could only be studied by the few.[27] From massive digitization projects like Google Books to period-specific digital archives like 18thConnect, eighteenth-century texts (including those that are out of print) have suddenly become easily available to students and readers. And just as the British House of Lords' 1774 deregulation of copyright made classic texts cheaply available to the masses (Martyn Lyons notes that "within five years of deregulation, Daniel Defoe's *Robinson Crusoe* sold more copies than it had done in the sixty years since its first publication in 1719"), eighteenth-century texts like *Robinson Crusoe* are getting a second wind as free e-book downloads (since the Kindle e-book was released in 2011, it has earned four and a half stars and well over five hundred comments on Amazon).[28] In these ways, we make the case that the eighteenth century presents the kind of ur-texts that beg for consideration in the public humanities context.

From within the ivory tower, there are other salient reasons to consider the mutually constitutive relationship between public humanities and eighteenth-century studies. The rise of cultural studies within English departments has spurred the recovery of voices excluded from the traditional literary canon. The original canon of eighteenth-century studies (the classic old-boys club of Jonathan Swift, Alexander Pope, and Samuel Johnson) has been reinvigorated by this shift to include, to name only a few, women writers like Margaret Cavendish, Charlotte Lennox, and Frances Burney, and voices of the poor and othered, including Ann Yearsley, Olaudah Equiano, and Ignatius Sancho. In addition, the temporal remove of an eighteenth-century British text—while still engaging relevant issues of access to education, human rights, or other contemporary concerns—provides a sense of detachment that offers a safe space for discussing complex issues in a classroom or the wider community. Most of all, literary history offers to the public humanities the sense that history and historical works are not simply of the past, but continually inform the present, and that conversely, our actions today can help us reevaluate the past.

Engaging the humanities in public life, we think, is not a new way of studying historical literature but a return to the core values and ideas that drive our field and that informed eighteenth-century writers and texts. For instance, while the eighteenth century often marks the rise of silent reading, reading collaboratively in public and private spaces was very much still in practice in ways that can inform twenty-first-century pedagogy. Although the idea of the humanities as a discrete field of study didn't emerge until the mid-twentieth century, many contemporary defenders point to eighteenth-century thinkers and writers, including Jean-Jacques Rousseau, David Hume, and Immanuel Kant, to justify the work and worth of the humanities.[29] The eighteenth century was host to the birth of national identity, the rise of coffee-house culture, and the professionalization of literary and artistic criticism—which was, for critics like William Hazlitt, written for public rather than specialized academic audiences. For all these reasons, the eighteenth century can be a model for humanists engaging in public life today. And the public humanities are, we think, distinctively in the spirit of much eighteenth-century British literature and thought.

Taking as our evidence case studies from the partnerships that we have forged among our own and our colleagues' classrooms and community agents and agencies, we focus our discussion on how publicly engaged activities in various places—libraries, literacy centers, museums, archives, and digital spaces—offer valuable opportunities for better understanding twenty-first-century issues and valuable spaces for reading, discussing, and interpreting the literature of the long eighteenth century. While we focus on this period because of our specific research and teaching interests, our techniques can be applied across cultural institutions and academic disciplines by those who are seeking ways to link community building with humanities teaching and scholarship.

In particular, we hope that this book will prompt an explicit and sustained dialogue between public humanities advocates and specialists in pre-twentieth-century literature and culture. In so doing, we hope that our discussions here will help practitioners of publicly engaged literary history improve our theories, methods, and strategies and revise problematic assumptions attached to individuals, institutions, and entrenched cultural hierarchies. Some scholars, like Laurie Grobman, have expressed concern that engaged work somehow dilutes the intellectual integrity of literary study and flattens complex issues faced in both literary and broader political analyses. According to Grobman, integrating public work with literary scholarship "can too easily encourage narrow interpretations of literature to fit or explain real-world situations, especially those related to race, class, gender, and other categories of difference, thereby erasing the complexities of literary interpretation."[30] Moving beyond the superficial approaches that Grobman warns against, this volume presents multiple case studies from our work, punctuated with and informed by many voices of the public, which collectively suggest that engaged forms of literary study can increase critical rigor while deepening the relationship between literary study and public engagement. By exploring a variety of projects and programs linked to particular types of cultural institutions, our goal is to offer a kaleidoscope of possibilities for doing public work with historical literature.

Doing the Work

We have structured this volume to privilege dialogue and collaboration, not just among ourselves but also with our many generous contributors. As a result, this book alternates between Bridget's chapters, which are grounded in public humanities work performed in particular places (the museum, the library, and the archives), and Danielle's chapters, which consider experiential classroom activities in related contexts (nonprofit after-school organizations and digital humanities projects). Throughout, we incorporate short essays by many contributors and agents who have made our work possible, because a fundamental principle of our work is that public humanities projects must be truly reciprocal and informed by the skills, interests, and needs of everyone involved.

Chapter 1 considers a partnership between one of Danielle's undergraduate classes on Jane Austen and an organization called 826LA, a regional offshoot of a nationwide network of literacy and creative writing centers founded by novelist and publisher Dave Eggers. Danielle connects the process of public humanities work to a particular issue encountered by civic engagement projects, particularly those structured by service-learning pedagogies: the dreaded savior complex that many students and people new to engaged work feel when they begin their experiences with community partners. This chapter argues that Austen's *Emma* is particularly well suited to helping students reflect on their impulses in this direction, and suggests that the novel affords opportunities to consider issues of race, class, and gender that are as prevalent today as they were in the eighteenth century.

Partly inspired by Danielle's approach to teaching *Emma*, chapter 2 describes a series of Jane Austen reading groups that Bridget hosted at public libraries. A revised understanding of libraries as public spaces and a shift in perspective on the myth of politeness surrounding Austen's work can help teachers, students, librarians, and community members engage with archival research *and* encourage politically engaged, intergenerational dialogue. For the novice public scholar, this project offers a form of community engagement that plays to the strengths of a literary historian.

Chapter 3 tells Bridget's story of collaboratively curating an exhibit titled Fresh Threads of Connection. In describing her experience of translating academic work for a public audience, Bridget articulates how the museum as a public space offers possibilities for connecting authors and texts usually housed in the academy to general audiences, and she suggests partner-based rather than project-based models of sustainability. In addition to creating meaningful alt-ac training within graduate education, exhibit curation also cultivates habits of mind more traditional to humanities scholarship and graduate education: making connections, explaining context, and telling stories.

Our fourth chapter straddles the physical and digital, detailing Bridget's work with the Newberry Seminar on Research in the Humanities, a program in which undergraduate students conducted original research in the Newberry Library in Chicago, one of the world's great archives. This chapter shows how archival experiences can translate into stimulating public digital humanities projects, opening up meaningful conversations about access, audience, and inclusion.

Chapter 5 explores Danielle's pedagogical collaboration with 18thConnect, a website that provides free access to images of original eighteenth-century publications along with plain text that has been extracted from each work through OCR, or optical character recognition. Danielle invited her undergraduate students to use 18thConnect's digital editing tool, TypeWright, to improve these texts' readability and searchability. This digitization project enabled students to perform what she calls "networked reading," or connecting ephemeral, noncanonical, and informational texts, both historical and contemporary, with canonical historical literature typically taught in an eighteenth-century survey course. In so doing, students become more informed and savvier readers of a range of texts from across the eighteenth century.

Chapter 6 develops points from the previous two, showing how Danielle's graduate students built upon the foundational engaged work of 18thConnect by creating the first digitized, annotated scholarly edition of Sarah Fielding's novel *The History of the Countess of Dellwyn* (1759). This chapter considers how such work encourages students to perform scholar-activist roles in their classes, their coursework, and beyond.

We hope this book will give you some concrete ideas about doing public humanities work with historical literature but also leave you with some nagging questions. What is different about doing public humanities work grounded in historical literature? How does working within a community change the way we see historical texts? How does this collaborative work help us redefine literary criticism and reimagine its practices? What is the impact of considering literary criticism, critical thinking, and analytical writing as public work? How does this reconsideration help prepare faculty and students for the ever-increasing challenges of finding a meaningful place in public life? We can answer these questions based on our experience, but we hope they're questions you'll also answer for yourself as you read. We invite you to ask not only how to do public humanities, but why and what it means for the future of literary history and our collective future.

1. THE STREET
🐚 🐚

What Emma *Teaches Us about the*
Savior Complex in Service Learning

DANIELLE SPRATT

When contemporary readers envision the places and spaces of works by Jane Austen and her contemporaries from the long eighteenth century, a flurry of BBC-inspired landscapes usually overwhelms their imagination: the bustling pump-rooms at Bath surrounded by the city's Georgian architecture, where *Northanger Abbey*'s Catherine Morland first experiences the frenetic qualities of public life; the precipices of Lyme Regis, where Louisa Musgrove falls on her head and *Persuasion*'s protagonist, Anne Elliot, comes into her own; the bustling streets of London that Marianne and Elinor Dashwood navigate in the wake of their displacement from their family home in *Sense and Sensibility*; and the candle-lit ballrooms of aristocratic homes, equal parts Pemberley and Downton Abbey, where Darcy first rejects Elizabeth Bennet in *Pride and Prejudice*. To put it another way, as Bridget discusses in the next chapter, "Jane Austen" connotes for many readers and fans a kind of mental travel that bridges time and space. These kinds of associations inform the stereotype of the escapist Janeite, as contemporary fans of her work are known. By extension, these associations contribute to the perceived disconnect between Austen's novels and the twenty-first-century world, one that pervades the media and haunts many of our students as they enter our classrooms. As Olivera Jokic has argued, some readers reject Austen outright because her novels seem concerned *only* with romantic narratives that end in marriage between upper-class people or with issues that many dismissively call "first world problems," a term that suggests the absurdly minor inconveniences that stymie members of the spoiled upper classes.[1] Likewise, many students and new readers of the period's literature bristle at the idea of reading canonical eighteenth-century works, which are almost always written by white authors who privilege the exploits of characters who exist in a culture that seems at once dramatically different and removed from our own and, perhaps even worse, fundamentally frivolous.

Of those readers who actively seek out courses or texts written in the eighteenth century, many actively indulge the Janeite stereotypes that Claudia Johnson, Deidre Lynch, and Devoney Looser have recently examined.[2] These enthusiasts often have their own barriers to engaging rigorously with the sociopolitical concerns that these cultural texts express; many have a hard time seeing beyond their admiration of Darcy's (or Colin Firth's or Matthew McFadyen's) proposal scenes. Marcia McClintock Folsom describes the obstacles to teaching Austen in this way: for many students, "Austen's legacy is so well known that using the words 'Jane Austen' is sufficient to evoke a whole world, and . . . no further comment is needed to know what world is being described."[3] In some ways, the problem that Folsom articulates is one that translates to the eighteenth-century literature classroom in general: since many students only know the eighteenth and nineteenth centuries as a period related to Austen's fiction, they often imagine her novelistic depictions of the Regency moment (1811–1820, when Prince George ruled for his incapacitated father, King George III) as wholly representative of the culture of the period (of course, reading Austen's own juvenilia, let alone works by — among others — Rochester, Swift, Equiano, and Sterne, quickly disabuses them of their visions of a sanitized long eighteenth century).

For differing reasons, then, many people come to the world of eighteenth-century literature — willingly or unwillingly — to explore what they see as a literary landscape of fairytale plots in far-flung spaces of economic privilege. For scholars and teachers of this period, the obstacles are well known: students find the culture alien or, perhaps even worse, irrelevant to their own intellectual, cultural, or social concerns. For students who resist engagement with historical literature, there are discipline-specific and broader intellectual consequences; students who are literature majors or minors lose access to the complex layers of allusion and revision, homage and resistance embedded in other literary and cultural works from across historical moments and genres. Imagine trying to interpret Joyce's invocation of Homer in *Ulysses* or Zadie Smith's structural allusions to Joyce's *Ulysses* in *NW* without these intergenerational, multigeneric references. At the same time, the intellectual project of accessing contexts and claims from a setting distinctly different from our own is crucial to intercultural and intracultural inquiry, particularly when we think about the relationship between literature and social justice. Indeed, if we rely too heavily on the notion that we have progressed so far from the dark ages when suffrage was denied to all but property-owning white men, we mistake the important work that still remains to be done for historically oppressed individuals. The recent #metoo movement has yet again reminded us of the pervasive and insidious violence of gender-based oppression and aggression and has simultaneously influenced the social media landscape and informed many of our most intimate, offline conversations. With this movement and other calls that #timesup for such behavior, we often run the risk of too quickly and easily congratulating our progressive, twenty-first-century selves that gender equality has been realized in all contexts and for all people. But just as the continual violence against people of color counters any claims that we are "post-race," any claims that we have fully addressed or achieved gender equality are refuted by news stories and governmental legislation on a daily basis.

Still, many students perhaps understandably have a hard time believing that historical literature from a cultural moment when people lacked knowledge about indoor plumbing can speak to our current cultural moment, rife as it is with complex technologies and rapid digital communications. This misconception resonates with a broader popular understanding of early modern and eighteenth-century culture. After all, although we encounter images of the eighteenth century passively but frequently—every time we use a quarter to feed a parking meter or pay for a cup of coffee with a dollar bill, we see George Washington, for instance—these representations nevertheless seem sanitized and restricted to a particular experience of a particular kind of privileged person. To the extent that communities of color or the economically disadvantaged register as part of the popular narrative of the eighteenth-century literary and cultural canon, they exist in liminal, subordinate spaces. As a result, the literary-historical record of the eighteenth century seems to exist in a cultural vacuum, one that is completely removed from the sociopolitical concerns that animate our public discourse today, even when we recognize that Enlightenment ideas continue to inform our political and legal systems.

But as this volume as a whole argues, we can engage meaningfully with contemporary issues by resituating literary and historical works from the eighteenth century in unfamiliar and unexpected places: not simply in our twenty-first-century classrooms but also in our wider communities, connecting twenty-first-century city blocks to eighteenth-century country fields. Likewise, seeking out community connections makes literary material that is often only experienced in the classroom or in isolated library cubicles more intellectually and academically rich. While Bridget's chapters consider eighteenth-century public humanities projects in the context of rural college towns, my chapter here explores what happens when we introduce Austen to the streets of Los Angeles, the location of my college campus. Bringing Austen to various Los Angeles community spaces, I argue, allows new readers to access the myriad ways in which her novels, seemingly dominated as they are by marriage plots and other seemingly petty concerns of the privileged classes, consistently respond to broader economic, social, and political issues from her time. In particular, I suggest that Austen's work is uniquely positioned to help participants in civic engagement projects recognize and address one of the most challenging issues in such work: the initial savior complex that many new participants feel when they go out to the community to right wrongs or "save" those who are members of underserved communities.

The benefits of addressing these points are manifold both intellectually and pragmatically. Studying historical literature with these issues in mind removes the supposition that reading such literature is itself an act of unthinking, escapist consumption, a privileged activity that is disconnected from reality in any meaningful way—to read Austen or other historical authors in this way asserts their continued relevance in the canon and the classroom. In addition, satirists like Austen are uniquely positioned to trouble the assumptions about privilege that many of her characters experience, and her ability to challenge such assumptions creates important possibilities for implementing the engaged, experiential learning activities that bring our students into often unfamiliar communities. To put it another way, reading Austen in the context of public projects can perform a decidedly activist function that not only addresses contemporary issues but also allows students to understand their place as members of a campus community and part of the community beyond the walls of the campus.

This chapter outlines how students, teachers, and general readers of Austen and other works of eighteenth-century literature can use the pedagogy of service learning—a vexed term that I use explicitly and consciously and that I will theorize more specifically later—to re-evaluate the biases that they knowingly or unknowingly espouse with regard to Austen, her novels, and their role in the community. In what follows, I narrate one of my attempts to create an experiential learning environment in a senior seminar on Jane Austen. My students and I combined traditional methods of literary study—close reading and historical-cultural analysis of Austen's novels and other prose—with experiential activities wherein each student spent approximately twenty hours providing support to literary and cultural projects at community nonprofits. Most students worked at the literacy and creative writing nonprofit 826LA, which serves the diverse communities in and around the neighborhoods of Echo Park and Mar Vista in Los Angeles (you'll hear more about 826LA from its volunteer manager, Mariesa Arrañaga Kubasek, as well as from Elizabeth K. Goodhue, later). This service work was part of the course content, and we reflected on the experiences of students in their work with children and adolescents (and read articles on demographics and issues of inequality in the Los Angeles educational system) at the same time that we considered Austen's heroines' encounters with unfamiliar settings.

Sending students to often unfamiliar geographic spaces in the communities surrounding the campus mirrors the British literary classroom's traditional academic focus, which directs students' attention to unfamiliar temporal and geographic locales; this joint displacement and replacement offers students the opportunity to revise some of their assumptions while also making them empathetic and savvy readers of themselves, others, and the connection between social inequality in the eighteenth century and in our own time. In other words, students engaged in service-learning activities can also see with increasing vividness the dynamic points of connection between Austen's early nineteenth-century Britain and our own historical moment, bringing into clearer focus significant sociopolitical issues in both contexts. Indeed, such an experiential approach to interpreting Austen's novels can help new readers access the complexity of her fictive worlds as they also locate a more active role within their own immediate and future academic and social communities. The service-learning pedagogical strategies that I outline here are focused on a case study involving Austen's novel *Emma* (1815), but they can apply to not only any Austen text but also any historical piece of literature.

In some ways, Austen's fourth published novel forges the most easily accessible connection to community work. Unlike other economically insecure Austen heroines, Emma Woodhouse, as a member of the landed gentry, has the financial resources—as well as an implicit societal obligation—to serve others in various capacities. Devoney Looser (who will say more about her own public work with Austen later) has noted that the novel "models the way elite women should wield power over less-privileged females through its protagonist's mistakes."[4] In the classroom, we build upon Looser's insightful claim by considering the ways in which the novel interrogates Emma's social responsibility to the broader Highbury community, including those impoverished and ostracized men, women, and children who live in the liminal space beyond the town's center. As students go out into their communities to tutor students in writing skills or offer homework help, they experience a process of defamiliarization that echoes Emma's own experiences, allowing them to become critically self-reflective at the same time that they are increasingly apt to critique Emma's experiences in more painstaking detail. In addition, the novel's setting registers concerns about the changing socioeconomic landscape of England. Laura Mooneyham White puts it this way: "The world of social flux is accurately rendered . . . in *Emma*, where almost every character is rising or falling or at least trying to rise or trying not to fall."[5] This volatility resonates with present-day students, many of whom face similar uncertainty upon graduation. Many wonder whether attending college will help them find a stable career and solid financial future; many more wonder if they will sink under the burdens of student loans. While not exact correlations, these comparisons allow students to forge illuminating connections between their assigned reading and service work.

A service-learning approach to studying *Emma* ultimately reveals to students a new and innovative reading of the novel, one that helps them analyze how Austen uses Emma to represent the plight of characters who have no discernible place within Highbury, a small, close-knit community just sixteen miles outside of London. I argue that by demonstrating the ways in which her heroine fails to assume her role as benefactress to those around her, Austen ironically links the privileged Emma to the impoverished outsiders that punctuate the novel's landscape, from the poor cottagers whom Emma fails to help in any substantive way, to the gypsies whom Emma's friend and philanthropic project Harriet Smith encounters, to the poultry-house robbers who frighten Emma's hypochondriacal father, Mr. Woodhouse, and facilitate the resolution of the marriage plot. As readers of the novel know, one of Emma's key failures is coercing Harriet into rejecting the tenant-farmer Robert Martin's marriage proposal on the grounds that he is an inferior social connection. Emma's failures with Harriet, along with Emma's failure to help (or even respect) her financially distressed neighbors Miss Bates and Jane Fairfax, combine to demonstrate the ways in which our protagonist increasingly finds herself a foreigner in her own community.[6] Emma's challenge in connecting with others in Highbury becomes all the more significant when read and discussed alongside students' own service experiences, a conversation that typically helps students realize that service work provides more intellectual and social rewards for those who serve than for those who are served. By discussing these issues in tandem, new readers of Austen can more readily understand the complex questions that the novel poses about the possibility — in both Austen's time and our own — of achieving social justice for those who have limited economic, political, or social agency.

In what follows, I begin by considering the concept and practice of service-learning pedagogy in the literature classroom. I then turn to an examination of how Austen's novels, and *Emma* in particular, offer a useful perspective for students who immerse themselves in their surrounding community, since these works address the savior complex that many students unknowingly espouse in their engaged work. Reading *Emma* via the framework of civic engagement allows us to trace Emma's increasingly fractured place within Highbury society, while it also enables students to understand better how Austen's novel engages with her world and ours. This approach relocates our focus from the romantic myth of eighteenth-century literature and the Regency-era dramas of our media-inspired imagination, instead retraining our critical gaze to reveal the significant connections between "the streets" of Highbury and those within and beyond our campuses.

Service Learning and the Street in the Literary Classroom

At most college campuses across the United States, clubs, groups, and offices that advocate various types of service activities have become increasingly visible. Caryn McTighe Musil observed this trend at the start of the twenty-first century, proclaiming that "there has been a quiet revolution occurring in the academy over the last two decades. Civic concerns have achieved new visibility alongside the traditional academic mission of higher education."[7] While these service activities are often referred to interchangeably as "volunteering," "community service," or "service learning," I suggest that we might productively employ the phrase "civic engagement" to encapsulate these terms. Jean Y. Yu helpfully defines civic engagement as "the actions of informed individuals and collectives to respond to the needs created by systems of social injustice in the communities in which they live and work. . . . [It] must be requested or approved by communities themselves, and executed in collaboration with community participants."[8] Here, Yu articulates civic engagement's emphasis on multiple levels of social justice, from the reciprocal partnership with community agents to the theoretical and political aims attendant to such ethical practices. Civic engagement, then, captures a range of activities performed in response to an articulated need of the community — from one-off volunteer cleanups of community gardens to a yearlong immersive experience that pairs course content with community work in order to create bilingual manuals on educational options for students and families new to a school district. What distinguishes these kinds of civic engagement is, in some ways, the level of engagement between an individual and the community. As Musil observes, while volunteering or community service is usually a fairly isolated activity that occurs once or sporadically, service learning involves a long-term project that allows for an immersive and often intercultural experience. In addition, while volunteer or community service work in academic contexts usually receives something like extra credit, we can distinguish service learning from these other activities because of its ongoing practice and its academic grounding; "like any test, paper, or research project, the service-learning experience must be integral to the syllabus and advance the students' knowledge of the course content."[9]

Although service-learning courses are especially prominent in fields like the social sciences, partly because many of these disciplines require fieldwork and partly because they have natural connections to people outside the walls of campus, the public-facing models of these disciplines can provide fruitful and effective formats for classes in literary studies as well. But while classes in social work can respond to immediate problems within the foster care system or urban studies majors can research and propose infrastructure projects that make cities more efficiently connected through improvements in public transit systems, literary studies needs to make its humanistic connections more explicit both alongside and beyond the concerns of structure, form, and theory that traditionally inform our scholarship. For instance, Mary Schwartz has recently argued that "the poetics of language draws students into imagined worlds that help them to question their own worlds and to begin to extend themselves to others."[10] Schwartz's point helps us rethink the imaginative Austen fan mentioned at the opening of this essay; rather than fostering a disconnect from real-life issues, such immersive reading practices might in fact create in readers an awareness of and sympathy for unfamiliar situations as well as skepticism toward the status quo of their own surroundings, as well as the capacity to identify and construct projects that address elements of social inequality in their nearby communities. Likewise, Anna Sims Bartel notes that the literary student's ability to understand narrative *as* construct, to analyze story rigorously, helps her critique the common narrative of a given demographic or place.[11]

The intellectual work of literary study is well suited for experiential work, particularly the kind that encourages self-reflective practices and helps disenfranchised people and populations recover agency over their own narratives. As experts on narrative and the articulation of the complexity of abstract issues (like equity and justice) and their relationship to individual people's memories of lived experiences, literature scholars are well suited to teach others strategies for and the value of harnessing narrative skills in ways that support civically engaged projects and have the potential to instigate changes in local, state, and federal laws. Put simply, engaged practices in the literature classroom can help reveal the important connection between narrative agency and other forms of political and social agency.

Still, there are aspects of service-integrated literary work that require careful consideration and caution, beginning with the term "service learning" itself. For many critics of the term, the word "service" connotes and in fact *encourages* the kind of savior complex that we must acknowledge and actively reject in community-based work, particularly at the university level, where such savior-based sentiments are easily fostered. The term "service" seems to suggest that well-meaning groups of students go out into communities surrounding their campus to help address social issues; the town-gown tensions surrounding many college campuses unfortunately further reinforce this perspective. In this mindset, the community's needs seem to be best addressed by those from outside, from the academy. Of course, no effective civic engagement can happen without respecting community partners as vital resources and the community itself as a group of active agents who know better than anyone else what methods will best serve their needs. Although "service" thus suggests a deep imbalance in agency and efficacy among the participants, it is nevertheless a disciplinary standard in pedagogy and is used widely both within the California State University system where I teach and at institutions of higher education throughout the country.

Laurie Grobman has expressed two important concerns with the institutional acceptance of the term: first, that service learning "can too easily encourage narrow interpretations of literature to fit or explain real-world situations, especially those related to race, class, gender, or other categories of difference."[12] In other words, such work can allow students to draw superficial, fleeting connections between literature and their surroundings. For example, Richardson's kidnapped heroine Pamela experiences a diminishment of agency that to some students might seem similar to that of women who are imprisoned in human trafficking rings, and if the comparison does not delve deeper into cultural and gendered assumptions and practices — if the connection stays simply at points of easy comparison — then we flatten the ethical concerns of both scenarios and devalue the brutalization of the women who are decidedly not fictional characters. Second, Grobman notes that "because service learning is for many students their first real-world encounter with some of the nation's profound social ills, it can be difficult for them to avoid seeing themselves as saviors despite the emphasis on mutual learning" (130). As I will discuss in more detail shortly, *Emma* presents characters and situations that critique or undermine the savior complex, an effect of what Ellen Cushman calls the "liberal do-gooder stance" that many students adopt when they begin service-learning activities.[13] In fact, as students in a service-integrated course trace the strategies that Austen uses to dismantle Emma's own pretensions of do-gooder glory, they must also recognize that service learning is not simply a system in which they, the privileged, smart students, sweep in to save the "less fortunate." In fact, two key insights that students learn in these courses are, first, that they gain far more than they give, and second, that no individual person, no matter how many hours she devotes to tutoring students, can overturn the systemic inequalities that perpetuate cycles of poverty and oppression.

One key challenge, then, is helping students question both the motivations that inform, as well as the effects that result from, experiential practice. At what point does service learning move from being a bandage on a gaping systemic wound (perhaps a bandage that allows, ironically, such systemic oppression to continue) to a practice that helps instigate the kind of broad intellectual and social change that leads to a greater sense of equality across communities? While I can't claim that any of my service-learning courses have led to radical revolution, a small victory is in moving students from the savior mentality to one that is open, inclusive, and aware that community work requires collaboration and reciprocity in order to effect incremental change.

To arrive at these conclusions, teachers and students must consistently write reflective essays and conduct reflective practices throughout the semester. These essays and practices require them not only to consider their service work from their own perspective, but also to imagine themselves in the role of the service partners and the population with whom they work. As Linda Flower suggests, through such acts of "intercultural inquiry," service-learning students can seek "rival readings of an issue"; while they may start out congratulating themselves on a successful afternoon helping grade-school students write personal narratives about their recent move to a new community, by asking our college students to revisit and narrate this experience from the perspective of the children with whom they worked, they might start seeing themselves not as authorities, but rather as learners and equal participants in this joint experience.[14] As a result, this process has "the potential to transform both the inquirers and their interpretations of problematic issues in the world."[15] Most service-learning classes won't topple fascist regimes or inequitable laws, but they can help create a cadre of more connected, savvy community members who find solidarity through these new connections. (And in an era that seems to encourage divisiveness based on regional and national difference, we might find the very ability to foster solidarity within and across communities a much-needed triumph against oppressive regimes.)

This is all to say that service-learning pedagogy is a complicated strategy precisely because it requires a series of radical encounters and confrontations between self and other. To emphasize both the rival readings — the benefits and the risks — of a practice that brings together people from often divergent life experiences, I find that it is helpful to recognize and discuss with students and fellow faculty how the term "service learning" itself demonstrates the tensions inherent in its practice. From the perspective of the educator, the links between service and learning are "interdependent and dynamic";[16] as multiple studies have shown, service learning is a high-impact practice that yields more sustained academic learning outcomes than traditional pedagogical approaches like exams and essays alone. Yet in addition to stressing the connections and continuities, the combination of words in "service learning" underscores some of the practice's intellectual and practical discordances. While students and teachers might reap the academic and intellectual benefits of service-learning courses, what long-term benefits do community partners receive? Are the community partners lost in the liminal space between the two words?

These are concerns that faculty and students can address by questioning the term "service learning"; ideally, faculty can invite community partners and members to reflect on the term as well in a discussion that promotes dialogue among participants.

The tension inherent in the term "service learning," one that I and other practitioners must acknowledge as deeply problematic for the reasons mentioned, can actually encourage faculty and students to move beyond what Gregory Jay calls a superficial "'celebrating [of] diversity'" that often unintentionally promotes the savior complex in service learners. Repositioning service learning in this way facilitates a practice through which we as teachers and students "learn to critique the assumptions [we] bring to the encounter and to respect the different virtues and assets each has to offer." In so doing, we allow for a multiplicity of perspectives and norms; we "proceed more beneficially when differences are accepted as assets rather than obstacles."[17] As I discuss later in this chapter, achieving this kind of self-reflection in practice is no easy task—but I suggest that the moral, ethical, and social dilemmas presented in using service-learning pedagogy to explore literary works like Austen's *Emma* help students make these sophisticated, complex connections in meaningful ways.

Crucial to such intercultural pedagogy is an acknowledgment of the complexity involved in connecting people from divergent backgrounds. Indeed, while many service-learning teachers use the rhetoric of harmony and collaboration when discussing service partners, I find compelling and significant Paula Mathieu's observation that, in some cases, the word "community" denies the challenges that our students and our service partner clients face on a daily basis. For instance, in the case of the after-school program 826LA, many student participants from the community are there because their parents signed them up, not because they themselves have opted into the program, leaving many service learners baffled at their lack of enthusiasm. Instead of community, following Mathieu we might productively use a more colloquial and perhaps more accurate term: "the street." Mathieu writes that this term "may refer to a specific neighborhood, community center, school, or local nonprofit organization. Like all the other possible terms (such as *community*, *sites of service*, *contact zones*, *outreach site*, etc.), *street* is a problematic term, but one whose problems, I hope, help illuminate the difficulties associated with academic outreach."[18]

Indulge me for a moment while I explain why I find the term "the street" more revelatory than other possibilities, particularly when it comes to addressing the savior complex in service learning. While terms like "community" and "contact zones" promote (in the former example) an abstract sense of place and belonging, or (in the latter case) connote contagion, the street offers an image that is at once quotidian and liberating (streets are important sites of travel and transport) and risky: we don't want to lose our homes and get thrown out on the street. The concept thus offers a significant "spatial metaphor for the destination of academic outreach and service learning";[19] not only do we want our students "out there" on the street, but we also want them to experience this space as one of connection and disconnection. The term also has connotations of action and protest: we "take to the street" when we demonstrate against a particular issue or incident. In recognizing these tensions and the role of place, service learners can have an important conversation about the distinction between classroom or campus life and life "out there." This approach allows us to "collapse harmful dichotomies that traditional university knowledge espouses: literary/vernacular; high culture/low culture; literature/literacy; objective/subjective; expert/novice."[20] Particularly in urban environments like Los Angeles, the street is often opposed to the enclosed space of the campus community. Considering the street in service-learning endeavors helps students recognize their assumptions and fears about the supposed dangers "out there" and also encourages them to think critically about the space and activities of the campus. Most importantly, the term "service learning" ultimately helps students realize that rather than being charitable agents, they themselves are the recipients of knowledge and skills from their work in the streets beyond campus.

Saviors on the Streets of Highbury and Los Angeles

Despite the increasing presence of community engagement initiatives, there are two particular obstacles that confront teachers who wish to pair service learning with an Austen text or any work of literature from the early modern period. First, while service-integrated pre-twentieth-century literature courses are rather rare, pedagogical scholarship on the practice is even less common.[21] As I prepared to teach a service-integrated class on Austen, I found myself sympathizing with Shakespearean scholar Matthew C. Hansen, whose comments also describe the availability of Austen service-learning pedagogy: "Almost no published scholarship exists on how courses on Shakespeare—a staple of nearly every college English department—might engage with the community through service learning that provides a genuine community benefit while simultaneously deepening undergraduate students' engagement with and understanding of Shakespeare."[22] Like Shakespeare, Austen is a pervasive presence in the Western cultural imagination and the classroom. This fact provides both points of access and, as mentioned in the introduction, myriad obstacles for twenty-first-century teachers of her novels, since many students arrive, whether gleefully or reluctantly, with certain assumptions about Austen and her novels. The second challenge becomes apparent from institutional data: studies by Ostrander and Portney and others have suggested that particular demographic groups—among them, women, persons of color, and those who are low-income—participate far less frequently in civic engagement activities, whether they are college students or adults living in a specific community.[23] While this underrepresentation is certainly troubling for all institutions of higher education, it is even more troubling at large public institutions like my own that focus on teaching underserved student populations. Although the obstacles to engaged activities for traditionally marginalized groups are deeply troubling, they offer an impetus for universities to confront the absence of diverse and committed participants in service activities. Indeed, for colleges that primarily serve the demographics just mentioned or for those that wish to address this imbalance, it is imperative to create a flexible and sustainable service-learning curriculum that encourages students to participate in experiential coursework, particularly when they are non-traditional students who, unlike many traditional college-age students, often have work and family obligations. Because service learning has been proven to be a high-impact pedagogical practice that deepens students' knowledge and enhances their success, institutions and faculty have an ethical obligation to promote engaged work in a way that is tenable for our diverse student populations.[24]

My first attempt to address these challenges came in spring 2013, with a semester-long undergraduate senior seminar entitled Jane Austen, Satire, and Society: A Service-Learning Course. In this class, students read all of Austen's major novels as well as *Sanditon* and selections from her juvenilia. In addition to primary and secondary readings, the coursework involved at least twenty hours of community engagement work, an amount that most experts agree allows for a sustained and meaningful relationship with a community partner and its clients. This engaged work included direct service activities like after-school and creative writing tutoring at 826LA; capacity-building work like sorting food and clothing donations at a local community resource agency, MEND (Meet Each Need with Dignity); and digital service activities in the form of editing and correcting the OCR of digitized rare eighteenth-century books via 18thConnect (more about this work in chapters 5 and 6).[25] Students also had the opportunity to locate an alternative service site either on or off campus that suited their interests and schedule. I allowed them to choose a site for two reasons. First, although "matching students to projects can be labor-intensive," like Schwartz I find that "students who exercise agency in their community adjust more creatively to the partnership setting than do those who are assigned a placement."[26] Second, as mentioned earlier, one reason that many nontraditional students and students of color do not participate in service activities is because their finances and other commitments prevent them from doing so; allowing students to tailor their activities to their own needs empowered them to participate fully in such experiential learning.

Before students went anywhere, however, I had to make sure that these community organizations were approved partners for our campus. Even when students work in the most seemingly innocuous of places—a mellow after-school program, an office adjacent to campus—they must complete important risk management forms that ensure all parties are covered with the proper insurance and liability forms in the event of an accident of any sort. Interestingly, although there are so many challenges in coordinating a service-learning course, it is often here—at the level of bureaucracy—that projects stall. Early that spring semester, my colleague in CSUN's Office of Community Engagement, Nicole Linton, connected our students and faculty with community partners and helped transform how our campus handles these challenging logistics.

DEMYSTIFYING RISK MANAGEMENT

Nicole Linton

California State University, Northridge, is an educational metropolis that is located in the heart of the San Fernando Valley. Our 356-acre campus is surrounded by organizations that have partnered with CSUN as coeducators in community service learning. Nearly 40,000 students contribute to supporting Cal State Northridge's commitment to engaging our community, while building connections between the two. This kind of work is a vital component in developing engaged citizens.

It is our goal to be an inclusive, cooperative community. We have over five hundred community partners with diverse and changing needs that allow faculty to collaborate with them to develop multidimensional sustainable partnerships. The community partners serve as cofacilitators in service-learning courses. They can provide the students with an in-depth look into the organization's mission and its role in the community. Developing meaningful relationships with community partners can have a positive impact on our region as well as students' learning outcomes.

As the service-learning coordinator, my commitment to comprehensive excellence has led me to streamline the risk management process, removing obstacles that prevented faculty from implementing proven high-impact learning practices such as community service learning. In the past, faculty who were excited about developing and implementing a service-learning project would frequently give up the moment they saw the stack of papers they had to manage: liability partnership forms to be signed by both community partners and dozens of students, student timesheets, site supervisor evaluation forms, pre- and postservice surveys, and more. On top of regular coursework and grading, these documents seemed just too difficult to manage.

So I put technology to work. In 2013 I began working with the systemwide California State University S4 team to develop a database that would function as a risk management tool to support community service-learning faculty, students, and community partners. The S4 database was widely embraced by faculty and students, who also provided feedback that led to the expansion of the database during the 2015–2016 academic year. By embracing innovation, Cal State Northridge worked with the systemwide S4 team to expand its S4 database into a risk management tool that supports not only service-learning courses but also field trips and internship programs.[27] The S4 database enables the campus to more efficiently capture students' community engagement activities while also providing

Community service-learning opportunities at California State University, Northridge

Community service-learning (CSL) data	2015–2016	2016–2017	Percent increase
Number of CSL courses or sections offered	77	159	107
Number of new CSL courses developed	7	41	486
Total student enrollment in CSL courses	1,795	3,557	98
Estimated total CSL hours in the community	33,229	121,207	265
Estimated number of community partner sites	137	538	293

students, faculty, and community organizations with a user-friendly interface for handling paperwork. The S4 database does the following:

- Adheres to CSU executive orders 1062 and 1065, which establish guidelines for off-campus academic experiences
- Removes the obligation for faculty to collect and store paper copies of students' risk management forms and evaluations
- Supports students' engagement activities
- Creates electronic forms in place of paper
- Authenticates users for e-signatures
- Maintains a list of approved community organizations for students and faculty to view
- Informs students and faculty of known risks at a community organization's site
- Captures student placements at community organizations
- Captures information for new community organizations interested in partnering with campus programs
- Supports campuses' sustainability efforts by reducing paper consumption
- Generates data for CSU reporting
- Holds procurement documentation of approved community organizations
- Allows faculty to view their students' placements and submitted forms
- Provides students with due date reminders

By leveraging technology, California State University, Northridge, made business processes more efficient and removed barriers that once discouraged faculty participation in community service learning. Since we simplified the risk management process, the number of new community service-learning courses has increased 486 percent.

As Nicole's essay shows, streamlining the logistics of service learning had a transformative impact on the number of partnerships that faculty at Cal State Northridge can create and implement. Once the partnerships are in place, it is important to nurture these campus-community relationships so that they grow over time. Indeed, whether students perform direct or indirect service activities, a sustained approach to service-learning activities is the bedrock of any well-designed public project. Mariesa Arrañaga Kubasek, volunteer manager for 826LA, explains that the participation of service learners over weeks, not hours or days, has significant impacts on both service-learning students and the primary and secondary schoolchildren who attend the variety of programs hosted at 826LA.

UPENDING EXPECTATIONS

The Impact of Service Learner Mentorship of Students over Time

Mariesa Arrañaga Kubasek

At 826LA, our volunteers not only support students with their creative and expository writing skills, but they also become mentors. In working together one-on-one, between editing an essay or finishing a math worksheet, we hope our students and volunteers develop mutual trust and understanding, which leads to a crucial mentorship relationship through which our students can grow into confident scholars and writers who recognize the power of their own voices.

Over the years, service learners have become an integral part of 826LA's community. As early adults immersed in academia, they are adept at connecting with our students (they both still have homework, after all!) and encouraging them to pursue their goals. In reflecting on their time at 826LA, service learners tell us that this is a reciprocal experience. They often recount discovering a deeper understanding of their interconnectedness with their community, a more horizontal relationship with the students. And throughout they develop confidence in their skills as mentors.

But this realization, of course, does not happen immediately.

I'm responsible for training new volunteers, welcoming them to the space, answering their questions, and helping them find a program that best suits their schedules and skill sets. When I train service-learning volunteers and greet them in our space, I can sense they're not always quite sure what to expect. Maybe it's because they're still in a classroom setting themselves, eager to really dig into a concept, to examine it, to feel like they're an expert in it, like they'll ace the test. When it comes to working with youth, though, study all you want . . . but who ever truly feels ready?

Our service learners understand the responsibility they carry and know that there is a level of unpredictability in their experience. That's good. This is the kind of space they should be in — not feeling unprepared but rather open to the possibilities the volunteering session will bring and ready to meet our students on their terms, to serve them as best they can.

It's also clear in the beginning that service learners can't yet see the role they're playing. Our students write stories about characters of their own invention — a dinosaur that's also a spy, a crime-fighting burrito, a llama in search of its fur, for instance — or they write stories based on culturally responsive prompts developed by staff. These can include spooky stories inspired by La Llorona (the weeping woman of Latin American folktales), brainstorming and then writing a pitch for a web series, or researching newspaper articles about the slime trend (a social media phenomenon that tracks the explosive popularity of DIY slime recipes on blogs, YouTube, Instagram, and elsewhere that yield customized batches of toy slime that students can replicate at home). At first, service-learning volunteers don't quite see how these activities are making that broad stroke "difference." They might even feel like they're not making any progress.

Each time the service learners come back, though, they become more comfortable in the space, more engaged, more willing to share their own stories too, more excited to talk about the topics they're learning about in class with our students. Sometimes, the service-learning volunteer will see that the student has the same required reading they did back in the fourth grade. Maybe volunteers and students will learn they both like to eat the same snacks. Either way, a relationship is being forged in these moments. As one of our service-learning volunteers wrote on our blog, "I've gotten to know the students, some more than others, on a more personal level. I've learned that some students really love bacon, *Diary of Wimpy Kid,* zombie stories, baseball, and hangman. I've been very fortunate to have the opportunity to see them work with their peers and their volunteers. I've listened to their personal stories, and I've learned to see and think about their world."

Through this kind of interaction, the service learner also starts to notice the small forward movements, for instance when students more readily return to doing their homework when asked. The service learner also sees that learning how to help guide our students is practical and deepens with experience, not underlining and annotating.

Most importantly, our service-learning students serve an active listening role. It's their responsibility to ask open-ended questions to better assess what the student needs in terms of homework or writing support. Through this listening and, as we say, meeting the students where they're at, our volunteers learn more about our students' lives. They hear how our students have support in some areas of their lives, challenges in others. Service-learning volunteers are able to connect these conversations to their coursework and see how they as volunteers play both a complex and crucial role in providing support to a student who might not have otherwise received that help.

"Ultimately, it is about the children, not us. It helps to put everything into perspective," one service learner wrote in a reflection. This realization is what I hope for: that at the very least, volunteering with 826LA helps service-learning volunteers upend an expectation, dismantle a preconceived notion, or create a small shift in perspective.

Mariesa's essay points toward the significant ideological transformation that occurs across the weeks—not hours or days—of service performed by student service learners. They move to a "horizontal," and thus less hierarchical (or savior-oriented) relationship with the students with whom they work, as well as with the broader community. Teasing out the nuances of this perspectival shift requires the faculty member (often in conversation with community partners) to design and implement what is perhaps the most important term-long practice in a service-integrated class: a sustained system of active reflection activities.[28] To encourage students to consider the social dimensions of Austen's novels even before their service activities began, I implemented a weekly online forum for students to discuss ideas and experiences related to class, service, and their own and their peers' work. Unlike traditional handwritten journals, the online component of the class helps students engage with one another more readily *and* offers a higher level of accountability, since it requires students to post about their experiences in real time. Most schools have secure platforms like Blackboard, Canvas, or Moodle; Google Groups is another useful option to encourage discussion in an online yet not fully public forum. If students are comfortable with online writing, public blogs may be more appropriate: Weebly, WordPress, and Wix are all excellent, largely intuitive, user-friendly platforms to explore.

Early in the semester, as students were beginning *Sense and Sensibility*, I prompted them to compare their initial understanding of Austen's social awareness with the views of critics. For instance, in the second week, students read excerpts from Marilyn Butler's seminal *Jane Austen and the War of Ideas*. On our discussion board, I summarized a main claim of Butler's work: although she admits that Austen "looks in her last few years like a social commentator" with novels like *Mansfield Park* (1814), *Emma*, and *Persuasion* (1816), she proposes that Austen's seemingly progressive representation of characters like *Mansfield Park*'s Fanny, William, and Susan Price merely critiques their higher-ranking cousins. For Butler, "This was no more a revolt on behalf of the underprivileged than it was a revolt on behalf of women."[29] Instead, she sees Austen as complicit in maintaining the status quo.

I asked students to evaluate and respond to Butler's argument via their initial impressions of *Sense and Sensibility* and *Mansfield Park*, which we framed through a further discussion of salient secondary sources, including Claudia Johnson's work about Austen's revolutionary tendencies, *Jane Austen: Women, Politics, and the Novel*. While some students agreed that the novels published before *Emma* lack social awareness, others argued that their focus on female agency and issues like the Dashwood sisters' inability to inherit or make legal claims to their father's estate suggests a keen awareness of at least certain social problems, especially those faced by women. At the same time, our class discussed inequalities that various groups still face. Students were quick to note that women receive less financial compensation than men for the same work; that poor children are less likely to excel in school; and that many states have official racial profiling protocols as part of their legal and educational systems. I paired this discussion with two articles that Susan Celia Greenfield published in popular online sources, both of which connect Austen to present-day issues: child poverty and the Violence Against Women Act (Susan talks about her experience writing these op-ed pieces later in this book).[30] As many students in my classes are people of color or from low-income backgrounds, these discussions were particularly engaging and important to them. Students began to see that while Austen's world may permit fantasies of Colin Firth's Darcy, it also reveals complex social and economic inequalities found in her time and our own.

We began reading *Emma* about halfway through the semester, when most students had just started their service coursework; this confluence helped build on earlier class discussions of Austen's street while it also immediately confronted students with the savior complex that Emma so keenly exemplifies. As Folsom has observed, the character of Emma—"handsome, clever, and rich"[31]—poses almost immediate challenges to student readers: "The opening page, with its famous first sentence, can repel students whose egalitarian values are affronted by Emma's obvious privileges. . . . How can a teacher help students understand Emma's position as a woman with power and Emma as a person whom readers love even when they behold her arrogantly interfering with other people's lives?"[32]

As I've mentioned, I suggest that there are a handful of key scenes that empower students to recognize the tension between Emma's perception of herself (handsome, clever, and rich) and her increasing psychic distance from the changing Highbury community. The first is an often overlooked passage in which Emma and Harriet perform a "charitable visit" to "a poor sick family, who lived a little way out of Highbury" (89). Just after the famous moment in which Emma explains that she refuses to marry because of her financial independence, she and Harriet approach and enter the cottage. Using free indirect discourse, which has the effect of moving seamlessly between the omniscient third-person narrator's voice and the characters' internal monologues, Austen writes,

Emma was very compassionate; and the distresses of the poor were as sure of relief from her personal attention and kindness, her counsel and her patience, as from her purse. She understood their ways, could allow for their ignorance and their temptations, had no romantic expectations of extraordinary virtue from those, for whom education had done so little; entered into their troubles with ready sympathy, and always gave her assistance with as much intelligence as good-will. In the present instance, it was sickness and poverty together which she came to visit; and after remaining there as long as she could give comfort or advice, she quitted the cottage with such an impression of the scene as made her say to Harriet, as they walked away, "These are the sights, Harriet, to do one good. How trifling they make every thing else appear!" (93)

Of course, Emma almost immediately forgets the plight of the poor cottagers when she and Harriet encounter Highbury's eligible parson, Mr. Elton, on their walk home, and Emma's desire for matchmaking soon surmounts any interest in poor relief.

Austen's use of free indirect discourse here can either encourage or undermine readers' sympathy for Emma, creating a tension that warrants intercultural inquiry between Austen's contexts and our own. For instance, if students contrast Emma's behavior with Mr. Elton's total obliviousness to the cottagers' plight, they might discover an admirable quality in the novel's heroine. As Laura Mooneyham White argues, because "Emma's sense of noblesse oblige is genuine . . . , [it] sets her above the clergyman whose charity is a masquerade."[33] For students who see clergy members as guides to moral and ethical behavior, this moment can elevate Emma as it demotes Elton.

Other students might read this moment as demonstrating Emma's obliviousness to her community as a result of her own savior complex: it's not the narrator who calls Emma "compassionate," but rather Emma herself. Read this way, the only positive effect that she accomplishes when she visits the cottagers is inflating her own self-esteem. The challenge of this reading is to get students to consider to what extent Emma herself might be enforcing and encouraging the inequality that she perceives.

Yet rather than encourage a reading that simply vilifies Emma for her privileged perspectives, I invite my students to analyze how Austen's use of free indirect discourse — how this complex balance of third-person narration with the ability to represent Emma's thoughts—might also be a means of encouraging an empathetic reading of her savior complex. It might, in fact, show us how Emma's often condescending attitude toward Harriet and others forces her into a position of marginalization. For instance, although the passage notes that "Emma understood their ways," readers know that one of Emma's continual mistakes is assuming that she understands people's motives. Reading this way, we might interpret the narrator to be representing (and laughing at—or with?) Emma's self-satisfaction with her public persona. Extending this line of thinking, I ask my students, "What real 'relief' can Emma offer the cottagers through her visit?" Students are quick to note that Emma eventually sends some healthful soup back with one of the cottagers' daughters. Generous, to be sure—but whatever relief the family gains from the soup is quite temporary. If we read these moments alongside Emma's almost instantaneous forgetfulness about the entire situation, we can see that Austen's narrator is using free indirect discourse to ironize Emma's abilities as an effective patroness. Rather than showing her integral role in the streets of Highbury, these events indicate her limited relevance. Whether cultivated or accidental, Emma's savior complex distances her from those in her community, from the poor cottagers to the women who are her friends, peers, and neighbors, like Harriet, Jane Fairfax, and the Bates family.

Reading this passage closely allows students to question the notion of saving others through service. When I asked students to compare their service activities to those of the characters in Austen's novels and to categorize both using Musil's service spectrum, which ranks students' understanding of their service involvement from a low point of "exclusionary" and "naive" to a high point of "reciprocal" and "generative," the majority used Emma's character—both her good and her problematic intentions—as a touchstone for their own experiences.[34] One student, Mary,[35] reflected that as she began her after-school tutoring service at 826LA, her mindset "was very much like Emma's. . . . I had a recurring and self-justified thought that 'at least I'm doing something, which is much more than other people of my generation can say.'" For Mary, linking Emma's behavior with her initial attitude helped her create a more active, less complacent, and, as Musil would categorize it, less "naive" model of civic engagement. Many of her classmates echoed this rethinking of their experience as service learners.

At the same time, students were able to understand that the narrator's opening description of Emma belies her increasing exclusion from the Highbury community. Anna, another student who was very attentive to Emma's class snobbery, argued that the character "see[s] the cottage as a separate zone in which her scheme for matchmaking can take place. It is not her land. It is the OTHER's land. . . . The narrator says that Emma 'enters into their troubles.' As much as she focuses on their troubles, she has not seen them as her own, and thus there is a major lack of interconnectedness." Anna's comments emphasize her awareness of the divide between those who serve and those who receive such service. This perspective helped her recalibrate her understanding of her own service activities: "While working at 826LA I was not seeing the children as deprived or 'ignorant,' as Emma describes her charity cases, but instead as fortunate. They are being empowered by attending 826LA. They are able to use their imaginations and think about school subjects in a new and fun way that they cannot experience in class." Rather than seeing the students she worked with via a deficit model, Anna was able to identify with the students and imagine herself in their place.

These comments demonstrate that there is ample room in *Emma* to discuss the construction of otherness as it relates to power. Emma treats the poor cottagers as others but in the process fails to enhance her own superiority beyond her own self-satisfied perspective; instead, she unknowingly distances herself from her community. The process by which Austen increases Emma's alienation from Highbury society becomes clear when students begin to see how the novel problematizes matters of race. *Emma* provides two such passages that teachers can effectively deploy in a sustained discussion of encounters with otherness. The first moment, at the end of volume II, arises when Emma observes a conversation between Mrs. Elton and Jane Fairfax. In this moment, Jane compares her potential role as governess to " 'the sale — not quite of human flesh — but of human intellect' " (325). Mrs. Elton, perhaps misunderstanding Jane's allusion to prostitution, instead links her words to the slave trade.[36] She attempts to vindicate Jane's intended employer and her own relatives by proclaiming, " 'If you mean a fling at the slave-trade, I assure you Mr. Suckling was always rather a friend to the abolition' " (325). Jane attempts to reject the explicit comparison by demurring, " 'I was not thinking of the slave-trade . . . ; governess-trade, I assure you, was all that I had in view; widely different certainly as to the guilt of those who carry it on; but' " — she then enhances the comparison by lamenting — " 'as to the greater misery of the victims, I do not know where it lies'" (325). The majority of this passage repeatedly delays an overt comparison between the working white woman's role as governess and the barbaric treatment of enslaved peoples; Austen waits until the end of the passage to let Jane indulge in such unthinking self-pity. Tellingly, in this passage both Emma's verbal participation and her interior, hypercritical evaluation of Mrs. Elton and Jane are missing; indeed, Emma herself is absent from this scene and indeed for most of the chapter. Her silence thus suggests her utter disinterest in the economic problems of lower-class women *and* the evils of the slave trade; she can't imagine herself as an agent in these narratives at all.

This passage offers a useful moment to remind students that the rhetoric of women's rights during the period was often linked to the cause of abolition. The conversation as Austen depicts it, however, underscores how problematic the comparison between abolition and women's rights was. Mrs. Elton both misreads and deflects Jane's lament about the necessity of her becoming a governess by stating that Mr. Suckling supports abolition; while the statement may be true, it in no way addresses Jane's fundamental concern. Likewise, Jane's comparison of the miseries involved in the state of slavery to those found in the condition of governesses seems, especially to modern readers, particularly hyperbolic and insensitive to the horrors of the slave trade. Because Emma routinely seeks out any reason to critique Jane, Emma's fundamental disengagement from this scene—both verbal and critical—suggests that she is entirely disconnected from the issues that Jane and Mrs. Elton discuss. Asking students to discuss present-day acts of omission and silence in the face of social ills helps emphasize the tendency in Austen's society and our own to ignore or suppress complex histories of social inequity.

Emma's silence regarding issues of economics and race reappears in telling ways soon after this incident, in chapter 2 of the third volume, when Harriet and a school friend encounter "half a dozen" begging "gipsie" children, "headed by a stout woman and a great boy" (361). Terrified and partially immobilized by a "cramp after dancing," Harriet offers them a shilling, but they follow her, "demanding more" (361). Happening upon the incident, Frank Churchill, the stepson of Emma's former governess and secret fiancé of Jane Fairfax, breaks up the scene; Austen narrates, "The terror which the woman and boy had been creating in Harriet was then their own portion" (361). Of this moment, Michael Kramp observes, "Austen often depicts Highbury as a microcosm of England, highlighting the disruption of its present, the nostalgia for the past, and the anxiety over its impending industrial future."[37] With no explicit comment on what the gypsies' presence or their begging indicates about the economic and social flux occurring in Highbury, the novel resolves the incident by the end of the chapter, when the gypsies, who "did not wait for the operations of justice" and "took themselves off in a hurry," leaving the "young ladies of Highbury" to walk "again in safety" (364). Kramp astutely observes that "the juxtaposition of Harriet to the gypsies helps expose a strong social desire to incorporate the former and the extant cultural fear of the latter."[38]

Perhaps tellingly, Emma's reaction to this incident almost perfectly mirrors her ruminations on the poor cottagers. Ignoring the range of implications (Harriet could have been harmed; Highbury is not supporting the most economically depressed people in its community), she turns her attentions instead to the possibility of a match between Harriet and Frank Churchill: "Could a linguist, could a grammarian, could even a mathematician have seen what she did, have witnessed their appearance together, and heard their history of it, without feeling that circumstances had been at work to make them peculiarly interesting to each other? . . . It seemed as if every thing united to promise the most interesting consequences" (362). Here, we again see Emma distancing herself from the broad, uncontrollable social issues that directly confront her by emphasizing the romantic schemes that she (incorrectly) believes that she can manage. Thus, while Emma encourages an element of change by imagining a connection between two people from disparate financial and social backgrounds, she simultaneously maintains the typical social order and represses a sustained confrontation with the unstoppable social, economic, and cultural changes occurring in Highbury. In other words, Emma refuses to see Harriet's tenuous financial circumstances, the references to Jane's need to work and the slave trade, and the poverty of the beggars as of a piece with broader economic shifts. Ruth Perry's insight that these incidents "reveal the deep contradictions of the Enlightenment itself" enables students to access and critique these tensions in Austen's own time as well as to think through how these confrontations mirror contemporary social injustices: "It was simultaneously an age of slavery and imperialist expansion; of wealth and poverty; of widening class division at home; of ancient lineages, great estates, and itinerant Gypsies; of expanding opportunities for educated men and continued dependence for educated women."[39]

The final scene of the novel further points to these contradictory social inequities and underscores the ironic distance between the romantic resolution of the novel and its unresolved class tensions. We learn in the last several paragraphs that the marriage between Emma and her dashing (if nearly age-inappropriate and cash-poor) neighbor Mr. Knightley, owner of the ancient Donwell Abbey, is expedited when Emma's father, fearful that his house will be burglarized after a spate of poultry thefts, demands Knightley's presence to protect the Woodhouse home and estate. In an unorthodox move, Austen tells us that "pilfering was *housebreaking* to Mr. Woodhouse's fears. — He was very uneasy; and but for the sense of his son-in-law's protection, would have been under wretched alarm every night of his life" (528). His only source of solace is Knightley's protection; and so Mr. Woodhouse, "with a much more voluntary, cheerful consent than his daughter had ever presumed to hope for" (528), permits Emma and Knightley to marry. Like that of the impoverished cottagers and the begging gypsies, the presence of poachers indicates the continuing economic inequalities of Highbury society; as a result of the increasing enclosure of property by the wealthy, fewer resources were available to non-landowning people.[40] No matter how diligently Mr. Knightley and Mr. Woodhouse send food to Mrs. and Miss Bates, no matter how frequently Emma offers soup to the poor cottagers or arrowroot to Jane Fairfax, these forms of charity provide only temporary relief that simply cannot address the fundamental causes of such structural and societal inequities. Nora, a student who was attuned to the short- and long-term impacts of community engagement activities, analyzed the novel and Emma's behavior in this way: "[Emma's] act of providing soup, perhaps a bit of money, and a compassionate ear have all the effect of making her feel good about herself, but very little lasting impact on the long-term health and prosperity of the family itself." Despite the many failures of Emma's encounters with people in and around the Highbury streets, students can also trace the initial steps that Emma takes to improve her standing in Highbury society, from her increased attention to Miss and Mrs. Bates to her attempts to loan Jane Fairfax her carriage.

To help students make connections among their service, readings, and their understanding of broad social inequalities and to foster dialogue among them, I created a two-part culminating project. The first part, a mock conference, asked students to work in groups of three to present the connections and challenges they found in uniting their Austen research (which involved traditional close-reading essay assignments, along with historical and archival research presentations related to references in the texts) with their service-learning work. Students were grouped based on their service site and their topics of interest: some wanted to discuss educational access, while others wanted to consider other forms of agency. The second part of the assignment asked students to write brief individual essays reflecting on their experience collaborating on their final presentation and on their work throughout the semester.

This final essay, composed after all other coursework was completed, allowed students to build on their reflection activities throughout the semester to see how their understanding of Austen and the street had developed. In her final reflection, Vanessa, who tutored at 826LA, demonstrated how combining service and research helped her understand Austen's novels and broader issues of social inequality: "In *Emma*, Emma's progression occurs based on her understanding of her social obligation to others. Hence the reader perceives her development from her initial, failed charitable attempt to perceiving Robert Martin as an educated man." For Vanessa, Emma's problem partly came down to exposure: she lacked experiential knowledge of others, an awareness that people from different backgrounds might be as intellectually and socially adept as she fancies herself to be. Vanessa continues, "In identifying [a lack of] education as a similar issue between the novels and contemporary society, it became evident that there is still progress to be made in ensuring educational access to all members of our community." In other words, Vanessa noted that both academic and experiential education were valuable to understanding the surrounding world.

Like Vanessa, Hannah Jorgenson, who worked with 18thConnect to correct digitized eighteenth-century documents and make them accessible for the visually impaired, also discovered a connection between academic work and the street beyond our classroom. She wrote that by considering Emma's character development through Musil's service spectrum, she began to reevaluate her understanding of Austen and her role in the academic community. Hannah, now a PhD candidate studying eighteenth- and nineteenth-century literature at the University of Minnesota, revised her original reflection essay to offer a new perspective nearly half a decade after her original experience.

Hannah Jorgenson

When I signed up for ENG495, the Austen service-learning course at CSU Northridge, I was mostly excited but a bit hesitant. I had always loved Jane Austen but was worried that studying her too closely would diminish the enjoyment I experienced while reading her novels. Additionally, I worried about finding time in my busy schedule to complete the community service requirement. However, over the course of the semester, my perspectives dramatically changed. Since taking this course, I have come to appreciate Austen in new and exciting ways. From working with 18thConnect myself to hearing about the many experiences of my classmates with organizations such as 826LA, I am amazed by the real-world, contemporary connections made with Austen's work. Since leaving CSU Northridge, I have become increasingly interested in the intersection of individual responsibility and civic duty. As I progress further in my academic career as a PhD candidate at the University of Minnesota, I often think back to this service-learning course and the texts we studied, and I contemplate my own responsibilities as an instructor and as a scholar of English literature. In particular, this course has influenced my dissertation work, and as I delve more deeply into the field of eighteenth-century studies, I am always seeking new ways to highlight the relevance of the important work we do in the humanities.

A particularly meaningful moment in this course occurred when we read *Emma*. This is perhaps my favorite of Austen's novels, and I was excited to read it again. I came into the class with a fondness for the titular Emma, and while she was frustrating at times, I always went back to loving her in a decidedly *non*academic manner. However, reading *Emma* in the context of this course changed my perspectives on both the character and the novel in fundamental and meaningful ways. Prior to rereading *Emma*, I read Caryn McTighe Musil's article, "Educating for Citizenship," in which she discussed six different types of civic engagement: exclusionary, oblivious, naive, charitable, reciprocal, and generative.[41] With this insightful work in mind, I reread Emma and actively focused on how civic engagement manifested in Austen's text. I began to look at the character of Emma more critically and spent time analyzing the structure of her community and her role within it, as well as how Emma dealt with the responsibility of being one of the community leaders, a position she was born into. As my engagement with the text increased, I began to see things that I had never noticed, and my understanding of *Emma* evolved.

I soon realized that Emma, though she provides assistance to people within her community, such as when she visits the home of the poor cottager, she largely practices a form of civic engagement that, on Musil's scale, would be called "naive." Musil states, "The naive face of citizenship is characterized not by civic detachment but by civic amnesia. While the community is seen as a resource to engage, the lack of historical knowledge about its residents or an analysis of its power dynamics limits the learning and the benefits of the experience."[42] While Emma does in fact aid the family, she doesn't fully engage with them and is unable to see outside of herself. She is unable to see them as individuals, nor does she fully understand their situation within the community, and consequently they immediately leave her mind when she leaves their home. Furthermore, Emma deems them worthy of assistance only to the extent that they fit into the narrative *she* has created for herself about her world.

Watching the moves Emma makes through the lens of civic engagement as outlined in Musil's article made me reconsider not only how I read Austen but also how I engage with my own community, especially my academic community. I often thought only about what I personally gained from college English courses and my own research and how the discipline fit in my own personal narrative, much like Emma and her engagement with her community. However, after working with 18thConnect to fulfill the community service portion of this course, I was forced to reconsider my position as a would-be scholar of eighteenth-century English literature. Being able to see myself through *Emma* in this critical way allowed me to realize that I had a larger imperative to fully engage with the academic community I wanted to belong to.

With 18thConnect I performed online OCR editing of scanned eighteenth-century texts. As a nontraditional student with a full-time job outside of school, being able to perform community service in the middle of the night and on weekends was crucial to my success in this course. Meanwhile, many of my classmates were out in the "real world" working with organizations like 826LA. I was grateful to have such a flexible option, but not traveling to a service site made me consider whether what I was doing truly qualified as a community service. I often felt that I was just sitting at home in my pajamas playing on the internet and that my classmates were doing the real work. However, the more I thought about Musil's article and the more I thought about what kind of scholar I wanted to be, I realized that the work I did with 18thConnect was important in its own right. While my editing could end up being an "exclusionary" form of service and I could work on just the texts I cared about, I wanted it to be more than that. I found great satisfaction knowing that the work I was doing would eventually make eighteenth-century literature more available to people without access to universities and expensive databases.

I was proud to contribute to 18thConnect, whose aims are so closely aligned to my own—making the humanities, and eighteenth-century literature specifically, accessible and usable for a larger population. Beyond the classroom, the work I did with 18thConnect became a bridge between me and others who previously didn't really understand why I want to study eighteenth-century literature. The conservation and accessibility goals of 18thConnect speak to larger social concerns than just those of academics. Other people that I spoke to not only understood the imperative to preserve and share these often obscure and rare texts but also why they are important to our culture. Through working with 18thConnect, I was able to see a point of engagement not only for myself within the discipline but also for those who are unsure of the place that the humanities do and should occupy in our society.

Now, as a graduate student at the University of Minnesota, I see the impact of this course still. In particular, this course has influenced my dissertation, in which I hope to trace the development of modern conceptions of consent, specifically as they pertain to the lives of women in the Enlightenment period. The topic of consent is particularly relevant in the twenty-first century, when what it means to give consent is a frequent topic of political and social debate. The

Jane Austen service-learning course showed me how the study of eighteenth-century literature can facilitate important discussions about the present. Through exploring the past, the work we do in English and other fields in the humanities is both important and relevant today. This course gave me the skills and the language with which to articulate why I chose to pursue a PhD in English to my sometimes skeptical relatives, and it is a course I will always look back to for renewed inspiration.

Reimagining the Eighteenth-Century Street

As readers, as teachers, as students — as *fans* — of Austen, we too can re-consider the connections that we make between the reading we do in our own homes and the reading we do in the street. Looking forward, we might use the following methods to integrate civic engagement and intercultural inquiry activities into our work on Austen, whether or not we can include semester-long service-learning activities in our classes. To start, we can direct our students' attention to passages that exemplify Austen's depiction of the relationship between the individual and society: how Colonel Brandon, Darcy, and Knightley are defined as gentlemen in part by performing acts that sustain their communities; how Anne Elliot's behavior toward the tenant farmers of Kellynch Hall contrasts with her father's obliviousness to his obligations; and how Mrs. Norris's and Lady Denham's acts of charity fail to work in *Mansfield Park* and *Sanditon*. We can also incorporate elements of community building by asking students to respond rigorously to one another's work through online discussion-board posts or in-class writing workshops that promote a sense of shared intellectual responsibility among classmates. Likewise, along with assigning traditional essays, teachers might facilitate a variety of forums that would allow students to share their research with one another and those beyond the classroom community. These assignments might include online blogging as well as conference-style presentations. Beyond the bounds of the classroom, there are important opportunities for engaging new readers of Austen and involving students in intergenerational dialogue about the books, as Bridget will discuss in more detail in chapter 2.

Along with these activities, we might also find more ways of incorporating service-integrated activities in our courses. Regardless of the specific site, forging meaningful partnerships with local agencies is key for a positive experience; individual people can start this process by becoming active at community organizations themselves and by reaching out to campus community outreach offices to seek out recommendations. Some teachers may find it useful to send students out into the street to tutor or to work in soup kitchens and homeless shelters. Others may invite the street to the campus, perhaps staging screenings and discussion of film adaptations of Austen's novels for senior citizens or creating workshops that invite local community members to adapt sections of Austen's novels for performance on campus. In so doing, we can help students understand how their particular position *as* students and their access to particular kinds of places (the campus, its libraries, its classrooms) has important implications for their own intellectual and everyday work. Underpinning all of these activities, we should ask our students to see how Austen's plots are informed by power dynamics that cut across gender, race, and class lines. As teachers begin to take Austen to the street—and bring the street into discussions of Austen—more conversations will emerge about how her novels remain relevant to the imaginative spaces and actual places within and beyond the classroom and campus.

With these ideas in mind and with these intellectual and practical tools at hand, we might redefine the collective cultural images of Austen and eighteenth-century studies themselves. I can think of no better way to underscore this point than ending this chapter by highlighting the innovative work of three scholars—Devoney Looser, Susan Celia Greenfield, and Elizabeth K. Goodhue—who offer three distinctive approaches to reinvigorating Austen's image with the public in mind.

JANE AUSTEN'S TALKING HEAD

Devoney Looser

Remember in 2014 when guys in clown suits were running around, trying to scare people and committing crimes? A scholar-friend of mine, Andrew McConnell Stott, had written a brilliant biography of a famous, pioneering nineteenth-century British clown. After twenty-first-century clowns started terrorizing American towns, he got to discuss the phenomenon with CNN, answering the questions, "Why scary clowns? Why now?"[43] Naturally, he took the long view. Although he hadn't exactly set out to become a scary clown commentator, he was ready when opportunity knocked. I admire that.

I had an inkling that opportunity might knock for me, as a scholar of Jane Austen (1775–1817) in 2017. With the bicentenary of her death, Austen's face was put on the ten pound note. Her novels were once again au courant. I elbowed my way into the news cycle because I'd just published a book, *The Making of Jane Austen*. It caught the attention of *Publishers Weekly* and was reviewed in the *New York Times Book Review* and the *Wall Street Journal*.[44] I published short pieces on Austen's reputation and celebrity in the *New York Times*, the *Atlantic*, the TLS, and *Salon*.[45] I talked Austen on the radio on three continents. Then, on the day itself, July 18, I was asked to be a talking head on CNN.[46] Jane Austen was, for a brief window of time, international news. I'm still pinching myself that I got to be a part of it.

That level of exposure may sound like a lot of good luck — for Austen and for those who study her — and it certainly was. But it's important, too, that people who speak about the eighteenth century to wider publics try to demystify how such opportunities come about. You can't exactly plan for them, of course, but I not only wanted these things to happen, I *worked* for them to happen. I set out to try to bring my passion for connecting Austen, then and now, outside the classroom and beyond the book, to thousands or even millions of readers, listeners, and viewers who might never have given Austen a thought. Making that transition meant reimagining what I was capable of. I needed to reinvent myself, not so much as a teacher or a scholar but as an engaging ambassador of the past, often in media that were new to me. I couldn't rely on my old skill sets.

My Austen-infused public outreach efforts were made possible by years of preparation and training and a lot of support. People who run marathons think nothing of working up to the goal in very disciplined, measured smaller steps over long periods of time. I don't run marathons, but I tried to break down the work of attempting to reach new, larger audiences into parts. My Austen odyssey began when I did the math backward several years from the anniversary of Austen's death to see if I might be able to complete a years-long book project in time to reach print at the most opportune moment. Starting that project at all involved listening to the advice of a visionary editor who challenged me to write for readers beyond academe. Then I visited and contacted librarians and libraries and sifted through previously untapped materials about how Austen was illustrated, dramatized, politicized, and schooled in the decades and centuries after her death. As I gave those stories a new shape, I tried to work some humor into my prose, because shouldn't material about Austen try to be a little bit funny?

Once the book was in press, I made myself the understudy of publicists and marketing representatives. I tried to learn that side of the book business, which I had long thought of as "their" side but realized I'd better start seeing as "my" side, too. My savvy publicist told me that the number one factor in a book's success is the author's involvement. It hit me like a lightning bolt in a Gothic novel. My Austen ideas weren't going to sell themselves. I was the chief huckster in charge. Fortunately, I believed in my product! I tried to be both amusing and informative. I wanted to emulate Austen's novels that way, so that you're learning almost without realizing that it's happening to you. I contacted newspaper and magazine editors, months in advance of the bicentenary, to pitch short op-eds and essays on Austen. (This was after years of learning how to pitch and write for public audiences. I wish I'd known earlier about the resources of the OpEd Project, which Susan Celia Greenfield discusses in her essay.) I carved out as much time as I could after my day job to devote to publicity and outreach. As part of the day job, I asked for help from my university. They gave it. I wrote the script for my three-minute video book trailer, but an Arizona State University office of research produced it.

This was no time for modesty or hanging back. I ignored my inner Fanny Price from *Mansfield Park* and boldly asked people for things, as directly and graciously as I could. As a valued colleague put it to me, a writer with a forthcoming book should just throw some darts, publicity-wise, every day to see if anything hits the board. I requested training from my university's media relations staff. I sat behind a camera and practiced short, digestible answers, echoing the tone and affect of the questioner. I studied the tape and tried to put the media people's advice to work. I deepened my professional use of social media. I scoured author websites and created one for my book.[47] I put audio and video clips of me talking about Austen on my websites (makingjaneausten.com and Devoney.com), so that I'd be findable by radio and news producers who wanted to vet me quickly for suitability as a talking head. When CNN contacted me, it was incredibly good luck, but it was no accident. The number of Austen scholars who had made easily findable audio and video clips of themselves turned out to be surprisingly small.

I've now been asked "why Austen?" dozens of times. I continue to refine my answer, and I can't imagine the question ever getting stale. I believe Austen and her fiction are still with us because her era's revolutions echo in ours. Her novels show, in moving scenes of everyday life, the influence of political revolutions (movements for fraternity, equality, liberty, the abolition of slavery), the industrial revolution (the shift from rural to urban life, the spread of colonialism), and what's sometimes called the longest revolution (women's rights). But the word "revolution" then meant more than political upheaval. It meant turning or revolving, and according to the *Oxford English Dictionary*, consideration or reflection. Revolution was also "the action or an act of turning over in the mind or in discussion; consideration, reflection; discussion, debate." These are Austenian bywords.

Austen's novels weren't advocating for overthrowing institutions or systems. But in the most wide-ranging sense, she was, I think, an eighteenth-century revolutionary. She was exploring how to effect change, how to turn, and how to reflect in a time of turmoil. Whether or not we consider ourselves revolutionaries — in the word's narrower or widest sense — those of us who know and care deeply about this period must reflect on how we too might reach new audiences, whether just beyond or well beyond our immediate, customary ones. Then we should encourage and mentor the next generation to see the possibilities and benefits of public humanities. Jane Austen wrote to her beloved niece about the challenges of finding time to write a letter, "I can command very little quiet time at present; but yet I must begin." We must begin. You must begin.

Susan Celia Greenfield

It was the fall of 2011, and I was feeling sorry for myself. A scholarly project on which I had worked for more years than I care to admit was floundering. The short fiction I had secretly written for decades was being roundly rejected from literary journals. From the sidelines, I watched my friends and colleagues complete scholarly and creative projects I envied and get promotions I might never achieve.

And then, out of nowhere, I received an unexpected boon. Along with roughly twenty other mostly female faculty members at Fordham University, where I teach, I was offered a Public Voices Fellowship with the OpEd Project. An organization whose mission is to "increase the range of voices and quality of ideas we hear in the world," the OpEd Project "scout[s] and train[s] under-represented experts (especially women)" to begin sharing their knowledge in the popular media.[48]

At the first Public Voices Fellowship meeting, Katie Orenstein, the founder and director of the OpEd Project, invited everyone to name their area of expertise. One woman described studying nonsuicidal self-injury in adolescents. Another was finishing a book-length theological and scientific analysis of the global freshwater crisis. Someone was doing research on HIV, another on American politics with a particular focus on black ethnic politics, a third was writing a feminist history of working mothers. Everyone's work had some obvious socioeconomic, political, and in some cases global significance. Meanwhile, what was my area of expertise? The early English novel, especially novels by women, and above all the works of Jane Austen. Of what larger significance was that?

Nevertheless, I announced my specialty with what I hoped was sheepish good humor and wondered if my fellowship would be rescinded. Instead, along with everyone else I was taught and encouraged to begin writing a standard 800-word op-ed. Almost immediately I loved the genre, partly because it was a welcome relief from my academic writing, partly because it offered the possibility of reaching a wider reading audience, and above all because it invited me to develop in writing the kind of entertaining, informative, and ideally intellectually inspiring voice I had spent years honing as a teacher — a voice that in itself was a kind of expertise. In an op-ed I could write the way I spoke in the classroom and perform that persona on a larger stage.

With fresh appreciation I realized that training students in the skill of textual interpretation is never simply about a particular work of literature. It is about teaching them to recognize the various permutations of linguistic representation, to read beneath the surface of literal meaning, to recognize the ironies, inconsistencies, and powers of persuasion and misdirection of words. The student who learns to read literature carefully can also begin to think critically about what contemporary politicians say, or how popular movies sell normative behaviors, or how different demographic, racial, and gendered groups are depicted in the media.

By the spring of 2012 I had published a few fledgling op-eds, each of which used a work of early modern literature to interpret the rhetorical and historical implications of a recent event. A piece called "Consent and Conception," for instance, addressed what was then a hot story: Representative Todd Akin's assertion that abortion should not be permitted in the case of rape, because, as he put it, a "legitimate rape" does not result in pregnancy (that is, if an impregnated woman says she was raped, she must be lying).[49] The claim, I noted, echoed the widespread early modern belief that pregnancy can occur only if a woman has an orgasm, which was seen as a signal of consent. It is in part because a woman's pregnancy could legally disprove a charge of rape that, in Samuel Richardson's sensationally popular novel *Clarissa* (1747–1748), the antihero hopes the eponymous heroine he has raped is now pregnant. Whether she is or not is never clarified. Instead, knowing that regardless of her physical status the law will disregard her right to justice, Clarissa declares her sovereignty over her own body by starving herself to death. If congressional opponents of reproductive rights like Todd Akin had their way, I suggested, American women would be left with a comparable lack of choices.

By the following fall, I had secured a permanent blog platform on the *Huffington Post*. That semester I was teaching an undergraduate course called Jane Austen in Context. At the same time, the 2012 presidential contest between Barack Obama and Mitt Romney was in full swing. I decided to set myself a challenge. Each week I would use the Austen novel my class was discussing as a springboard to blog about the election or another current event. From a personal perspective, I wanted to develop my op-ed voice under the pressure of a deadline. More publicly, I had several goals: I wanted to bring my expertise on Austen to a wider audience. Popular culture so often featured her as the consummate romance writer, pumping out page-turning affirmations of heterosexual happiness. Like countless Austen scholars I wanted to detonate this stereotype and highlight her narrative brilliance, wit, and ideological complexity. I also wanted to use Austen to guide readers in the basic art of literary interpretation. And I wanted to draw on the presidential election to prove the broad-based political relevance and power of literary critical analysis.

That I would be doing all this from a progressive perspective was something I announced in the first column of a series I called "The Jane Austen Weekly." "In the next few months," I wrote, "as the presidential election approaches, occurs, and recedes, my class will be reading all of Austen's major novels. I'll be writing a weekly column about that overlap and about other current events and concerns. My own political views are (prepare to be shocked) very liberal."[50]

For that week's column, called "*Northanger Abbey* and the Presidential Election," I compared Obama's and Romney's competing truth claims to the linguistic ambiguity that mystifies Catherine Morland when she arrives in Bath. In one instance, when she and John Thorpe take a carriage ride with Catherine's brother James and Isabella Thorpe following behind, Thorpe attempts to elevate the status of his own carriage by denigrating James's as falling apart. When Catherine expresses alarm at the danger to her brother and Isabella and demands that they turn back, Thorpe asserts that James's carriage "will last above twenty years." A hopeless literalist, Catherine does not understand how to "reconcile two such very different accounts of the same thing."[51] The challenge for Catherine, I wrote, "is to sift among the verbiage [in her society] and know how to think beyond it. Sounds like the task facing the current electorate." My conclusion—that Catherine succeeds in doing this when she recognizes the duplicity of General Tilney and that Americans needed to recognize the same about Mitt Romney—earned me a stinging attack in the comments section of the blog post. I was accused of cheapening Austen by politicizing her and of other things that I don't care to remember.

That was the first night I didn't sleep because of my public writing—but by no means the last. Each time before my weekly column was due (a deadline, I might add, that was entirely self-imposed), I pulled an all-nighter. Week after week, the same ritual occurred. At some point between two and five in the morning, my husband would appear bleary eyed in the doorway of my so-called study (the bedroom of my daughter, who was away at college) and say, "What, are you still up? This is crazy!" My cat would pace in circles, meowing pitifully at my abject neglect of him. I would not respond, would not get up—no bathroom, no food or water, no staring out the window at the lonely souls on the Manhattan street—until the article was finished and posted. By the time the semester was over, I had written twelve columns with titles such as "*Sense and Sensibility* and the Occupy Anniversary," "Mitt Romney is No Mr. Darcy," and "Child Poverty in *Mansfield Park*."[52] I had written about the technical richness of irony and Austen's magnificent and morally complex use of it. I had described the art and psychological (and even neurological) implications of her deployment of free indirect discourse. I wrote about the brutal coercion of gratitude in *Emma* and about the emotional hollows and lyricism of grief in *Persuasion*. If "likes" on my *Huffington Post* blog and Facebook page were any indication, I had gathered a following of a few hundred readers. *New York Times* columnist Maureen Dowd I was not. But compared to the readership of scholarly articles, this number seemed massive.

From 2012 to 2014 I wrote a number of other articles, mostly but not exclusively on Austen, for other online outlets.[53] Throughout this time, I was also running memoir-writing workshops for homeless and formerly homeless individuals participating in a New York City life skills program.[54] I have always had a kind of addictive (one might say nosy) desire to know people's life stories; indeed, this craving led to my love of novels and my decision to study their so-called rise in the eighteenth century. Running these writing workshops, like my op-ed experience, showed me that I could put my professional skills to a broader social use. As a result, I undertook a project I doubt I would have ever considered before developing a public voice. I began interviewing formerly homeless people from the program for an edited book of their life stories published by Fordham University Press.

Since 2014 much of my writing life has been consumed with this project (and with my secret fiction writing), but by August 2017 I felt compelled to produce another op-ed about Jane Austen. At the time, the entire world (and I mean *world*!) was exploding with celebrations of her bicentenary. Meanwhile, in America, Republican senators had just failed to repeal the Affordable Care Act (ACA). As I wrote in my op-ed for *BLARB*, the blog of the *Los Angeles Review of Books*, probably few people saw any connection between these subjects. "But for an Austen scholar like me there was an eerie overlap. Despite the festivities and media hoopla surrounding it, Austen's bicentenary marked the anniversary of her death. Her novels satirize people who do not care about other people's lives. At the end of July [when Republicans were trying to kill the ACA], the same seemed true of too many Senate Republicans."[55]

The op-ed outlined the many ways Republican efforts to repeal the ACA seemed to ignore the millions of people, especially low-income and marginalized people, who would be at greater risk of illness and death without it. I compared the repeal vote to the moments in every single Austen novel when she skewers characters that "do not care about the well-being of their dependents. In Austen's novels such inhumanity is common in a society based on socioeconomic advancement and self-interest."[56] The same inhumanity, I implied, was driving Republican attacks on the ACA.

I ended the article with guarded optimism. The attempt to repeal the ACA had failed, thanks to Republican Senator John McCain. Though suffering from brain cancer, McCain took to the Senate floor and in an act of heroism worthy of Mr. Darcy, voted against the measure and declared the importance of preserving the "liberty and justice" of an American political system designed to mitigate the corruptibility of "human nature."[57]

Back then, I had some hope that maybe this country could preserve its democratic ideals despite the catastrophe of the current administration. As I sit here months later, I am less sanguine than ever, forced to agree with what Elizabeth Bennet tells her sister Jane:

"The more I see of the world, the more am I dissatisfied with it" —
indeed, I would have to add horrified.[58] But that dissatisfaction need
not be our only recourse. Now, more than ever, we need to have
public voices.

PUTTING LITERARY HISTORY TO WORK

Elizabeth K. Goodhue

For several years, I have collaborated with Los Angeles schools
and educational nonprofits to offer a community-engaged course
on children's literature and childhood literacy for undergraduate
students at UCLA. The reading list for the course stretches across
more than two centuries — back to the earliest days of printing and
marketing books specifically for young readers (often dated to John
Newbery's publication of *A Little Pretty Pocket-Book* in London in
1744) and forward to encompass a wide range of popular and lesser-
known titles from the twentieth and twenty-first centuries (including
several texts honored with the American Library Association medal
that bears Newbery's name to this day). While my undergraduate
students study the history and future of children's literature on
campus, they also examine past and present trends in literacy
education and work to support literacy in Los Angeles by reading
with preschoolers and K–12 students each week. Collaborating
with local teachers, librarians, and education activists allows my
undergraduate students to gain a richer understanding of how
publishing and reading practices evolve over time — which is to
say, they gain a richer understanding of literary history. But above
and beyond that, the students also put their growing knowledge of
literary history to work to help local leaders address educational
achievement gaps and cultivate culturally responsive learning
environments. These reciprocal academic and community benefits
keep me coming back to engaged teaching and research year after
year, and they keep UCLA students and community partners engaged
as well.

Admittedly, although community-engaged teaching offers
substantial benefits for all stakeholders — students, faculty, and
community partners — the pedagogy can also bring significant

challenges. All too often, those of us who teach historical literature already find ourselves facing real and imagined pressures to justify the relevance of our fields to contemporary college students and their parents, and these demands can intensify when we attempt to articulate the value that literary history can bring to wider publics beyond campus.

While at least some college students and their parents may be persuaded by common claims that the liberal arts, including classic historical literature, should be valued for their own sake, many of the K–12 students that my undergraduates tutor and the schools and nonprofits that serve them have much less philosophical and far more practical goals at the forefront. Many of the students we work with are the first in their families to attend US schools, and a large portion are learning English as a second language or have parents and caregivers who work long hours to make ends meet. Introducing these students and families to classic works of eighteenth-century British literature might stand a slim chance of increasing their cultural capital in the United States, but research suggests such stakeholders benefit at least as much if not more — in both the short and long term — from programs that affirm and enrich the cultural wealth that is *already* present in their communities.[59] Because I recognize this, as do my community partners, the undergraduates in my class rarely (if ever) read the eighteenth-century texts we study in class with the children they tutor. Instead, they support classroom and after-school activities that our community partners have identified as best suited to helping their young learners thrive in the twenty-first century.

As Bridget's discussion of exhibits at Iowa City's Old Capitol Museum in chapter 3 so aptly demonstrates, bringing literary history directly into public venues tends to work best when such partnerships are designed with the assets and interests of community stakeholders at the forefront. But through public humanities pedagogy, the practice of literary history can inform and enrich community partnerships in indirect ways as well as direct ones. In my children's literature course, for instance, undergraduates study how eighteenth-century booksellers like Newbery used toys and play to market books to young readers, and this historical context helps the students appreciate and critically analyze trends they observe in their contemporary community, such as the predilection many young readers exhibit for books that tie into movie franchises and video games. In a similar vein, while the gruesome fates of stepmothers and stepsisters in eighteenth- and nineteenth-century fairy tales are not common fare in local first-grade classrooms, my college students can and do learn a great deal from reading modern adaptations with younger students and then comparing those retellings to the historical texts from our syllabus.

In the limited space I have here, I'd like to offer a more extended example of how community-engaged approaches to teaching literary history can enhance undergraduate learning while simultaneously supporting the work of K–12 schools and educational nonprofits. This case study centers around the first full-length novel that undergraduates read in my children's literature course: *The Governess; Or, The Little Female Academy*, published by Sarah Fielding in 1749. Often touted as the first fully realized novel for young readers, *The Governess* centers around a small boarding school where young girls spend much of their time reading and discussing various interpolated fairy tales and other texts. Fielding's preface highlights "the true use of Reading" as a key theme of the novel and goes on to define that utility as "to make [the reader] wiser and better."[60]

In the world of Fielding's novel, advancing the disciplinary and moral education of children requires careful supervision by their adult governess, who oversees the selection of texts and stresses that the girls are free to read "any Stories to amuse [them], provided [they] read them with the disposition not to be hurt by them" and focus on the morals they can draw out from "even the most trifling Things."[61] My undergraduate students are often quick to note that adults still curate much of what children read in the twenty-first century—and even though the stories available today tend to be less overtly moralizing than the texts available to Fielding's schoolgirls, debates still rage around what sorts of content are suitable for readers of different ages. Learning about the long history of adults regulating the publication and dissemination of literature for children helps my undergraduates understand just how much is at stake when they help a child choose what to read.

What criteria should one use to determine which books children read, for instance? Should the same criteria apply universally for all children in all settings? Fielding's governess presents these questions as if their answers are straightforward, but the issues at stake quickly prove far more complex when my students begin examining reports by the American Library Association (ALA) of recent efforts to ban children's books from circulation. Together we learn that it is not just the modern equivalent of Fielding's "trifling" fairy tales — such as comic books — that face frequent challenges. Indeed, the ALA's Office of Intellectual Freedom has found that a disproportionate number of banned and challenged books are "by or about people of color, LGBT people and/or people with disabilities."[62] Exploring this more recent — and troubling — history of adults attempting to restrict access to books they deem unsuitable for children helps my students recognize that there are *also* ethical and political implications in the moralizing impulse that guides how Fielding's governess regulates the "trifling" stories available to the girls attending her school. Moreover, connecting past and present reading trends makes my students more aware of how their own histories and values not only shape their personal reading choices, but also inform — and potentially limit — how they interact with younger readers who have their own specific cultural backgrounds. These issues are deeply connected to questions raised by many essays in this collection, perhaps most notably Danielle's discussion of the savior complex.

The community organizations that partner with my class are acutely aware of how important it is for *all* young children to have access to books that reflect the diverse range of identities, experiences, and family structures that abound in the twenty-first century, and my students benefit greatly from talking with community leaders about these issues.[63] But our partners also often struggle to build and maintain book collections that are in keeping with their values and reflect the diversity of their constituencies. These struggles stem from a wide range of causes, including (but by no means limited to) lack of staff time to research new titles and insufficient funds to purchase materials that could help update library collections.

I close by noting that public humanities pedagogy has allowed my undergraduates to assist our partners with the goal of diversifying collections through both service and research. During tutoring sessions, my students have been able to supplement onsite collections by bringing diverse texts with them to read with younger students, and in their final research projects for the class, they have been able to dedicate the time our partners often do not have to research best practices for curating collections and identifying book titles that could be worth acquiring when funds become available. In future iterations of this course, I hope to put my undergraduates to work researching grant opportunities or writing proposals to donors who may be interested in funding efforts to diversify the libraries at our partner agencies. By incorporating these sorts of projects as part of the graded work for my course, I am able to offer our community partners an opportunity to shape the aims of academic research, and at the same time, these public humanities projects help my undergraduates see that their knowledge of literary history can have tangible impacts in the present and future.

2: THE LIBRARY
𝕬𝕾 𝕾𝕬

Productive Failure and Politicizing Silence

in Community Reading Groups

BRIDGET DRAXLER

Libraries were my first love. I was not only the introspective child of a librarian, but I was also the child of a librarian who worked for a books-by-mail program at a closed-stacks county library. This wasn't a community gathering place. There were no story times, no evening classes, no public restrooms. It was an almost parodic exaggeration of the quiet, solitary space of the library. It was, for an awkward bookish kid, more than anything a place to hide. And I did, for hours at a time, reading the Baby-sitter's Club and the Boxcar Children books. At the time, books and libraries were synonymous with solitude.

Later in college, the solitude of the library was what initially drew me to study literature. But at the same time, I started noticing that talking about books with my classmates and professors became almost as delightful as reading the books themselves. It turned out that I liked people, much to my own surprise. I found that literature could be a way to connect as well as a way to escape, and before I knew it, I found myself quite contentedly in the midst of a community of scholars. When I chose the University of Iowa for graduate school, it was largely because of the cohesive sense of community among the graduate students in the English department. That sense of community became not only intellectually nourishing but a professional priority for me.

As I found my footing as a public scholar halfway through graduate school, the quiet and solitude of a library became a symbol of what I was working against—the shell I was outgrowing. I was in awe of other graduate students who were empowering victims of domestic abuse through art and fighting cancer by demystifying the early screening process. In these circles, I was somewhat embarrassed to introduce myself as a student of eighteenth-century literature; it felt small, quaint. I had always believed that teaching literature was meaningful and empowering, but I started to feel that it wasn't enough. When I landed a tenure-track job that was more

[65]

focused on writing than literature, I decided to let go of my work in historical literature so that I could tackle "real" problems in my new community. (If that last sentence is giving you the sense that this paragraph is an epic setup to an epic disaster, you are right.)

Soon after arriving in my new home, I befriended Susan Twomey, the director of the town's community arts center. After closing a successful Smithsonian exhibit titled Journey Stories, she was collaborating with community and college partners to develop an exhibit on movement and migration between Mexico and our community, which has had a large Latinx population in town for generations. She had just received a $5,000 grant from the Illinois Humanities Council, and there was broad community interest and support. It was an exciting and meaningful project, and just the kind of thing that I wanted to be involved with. One of the partners who had planned to provide the research wasn't following through, so I saw my chance; I quickly volunteered to integrate local research into my syllabus for an interdisciplinary writing course I would be teaching the next semester. I thought it would be a great opportunity for the exhibit planning group to get the local research they needed and the students to do meaningful research and writing.

We planned to have the students interview, collect objects from, and write biographies of Latinx community members: artists, small business owners, and community volunteers who would share their arts, culture, and stories with the broader community. Susan had already established connections with Latinos Unidos, a local Latinx activist group, and we worked hard to let this group control the narrative. As artifact donations started coming in, we had long conversations about making sure our choices didn't exoticize, exaggerate, or erase difference. We found ourselves grappling with how to publicly acknowledge individuals whose documentation status was unclear. We wanted so badly to celebrate our community's rich diversity while recognizing the complexities and challenges that immigrants face carving a space in a rural midwestern town. But this nuance was a lot to handle for twenty undergraduate students in a general education course who had never done original research, had never taken a civic engagement course, had little or no experience with immigrant communities, and lacked the time, disciplinary knowledge, skills, and interest to do their best work. I was so earnest! I was so optimistic! I was so clumsy!

In the end, despite significant hours of effort on the part of community members, staff, and students, the exhibit never opened. I am telling you this story that I would rather forget because I think we can all learn as much from mistakes as successes, and I want productive failure to be part of the discourse of the humanities. There are important generative ideas that come out of things that don't go right. For the collaborators, this failure taught us, among other things, that there is no single Latinx community in our town, and there is no common immigrant experience, no tidy story to tell, even within a handful of families with long histories in the same small town. For myself, I learned the limits of what I can expect undergraduate students to do, and I learned to recognize my own white privilege shrouded in good intentions.

I wanted to be the kind of public scholar who could tackle issues of race and racism, who could create an exhibit that would be the site of sustained dialogue in a community on the issues of power and prejudice that fracture it. My interest and investment in the project weren't even really about the exhibit; they were about the people, the process, and the conversations I imagined we would have as a community. There were some important connections made and conversations held as part of the planning process that had a positive long-term impact, especially among the Latinx participants. There was a general sense of goodwill and best intentions among those of us left at the end. But there was also a lot of disappointment and, in some cases, as Susan notes in her essay for this chapter, deep distrust sown among other members of the campus and community. For myself, I don't think I caused any lasting harm, but if I'm honest, I'm not sure I did any lasting good either.

Creating a sustained dialogue on complicated issues like race, class, and gender is really beautiful, important work, but as I learned, it's also difficult work. I started asking myself questions: How do you find spaces where members of the campus and community can meet on common ground? How do you moderate a conversation that is respectful of individuals' stories while moving beyond anecdote? How do you respond to contributors who are racist, sexist, or xenophobic, especially if they are unaware of it? How do you get participants to talk to one another rather than just the moderator? And most of all, how do you make everyone feel welcome to attend and participate — even, or especially, those who don't feel comfortable having these conversations?

That last question is a particularly sticky one. When I've attended events to promote civic dialogue on the wage gap or the Qu'ran, the self-selected participants are often a homogenous group of advocates who are invested in the topic, know a fair bit about it, and tend to agree with one another. The choice to attend an event that asks participants to grapple with social injustice narrows the pool of participants dramatically. Civic dialogue can easily turn into the choir preaching to itself.

The more I thought about these questions, the more I realized that these are the same issues I grapple with in a literature classroom: finding common ground, moving beyond anecdote, and getting all students — more than the half-dozen regular speakers — to talk with one another rather than to me. I didn't need to run away from the safety of books and the safety of libraries to tackle "real" problems. I didn't have to try to be something else or someone else. My background in teaching literary history could be an asset here.

More importantly, in terms of the problem of self-selection, historical literature could be something of a Trojan horse. The presumed safety of books and libraries is what makes them uniquely positioned to draw unlikely participants into important community conversations about social justice. Instead of separating my identities — public scholar on one hand, literary historian on another — I needed to start thinking of myself as a public scholar in literary history.

As Danielle discusses in chapter 1, at face value Jane Austen's novels seem like the last place to turn for conversations about social justice. They chronicle the lives of privileged white women who always get married off in fairy-tale endings. Right? Supposedly timeless novels like Austen's can reinforce the oppression of women, minorities, LGBTQ+ people, and those with disabilities, partly by normalizing oppression within a historical moment and partly by erasing unprivileged groups from history altogether. The literary canon and Austen in particular are part of the problem.

But Austen can also be part of the solution. In fact, among audiences most uncomfortable with conversations about race, class, ethnicity, ability, and sexuality and sexual identity, the seeming politeness of Austen can make these topics feel safer — safer because of both the historical and geographical distance and the subtlety of her writing. In so doing, we must remain mindful of presentism; allowing modern-day perspectives to collide with eighteenth-century literature and culture and mapping contemporary perspectives on diversity onto these texts can raise ethical concerns about how this process is reductive of both past and present. At the same time, issues of presentism introduce the generative *imperfections* of the comparison. In fact, exploring a cultural setting that is different from our own can allow us to engage in intercultural inquiry on the sly, taking an outside perspective on our own cultural context. Reading Austen can draw in participants who would never attend a civic dialogue on issues of systematic oppression to engage in exactly these sorts of conversations, because reading Austen in a group outside of the classroom is usually called something else. It's usually called a book club.

I got the idea of a Jane Austen reading group early in my career. As part of a general education literature class, I required students to participate in (not just attend) a community event related to literature. Some students volunteered to pass out programs at a theater production; others went to a book reading and asked the author a question during the question and answer period afterward. A handful tagged along with me to a series of conversations I was leading about Austen and her contemporaries at the local public library; we read short excerpts from Austen alongside pieces from writers like Margaret Cavendish and Mary Wollstonecraft. The intergenerational conversations between my students and the mostly retired attendees were a highlight on both sides.

Over the course of the next decade, I developed variations on this reading group project in which the students were facilitators rather than participants. The basic formula (described in more detail shortly) was to have small groups of students research an Austen novel, develop contextual materials and discussion questions for general readers, and then lead a series of community conversations about the book. The polite veneer of a Jane Austen book club, with all the tea and trappings, became a covert way to have meaningful dialogue about privilege, oppression, and human dignity.

The seeming politeness of Austen, as many enthusiasts know, is a myth. Austen was a brutal satirist who was astute, pointed, and political in her criticisms. And in her own way, she opened space for her readers to confront oppressive systems in Great Britain and its empire, from slavery to the British class system to women's rights. The Bertrams' wealth in *Mansfield Park* was earned through the slave trade in Antigua; the standing army of heartthrob soldiers in *Pride and Prejudice*'s rural setting signals the constant fear of imminent conflict with revolutionary and Napoleonic France; Austen talks openly in the early pages of *Sense and Sensibility* about death and, worse yet, money. I have heard Austen described in scholarly contexts as a rebel, a radical, a revolutionary, a protofeminist, and, reverently, a bitch. (May I add "nasty woman" to the list?)

This myth of Austen's politeness can be traced to a particular biography, the 1870 *Memoir* of "dear Aunt Jane" written by her nephew, James Edward Austen-Leigh.[1] While this family-approved biography regrettably framed Austen as a saintly maiden authoress, the daughter of a clergyman who wrote well-mannered, moral novels that were appropriate even for Victorian ladies, it also recovered Austen from relative obscurity and delivered her to a broad and devoted public readership that has been sustained for a hundred fifty years. It's the biography that simultaneously made and undid Jane Austen.[2]

The myth of politeness, then, is critical to the supposedly timeless success of the novels. The myth (the romance, the empire waists, the tea) is what pulls readers in, even if debunking the myth (the sex, the violence, the satire) is sometimes what keeps them hooked. Inadvertently, the myth of politeness is also what makes Austen the ideal platform to discuss contemporary issues of social justice.

Jane Austen is often quoted as describing her writing, with ironic false modesty, as a "little bit (two inches wide) of ivory on which I work with so fine a brush."[3] Using her novels to talk about complex social problems is a bit like wielding that fine brush. It's not a jump-in-the-deep-end, hit-them-over-the-head-with-a-hammer, bring-your-pitchfork kind of conversation. It's more careful, more cautious, more polite, more midwestern.

When I was trained in facilitating community dialogue through the Project on Civic Reflection, the facilitators emphasized the value of "third things" to triangulate or refract conversations.[4] Rather than talking about local issues of rural poverty directly, for instance, you could talk about a poem that describes a homeless child, bouncing between shelters and relatives, trying to learn math. It gives participants common ground, a concrete shared framework, and crucially, a bit of distance. First, you might ask everyone in the group to share one word that the poem brought to mind. Then, you might open a conversation with some general questions: When did you try to help someone you weren't sure you should try to help? Why weren't you sure you should help? Why did you do it anyway? Move from narrow interpretive questions to bigger evaluative questions, they told us, and don't be afraid to let things get personal. Talk about experiences. Talk about values. This model of community dialogue is really a form of close reading, moving from understanding to opinion to analysis in the service of building empathy and common ground; here were the skills of literary historians at work making real community change. The fictional or hypothetical ideas raised in these third things can help us address local problems more effectively and more inclusively, the facilitators explained, by coming at them indirectly.

Coming at things indirectly is, of course, Austen's forte. Because she addresses war and slavery implicitly, in a passing, glancing way, it can be easy for first-time readers to miss her hints. However, it's also what makes her novels ideal third things for talking about these issues in our own communities. Because of this double layer of indirectness, the Jane Austen in Community project I've developed has two parts: first, identifying the social and political context of Austen's novels in Regency England, and second, carrying those lessons forward to today. We start with Jane Austen in her community, then bring her to our community.

The first iteration of Jane Austen in Community began as part of a summer undergraduate program at Monmouth College designed to give incoming first-year students the chance to work on collaborative research projects in teams with faculty.[5] Participating students and faculty earned a modest honorarium for the three-week session and had a small budget for research materials or travel, which we used to purchase copies of the novels for participants in our reading group and hire experts in Regency-era food and dance to help us prepare refreshments and lead country dancing at our planned Jane Austen Ball. Exceptional students were invited by their admissions representatives to apply to particular projects, and faculty mentors in the program chose applicants for their teams during late spring. The teams also included one returning upperclassman.

For the research component of my project, I capitalized on the way that digital archives offer new opportunities for students to fully immerse themselves in Austen's literary context. Students chose a social or political issue in Austen's novels and conducted research on its biographical and historical context, to both give a broader frame of understanding the issue and offer an interpretation of Austen's position on it. While they read some secondary literature, I emphasized using primary sources from online archives to immerse themselves in Austen's world.

As a practice of literary instruction, this assignment was fairly conventional: students read literature and then conducted research to provide a cultural context. While the digital project they created was formatted differently from a term paper and the intended audience was a specific and local group of nonspecialist readers, the research process itself (drawing on various literary, historical, and biographical documents to provide an interpretation of a text) is not unlike what you'd see in a more traditional literature class.

In addition to these new possibilities for conducting undergraduate research, digital tools also provide new ways for students to collect and present their research. Because primary research can include a large number of small items—including book reviews, personal correspondence, maybe even tightly rolled laundry lists—students may struggle to organize the materials to produce an effective argument. How might students researching Austen's letters, which may be scattered across various sites, go about finding a pattern and building an arc for their argument? They could benefit from creating a digital storehouse to collate such materials.

For many undergraduate students who are embarking on their first research project and certainly their first multimodal research project, one primary obstacle they face is organizing their research in a coherent way. I found that a timeline can help students visually organize their archival research, in both the process of forming a hypothesis and compiling their research and presenting the finished argument. By creating a digital timeline, students can supplement a basic chronology of events with images, links, scans, and maps, drawing a virtual path through their research to tell a multimedia story of their findings. The timelines also served as an image-centered way for our book club participants to access the student research.

The digital timeline idea has a bit of backstory. I began experimenting with digital timelines as part of my own research process at Chawton House, where I spent the summer of 2011 tracking the literary friendship between the Scottish playwright Joanna Baillie and the Irish novelist Maria Edgeworth. In preparation for the public lecture I gave at the end of my stay, I created a timeline of my research to organize relevant biographical details, correspondence between the two writers, and publication dates for their works into a meaningful chronology culminating in a subtle gesture of solidarity and empathy. In her essay, Gillian Dow offers more on this institution's twin commitments to scholarly research and public outreach.

A Unique Heritage and Research Library

Gillian Dow

The sixteenth-century manor known as Chawton House, its appearance and surroundings still recognizable from Jane Austen's time, was owned by the Knights, relatives of the Austen family, in the late eighteenth and nineteenth centuries. Jane's elder brother Edward (1768–1852) was made the heir of the childless Knights, taking their name. After inheriting the Chawton estate, Edward loaned the nearby cottage to Jane, her mother, and sister Cassandra, and Jane spent the most productive years of her literary life there. From 1809 until her death in 1817, Austen came and went along the road between her cottage, where she wrote in the dining room, and the Elizabethan property a five-minute walk away, a place she always called the Great House.

The house remained within the Knight family, following the typical trajectory of the fall of the English country house throughout the nineteenth and twentieth centuries. The situation became critical in the 1980s, when Richard Knight inherited the house and estate without the money to carry out the extensive repairs that were necessary to ensure the fabric of the building survived. Various ventures were attempted—including a country house hotel and golf club—as the family endeavored to ensure the estate's survival.

In 1992, a 125-year lease was bought from Richard Knight by the American philanthropist Dr. Sandy Lerner, OBE. A passionate Austenite herself, she had heard about the sale of the house at a meeting of the Jane Austen Society of North America. She set up a charity, Chawton House Library, donating her own collection of early women's writing, a collection that was inspired by second-wave feminist writing on Austen and her contemporaries. Chawton House became Chawton House Library: a place where scholars and general readers could, in these atmospheric surroundings, study, celebrate, and publicize the work of Jane Austen's unfairly neglected women contemporaries and foremothers. Dr. Lerner's core collection was expanded and enhanced, and—in a world of increasing digitization—the rare books at its heart formed a unique resource.

From its opening in 2003, Chawton House Library became respected in the academic world as a flourishing venue for study, literary talks, and conferences, as well as a hub for Austen scholars. A visiting fellowship program—run in partnership with the University of Southampton—started in 2007, enabling scholars to live on the premises and carry out their research. This community of readers brought a great deal to the institution, not least engagement and interaction with each other and with the local community. Chawton House Library has benefitted from close links to the University of Southampton since before the library opened to the public. Two posts, including my own as executive director of the library from 2014, are seconded from the university. Part of a UK-based academic's remit must now be focused on public impact and engagement; Chawton House Library provides a perfect forum for this work.

The program of evening talks at Chawton House Library was always designed with outreach in mind and attracted a committed and devoted audience who came to hear authors and scholars on eighteenth-century literature and culture. A thriving book group meets monthly (reading Austen alongside authors from Mary Astell to Susan Ferrier); tea and cake are always part of the offering. In recent years, the library also developed into a thriving, if small-scale, visitor attraction. Since 2015, the staff, with much help from volunteers, has welcomed increasing numbers of nonspecialist visitors into the house and grounds and made a name for itself with garden walks and activities alongside the Austen-related heirlooms and library.

The need for a renewed vision securing Chawton House Library for the future became critical in late 2016, following the cessation of her generous funding by Dr. Lerner as she—understandably, after many decades of support—turned her philanthropy to other organizations. Without an endowment to maintain its activities, Chawton House Library had to revise its business plan at speed. Almost immediately, the visiting fellowship program was suspended, as we looked at ways to maintain our core programs as well as develop sustainable, income-generating activities. The restructuring that will be essential to keep the house open is an opportunity to welcome many more families, scholars, and lovers of Jane Austen's work to explore this beautiful place. We will be working with the Jane Austen House Museum and residents of the village of Chawton to make sure that the growing popularity of this destination works for everyone in the area. The reimagining of Chawton House Library as a much more widely recognized, more visited, commercially viable destination will help secure the library founded by Dr. Lerner and the associated cultural, academic, and literary events that, in addition to its Jane Austen connections, give this manor house its special character.

One of the casualties of the reimagining of Chawton House Library, however, is its name. Research demonstrated that the casual visitor to the village of Chawton was put off by the word "library," suggesting, as it does, not a visitor attraction but a place of solitary confinement. And so in January 2018, Chawton House Library became Chawton House, in the hopes of attracting more of the visitors who will ensure the organization's survival. What is clear as we start on this road is that we will need support from lovers of literature and reading to help us maintain our programs. Jane Austen herself knew the value of a good library, and it is in tribute to her and her contemporaries that we continue to create a place where "the work of many generations"—as Darcy said of the library at Pemberley—can continue.

In order to organize decades of correspondence between Joanna Baillie and Maria Edgeworth, two women with prolifically long literary careers, I created a timeline from May 1813, when the two writers met at a dinner party, through the late 1840s, by which time Edgeworth addressed Baillie as "my dear and constant friend in weal or love ever tenderly and cordial by sympathising!"[6] I organized the letters, secondary criticism, publication dates, literary excerpts, and biographical notes into this time-line using the visual presentation tool Prezi.[7]

Depending on which threads I followed, I found a different version of what their friendship meant to these women. By resizing items according to importance, highlighting key ideas with corresponding colors, and weaving a path along the central points, I told a story that traced Edgeworth's eye troubles, which began in her childhood, through to her friend Baillie's 1823 poem "Sunset Meditation, Under the Apprehension of Approaching Blindness."[8] I speculated that the poem might allude not only to a literary inheritance, in the tradition of the blind bards of Homer and Milton, but also to her literary friendship with Edgeworth, in promising that friendship has "the power to console" the grieving speaker through her impending blindness (229). The timeline helped me to see patterns, intersections, and themes in a vast body of research, and it gave me a way to present this research to an audience at Chawton House like so many breadcrumbs along a trail.[9]

The following summer during the NEH seminar Jane Austen and Her Contemporaries, I developed a timeline that juxtaposed Austen's composition of *Northanger Abbey* with her exposure to Gothic drama in London and Bath. However, this time the top half of the timeline traced Austen's writing process and the bottom half was a student tutorial that chronicled the process of creating a digital timeline and would help my undergraduates organize and share their own discoveries in the archives. This tutorial became the basis for student research in Jane Austen in Community.

I first assigned students to create digital timelines in the 2013 iteration of Jane Austen in Community. The students' approaches to contextualizing Austen's *Pride and Prejudice* varied as widely as their approaches to visualizing their research. One student explored the paradox of early nineteenth-century American hostility to English social stratification and the simultaneous popularity of Austen's novels after the first US edition was published in 1832. Another student researched Austen as a social satirist, while a third examined conduct books in order to explore late eighteenth-century "portraits" of the ideal woman. The student framed her argument as portraits on a digital wall.

For each of these students, the ability to include multimedia components (such as images, graphics, and videos) and to use an overarching spatial metaphor (such as a book, picture frames, or footsteps) guided and informed their research process. The task of populating a timeline that tells a story seemed less daunting to them than researching and writing a thesis-based paper, though the process and outcomes were similar: they gathered evidence, synthesized sources, identified themes, and formed arguments.

This research then became the springboard for a series of community events related to *Pride and Prejudice* in celebration of its bicentennial anniversary, including a weekly reading group in partnership with the local public library and community arts center and an evening of English country dancing and Regency-era food open to the public at a downtown theater.[10]

The intergenerational exchange was, as it had been in the project's nascent iterations while I was a graduate student at Iowa, the highlight on both sides. My students saw models of lifelong learners who read the same books as the students, reading simply for pleasure and an eagerness to share their ideas and interpretations with others. Community members got to see college students discovering parts of our downtown space for the first time. They praised the students' thoughtful discussion questions, asked for their opinions, and eagerly shared their own stories with a rapt audience. The community members' enthused participation and willingness to return week after week was, I could tell, at least partly motivated by a desire to support these young people's efforts.

At each discussion, students shared a bit about what we read together (Edward Said and Ruth Perry's debate on Austen's position on slavery, for instance)[11] or what they were finding in their research and then posed discussion questions to dig deeper into these topics. The community members who attended our reading groups all received a free copy of the novel (Norton Critical Editions, of course, at my aspirational insistence, so they could do some secondary reading if they were so moved), and we circulated some contextual reading and discussion questions in advance. The reading group was mostly but not exclusively white women of a variety of ages but dominated by retirees. In many ways, it was a group you might not see at a civic dialogue about contentious political issues like the status of refugees in this country. In that way, my Trojan horse worked.

Our public library, like many public libraries, had a vibrant series of children's programs, from summer reading programs to story times. But it's sometimes harder to drum up interest in adult reading programs. This gap is where Austen comes in. When I hosted the first Jane Austen book club, we had waiting lists for every weekly meeting. The same pattern proved true in Monmouth. We consistently had fifteen to twenty participants in our reading group, ourselves included, when we met at the Buchanan Center for the Arts each week to discuss one volume of *Pride and Prejudice*. In the essays included in this chapter, students and community partners describe their experiences with the Jane Austen book club.

Larisa Good

Partnering with a faculty member of Monmouth College for themed book discussions was an opportunity to elevate the Warren County Public Library District's programming. By teaming with the college, we were able to provide an educational component backed by an expert in the field. The students leading the discussion were guided by the faculty member and therefore created an academic environment similar to the college experience. As many of the attendees were retired individuals, I think they enjoyed immersing themselves in academia once again. But there was plenty of levity in our discussions, and supplemental activities (movie night and the Jane Austen Ball) made the whole experience both educational and fun.

For a library and a college in a small community, partnering was natural and easy. Adding partners, such as the Buchanan Center for the Arts, meant greater access to our community. This alone is attractive to libraries as we are always searching for ways to reach our nonusers. In addition, partnerships such as this one are opportunities to bridge the so-called town and gown divide that exists in many college towns. The more we minimize the separation, the better it is for us as a community. And, of course, these partnerships tend to provide fertile ground for more collaboration to take root.

I don't have much advice except to say, "Go for it!" As long as all parties communicate and participate, the experience is rewarding and unique.

TOWN AND GOWN, UPS AND DOWNS

Susan Twomey

In my former position as the executive director of the Buchanan Center for the Arts, an art gallery and center in west central Illinois, I had many experiences partnering with various departments and professors working at our local college. These partnerships were sometimes successful, other times not.

My experience with a professor from the drama department was excellent. The Buchanan Center offered a variety of theatrical opportunities for children and adults. In our collaboration, the professor wrote her curriculum to include children's theater. Her students came to my center and gave acting classes, script writing classes, and a host of other activities, including a spring performance that featured local children as the actors and the students as director, lighting designer, costume designer, and so on.

This venture was hugely successful for both my art center and the college's theater program. The college often cited our partnership in its promotional materials for prospective students and in testimony to its board of trustees as a tangible result of efforts to bridge the divide between town and gown. As the director of a rural art center, I had limited resources to deliver quality programs to our citizens (among whom are the same professors teaching at the college). Collaboration with the college was a huge component of making programming like this possible.

Not all of our collaborations went equally well. I often found that many professors who provided their students with an internship with me felt as though they were then no longer responsible for their students. I was asked to monitor their schedules and in one instance to give grades. In another case, I worked with several faculty on an exhibition to focus on migration from Mexico. I was excited about the prospect. We worked faithfully to build a coalition with members of the Latinx community. Sadly, when the project failed, some trust was broken. It was a long climb back to regain the Latinx community's confidence.

Through all my experiences working with the college, I suppose my overwhelming feeling was frustration. I would often find myself either throwing up my hands and wondering just who these professors thought they were, or wondering how we could find ways to help them feel like members of the community in which they lived and worked.

What I really found interesting, though, was an opportunity to go to an academic conference in Atlanta a few years ago with Bridget

Draxler. The conference focused on community engagement, and when she asked if I would be willing to attend, I jumped at the chance. I was hopeful that this experience would finally help me to be more effective at these partnerships. I felt as though there was very little I was doing right. The conference was an amazing experience that really opened my eyes and allowed me to see things in a way I would never have imagined.

The more I listened to the academics from all over the country, the more I felt as though colleges and universities were such insulated and isolated places. In a strange way, learning this fact made me feel better on many levels about the failures of many of our attempts to work together. The faculty just didn't seem able or ready to engage in the greater community because they were struggling to engage in their own campus community.

After this conference, when Bridget broached the subject of putting together a book group on Jane Austen, I jumped at the chance to work with her again. Why? She was a diligent, open, caring, motivated partner. I understood her commitment to our greater community; I had witnessed it time and again. Even when her students' research didn't work out as planned, she was always optimistic and understanding. She had honorably made the most efforts to bring the failed exhibition on migration to fruition. She persevered.

I also knew that Jane Austen was her wheelhouse and that the book club would be fabulous, even if it was just the two of us. I still remember with such fondness one of her students marveling at how people from the community read a book just because they wanted to.

As part of the reading group, Bridget and I managed to bring a country line dance event to town to celebrate the end of our reading of *Pride and Prejudice*. People came from all around. The dance was held in a local venue that is most often patronized by college kids and those a bit down on their luck. One of the bartenders was so excited, he researched eighteenth-century cocktails and made a special punch for the event. The owner of the bar adapted his food menu to include references to the book. It was more than just charming; it was inspiring.

As to what advice I would give to faculty embarking on a partnership with a community entity, I guess I would remind them that such a partnership can often be like a marriage. Sometimes the partners share the responsibilities fifty-fifty, sometimes more like ninety-ten, and sometimes the relationship is for better or for worse. Successful college partners have valued the community in which we live and wanted to share their expertise with it. That authentic desire to make the place in which you live better for others seems to be a common thread. The faculty who were easiest to work with knew their subjects, knew their desired outcomes, and were flexible enough to adapt. I think truly a commitment to engaging in the community in which they live and work will make professors' lives and jobs more meaningful.

I would also caution faculty to really check their egos at the door when they come into these partnerships. As a "local" (as I still get introduced by professors), I encounter an inherent and often insidious perception that people like me are a level or two, or hundreds, below their own level. I can promise this attitude is very easy to spot and feel. It puts up another set of barriers that can really slow things down. Acknowledge the work done by all, whether it feels like a little or a lot. Almost everyone involved in these projects is doing them on top of busy work schedules. And be forgiving.

MORE LIKE CONVERSATIONS

Tiffany Ouellette

Growing up in rural Illinois, I found myself surrounded with people who all pretty much enjoyed the same things. However, Jane Austen was not one of them; when I happened to pick up *Pride and Prejudice* from my high school library's bookshelf, I could not understand why more of my friends, family, teachers, and everyone else I knew did not love this book as much as I did. Instead, I was usually met with something like, "It's just a boring love story." It was not until I reached college that I met other people who appreciated Austen's work and saw that it was so much more than a dull romance novel.

After graduating from high school, I felt called to education. As I completed my first year at Monmouth College, it became clear to me that teaching English was my passion. So when I heard one of my professors was interested in doing an independent research project about Jane Austen during the summer leading into my senior year of college, I jumped at the chance to work with her. Since I would begin student teaching at the start of the fall semester, I found this project, called Summer Opportunity for Intellectual Activity (sofia), could not have come at a busier or more perfect time in my college career. The project allowed me to practice many of the key elements of teaching that I would be diving head first into in the coming weeks. I was able to read material through a new lens. I was not reading *Pride and Prejudice* to understand it myself, as I had already read it multiple times previously; instead, I was able to comb through Austen's novel to find the hidden gems I had missed before. As I found these bits of information, such as the commentary about slavery hidden ever so shallowly underneath the surface of Austen's constantly moving lines, I asked myself how could I get the members of our book club to see this without undertaking multiple readings.

Sofia was the first time I would be teaching people older than myself, and I was concerned with how I would speak to them. I wanted to have a discussion, to create a safe place where we could discover and learn together, without making anyone feel inadequate or lost. So as I was planning and thinking about discussions, I thought of the experience less and less like teaching and more and more like a conversation. A couple months later, when I had full control of my student teaching classes of high-school sophomores and juniors, I realized that my teaching became much more effective and engaging to them when I treated and instructed my students the same way as I had treated the adults in our sofia project. The more I set up my classroom discussions to be more conversational and less like a list of bullet-pointed questions we needed to answer, the more my students flourished and shined.

Had I never signed on for this project, I would probably never have realized the implications of "new money" and where it came from in Austen's world and all of the social commentary Austen makes in talking about it. I would never have thought about having a conversation about this topic with strangers, let alone our book club. In those conversations, I learned things about what it means to be human. I learned how literature impacts people differently based on different backgrounds, age, and gender in a way that I could not learn in a college education or English course. These were things that I could only learn through experience and exposure, and I am thankful that I had the chance to figure them out before entering the classroom as a teacher.

While participating in the project in many ways added exponentially to my workload, the amount of enrichment, the quality of research and instruction, and the opportunity to work with and help the community made it worth all the extra work and stress because it made my whole educational experience more engaging. It allowed me to develop into the person I wanted and needed to be, not only as an English major, not only as future educator, and not only as a liberal arts student, but as an individual as a whole. It helped bring my whole educational and liberal arts experience full circle because I was no longer sitting in a classroom absorbing information like a sponge; instead, I was using the information and doing something with it that had implications outside the classroom, another lesson I have implemented in my own classrooms whenever I can.

Being able to wrestle with information with people of varying backgrounds, educational levels, and experiences allows students to find the deepest meaning and understanding of the topic they are trying to comprehend. If given the chance and the time, students will find that moments and experiences like these will redefine and inspire them to do, strive, and achieve more while perhaps realizing for the first time that their education can make a real difference, but only when shared with others.

MY COMMUNITY

Rachel Lynne Witzig

As a first-year student at Monmouth College, I was nervous to enter the higher education world. Because I had been homeschooled since my kindergarten days, I felt timid about the idea of the college classroom. Upon my enrollment at Monmouth, the admissions office notified me that I had been nominated to participate in a three-week precollege program called Summer Opportunity for Intellectual Activity (sofia). I chose to work with Dr. Bridget Draxler and three other students on a Jane Austen program dedicated to integrating the work of the famous Regency-period author with the Monmouth community. Engaging with Austen's work with modern-day readers and learning to do college-level research prepared me not only to enter college with confidence but also to find the relevance in Austen's novels and apply it to my community.

The characters' complexities and the social commentary present in Austen's work enchanted me. We spoke of terms such as "free indirect discourse" and discussed Austen's use of letters as tools for character formation and development. My mind whirled with questions and ideas unleashed by challenging discussions. These experiences solidified my desire to declare an English major.

At first, the thought of sharing with the Monmouth community what I was learning about Austen was fear-inducing. On the day of the public discussion, I seated myself at one of the large white tables in Monmouth's Buchanan Center for the Arts. To my left was one of my fellow students; to my right was an elderly woman who immediately began asking my opinion of the novel and my plans for the future. By the time Dr. Draxler launched us into discussion, my nervousness had largely subsided. I was surrounded by members of the community who had just as many questions as I did and, like me, spoke quietly at first, due to timidity. I only spoke up once during that first discussion; in the following two weeks, however, I contributed regularly to the conversation as my courage began to grow. What I discovered was that I had a gift for listening and mediating discussion—deciding when the conversation began to lag and when to encourage other individuals in the group to voice their opinions.

At one point in our discussion of Mr. Darcy, I mentioned that I remained unimpressed by how infrequently the man seemed to be attempting to gain Elizabeth Bennet's attention and trust. Almost immediately, one of the quieter members of the group spoke up and pointed out instances in which Mr. Darcy had tried—and failed—to earn Elizabeth's approval. At first, I was miffed. I had mustered the courage to declare an opinion on the subject, and I had been countered. Yet as the conversation continued, I realized that the woman had not been trying to invalidate my viewpoint as a reader; she had simply been pointing out that the particular bit of insight I had shared was not consistent with the text. It was then that I began to learn what often constitutes a meaningful discussion of literature: the exchange and testing of ideas, considering some opinions and knowing when to disagree with others. And it was not another English major who had taught me this; it was a woman who, as she made clear during our several discussions, had learned throughout her lifetime how to disagree and debate productively.

Furthermore, I learned throughout the three-week project that meaningful exchanges of literary opinions and concepts are not confined to classrooms, nor does insight belong solely to experts in a given field. Our discussion group laughed with one of our community members when, during discussion of one of the dances that takes place in *Pride and Prejudice*, she described one of her previous beaus as a "crashing bore who sure could dance." Leading group discussion helped me in my own learning, as I had to become familiar with the topics of interest in order to be able to share insights with people who had not studied the novel as extensively as I had. Perhaps most important of all was the awareness that the enjoyment of Jane Austen's novels is not, and should not, remain strictly in an academic setting; her work is made even more meaningful by the interpretations of readers who express their opinions without worrying about English-major jargon or essay deadlines.

Much to my happiness, Dr. Draxler asked me to work with her on another Jane Austen project shaped in a way similar to the first, this time focused on *Emma*. A junior by this time, I was far more confident in the skills I had acquired during my two years in the English department, and I was able to lead the community discussions with even more enthusiasm and energy than before. Doing so without the pressure of earning a participation grade or performing well in the classroom enabled me to discover further the joy of examining a text with other readers who had chosen to be a part of the conversation solely for enjoyment. This sort of environment has remained unique throughout my college experience. Due in large part to these two Jane Austen projects, I learned confidence and motivation, how to lead a discussion and how to listen. I learned to be a literary citizen not only in an academic environment but also in the community in which I engage daily.

Working with a public library was, in some ways, natural and easy—which, it's worth remembering, isn't a bad thing. A lot of the time we think about community engagement as really challenging and complicated, and a lot of the time it is (see the introduction and the first few pages of this chapter). But sometimes—though this may be difficult for academics to accept—community engagement doesn't have to be difficult to be meaningful. Part of the reason this project worked, as Susan Twomey notes, is because everyone was in their element. And on all sides, a love of books and a desire to cultivate community literacy were important motivations for our work. We had a really unusual advantage, one that is rare in civic engagement projects: the campus and community shared the same goals. It's an asset not to overlook.

Pivotal to the project was connecting the community events (bringing Austen to our community) with the student research (contextualizing Austen in her community). As much as I could, I tried to have the students use their research as the springboard for leading discussion at our reading group, though the tight time frame made this part challenging, because it was not possible to complete the research before the meetings. In order to have three community discussions covering the three volumes of the novel, the students had to conduct their research and build their timelines while concurrently planning discussion questions and leading the reading groups. Students would essentially read, research, write about, and lead discussion on one volume of the novel each week.

It was difficult to get the research polished early enough to be distributed to readers before each meeting. And on this tight time frame, it was also difficult to do primary research on Regency England with much nuance. Students essentially had to choose a topic before they finished reading the novel, and they would have only a few days of research each week. And while the experienced student had some research skills coming in, the first-year students were using our library database for the first time, and they had rarely worked with primary documents before. These factors conspired to limit how much primary research made its way into the reading group discussions. And in truth, the reading group that first year was pretty tame. We talked about morals and manners, what it means to be proper. We had tea, and it was all very civil.

The next spring, students from the first project volunteered to host another reading group for the bicentennial of the publication of *Mansfield Park*, and I made a concerted effort to focus our conversation on its designation as Austen's most political novel. Austen, I argued, was a master of meaningful silence, and reading her well requires paying careful attention to what she *doesn't* say. We talked about what Austen leaves unsaid in the passing references she makes to war, imperialism, and the slave trade. A good example is Sir Thomas Bertram's return from Antigua. Although he is "ready to give every information as to his voyage," he is interrupted by the meddling Mrs. Norris: "In the most interesting moment of his passage to England, when the alarm of a French privateer was at the height, she burst through his recital with the proposal of soup" (123-125). The narrative interrupted, "there was a pause," and the conversation changed topics (125). Later, Fanny expresses curiosity and pleasure in hearing her uncle's stories of the West Indies. After asking him about the slave trade, she is disappointed by the "dead silence" she receives (136). In both cases, the silence in Austen's narrative is conspicuous.

Acknowledging meaningful silence is a powerful tool, both in the novels we read and the communities we inhabit. It opened a door to talking about Austen in a different way than we had with *Pride and Prejudice*, and it let my political self peek into the seemingly apolitical space of the library book club.

I rebooted Jane Austen in Community in 2015 for the bicentenary of *Emma*, this time (inspired by my coauthor Danielle) with a more explicit focus on issues of philanthropy, class, and nationalism—and this time with messier, more conflict-ridden conversations. We talked about homelessness, poverty, and the stratified class system in Austen's novel, whose servants, sick cottagers, gypsies, and poachers make pivotal incursions from the lower classes into high-class Highbury life. We even talked a bit about homelessness, poverty, and the stratified class system in our community.[12]

Borrowing from Devoney Looser's NEH seminar, we read Hannah More's *Betty Brown* (1795),[13] whose eponymous protagonist serves as a parallel to Austen's Harriet Smith, the character in *Emma* described as "the natural daughter of somebody" (18). We talked about illegitimate children and unwed mothers in the Regency period and noted how far we've come, and how far we haven't come, in supporting single mothers. With a group of locals, most of whom have always lived in or near our small town, we talked about Emma's love of home and how that both enriches and limits her worldview.

Most of all we talked about charity, from Emma's supposed charity to the sick cottagers to her presumed generosity to Harriet Smith (63–64, 18). Debates about whether Emma dismantles or perpetuates social stratification through her philanthropy dominated the conversation week to week. The tide of the conversation turned from collective confidence in charity and Emma during the first week to a much more complicated, skeptical, and nuanced perspective on philanthropy and the title character by the end. We talked in thoughtful and nuanced ways about charitable acts that reinscribe social hierarchies in our own day, leaving participants unsettled and maybe uncomfortable but still safe within the bounds of polite conversation. Austen's politeness let us have a conversation we couldn't have had otherwise.

It was fitting in the end for me to guide a community discussion on the dangers of good intentions gone awry. Several years after the exhibit debacle, there I was back in the quiet, solitary space of the library reading old books, but this time in a community of readers and with a welcome political edge. The conversation became a metanarrative of my own failed attempt to be of service, and like Emma I was lucky enough to have the chance to redirect my efforts toward reciprocal engagement rather than mere (and misdirected) service. Just as Emma absolves herself by supporting Harriet's union with Robert Martin, I made peace with my own more modest matchmaking and acknowledged that my political ambitions are best paired with books and libraries.

We didn't march, we didn't fight, we didn't occupy the courthouse or make front page news. It wasn't flashy. We sat together and had an honest and open conversation about how some forms of service only benefit the patron. We had a few moments of pregnant silence together contemplating our own community, our own charitable efforts, our own similarities with Emma, our own mistakes. Those moments of silence opened space for us to listen to each other more carefully. And for that moment, quiet time in the library was enough—was just right. A bit of silence in the library, I realized, could be something to fight for rather than against: something that, in its own way, does a bit of good.

This story has one final iteration and one final twist. I'm living in a new community now, and I'm discovering that one version of sustainability is to have an ongoing project with multiple community hosts. After taking a new position at my alma mater, St. Olaf College, I brought the community reading group project to the public library in Northfield, a small, well-mannered midwestern community (do you know the phrase "Minnesota nice"?). The Jane Austen in Community project celebrated one last bicentennial anniversary, honoring Austen's death and her final posthumous publications.

I received formal approval for the last iteration of the project on January 20, 2017. I remember a heavy silence on the day of the new US president's inauguration, a silence of powerlessness, a silence of grief. At the same time, it was a silence that transformed into solidarity. The next day, I attended my very first political march, shoulder to shoulder with a bunch of polite midwestern women who (like Austen) are radicals and revolutionaries who are fired up about politics, if you take the time to look close enough. The cohesive voices of women chanting together in the streets were strengthened by that shared silence.

This time around, I was better equipped to dig into the tough questions, using the novels as third things to get at bigger questions and contemporary concerns. How can *Northanger Abbey*, for instance, help us think about the role of parody and satire in contemporary political discourse? What can Austen's famous defense of the novel early in the book tell us about the way we read today and whether "solitary acts of reading might be regulated by the presence of coercive models of pedagogy"?[14] Given the state of slavery and empire in England in the early nineteenth century, what do we make of the heroine's entrée into Bath society, when she describes the "mob" of the assembly room as an "imprisonment" with "fellow captives"?[15] As Catherine is courted by the insufferably bombastic John Thorpe, what do we make of General Tilney's rapacious eagerness to believe Thorpe's misinformation about Catherine's inheritance, twice—first to seize the supposedly wealthy woman for his own son, and then, when Thorpe paints her as penniless, to abruptly avert it? And is it significant that the narrative hinges on a high-level government official's reliance on an untrustworthy news source? How can Austen's only Gothic novel open a broader conversation about feudal spirits, reckless authoritarianism, and violence against women? And how does her satire of imperial consumerism fit into this violence?

The 2017 project had some assets: in addition to having a team of three upperclass students (studying combinations of English, women and gender studies, political science, religion, and digital media), we also had a full ten weeks for the project, access to more primary source databases, and grant-funded time and support from staff in our library and our digital studio. I also had a clearer vision for the project and its purpose, having done it a few times and knowing more about the community. These changes made a difference in the kind of research students were able to produce and the kind of reading groups we could host.

The students created a website broken into three parts: first, background information that included a reception history of the novel, advice for reading Austen, some literary context on Romanticism and Gothic novels, and a brief history of English politics in the context of the French Revolution; second, research on volume I of the novel, including access to a conduct magazine mentioned by the heroine's mother Mrs. Morland, excerpts from Bath newspapers, a miniexhibit on Bath society, and a rich history of the muslin trade traced through India to London to Bath; and third, a guide to volume II covering the Gothic Revival in everything from architecture to fiction, along with a dark take on the political Gothic, exploring the repressive and suspicious government of Regency England through period political cartoons.[16] Instead of one reading group, we hosted three: one at the local public library, one at the senior center, and one for St. Olaf alumni.

Another key difference with this project was working with an Austen novel that isn't beloved and doesn't have a feisty, likeable heroine like *Pride and Prejudice*. Far fewer reading group participants had read the novel before, and those who had universally disliked it and its heroine. This hurdle actually turned into an asset, as readers avoided the tendency to idealize Austen's world and Austen's women. It opened up new space for critique.

While I expected a degree of dislike for the novel and for Catherine Morland, I was surprised by how much the reading group participants and students shared a distaste for the novel's romantic interest, Henry Tilney. Sure, the novel is more of a social satire than her other works; sure, Catherine is a bit of a naive pushover. But Henry Tilney? The witty wordsmith who is the character in Austen's canon who most reminds me of the author herself? Of what can you possibly complain?

In the most memorable conversation of the summer, at the senior center (whose group turned out to be most politically engaged and opinionated about the novel), we talked at length about a passage that I had never given much attention. In it Henry Tilney takes pride in being able to recognize (and pay a bargain price for) a "true Indian muslin" and remarks that he not only chooses his own cravats but also that "my sister has often trusted me in the choice of a gown" (16).

One student read the passage through the prism of secondary literature, including Sarah Eason's "Henry Tilney: Queer Hero of *Northanger Abbey*," which cites this passage to argue that Tilney's "knowledge of fashions, fabrics, journal writing, and even feminine internal dialogue" marks him as "feminine-identifying."[17] Another student, drawing on research about England's muslin trade with India and the national pride tied up in the East India Company that ran the trade, read a more sinister patriotic imperialism into Tilney's knowledge of fabrics. In both cases, the students were bothered by the hero's entitlement to choose what his sister would wear. In a world where, as Tilney himself notes, "man has the advantage of choice, woman only the power of refusal," his choosing his sister's gown felt like a final indignity (51).

If we were reading this passage in a classroom, the discussion might have ended there. But then one of the reading group participants chimed in with a relevant weekly headline: the debate over whether sleeveless dresses are appropriate attire in the US Congress. The conversation that followed could be called tangential; it digressed into personal examples from sweet sixteen parties to proms to private schools, ranging from the 1930s to the early twenty-first century, of ways that women's bodies are circumscribed by what we wear—whether through overt control of clothing choices or the shaming of women for their own choices. I think the participants on both sides were surprised by the similarities of their experiences. They were surprised by how little had changed in such a long time. The intergenerational connections, from Austen to retirees to students, made the indignity against Miss Tilney carry a kind of historical weight. Henry Tilney's control over his sister's wardrobe became personal and then political.

As a Henry Tilney enthusiast, I was reluctant to go along at first. I have always read that passage as Tilney indulging himself, as Catherine notes, with "the foibles of others"—in this case, with Mrs. Allen's ridiculous interest in muslin (17). This passage shows his sense of humor, I thought, and his critique of frivolities like fashion. It represents Tilney's sharp wit properly applied. Like Miss Tilney, I thought that he only *seemed* "intolerably rude" and a "great brute"; he only *seemed* like a John Thorpe (78). Tell them, Henry, I wanted to plead, "that you think very highly of the understanding of women." But he replied, as usual, that nature has given women so much understanding "that they never find it necessary to use more than half" (79).

I still read the tone of the muslin exchange as tongue-in-cheek, but after that conversation, it seemed less benign. This conversation made me regard other passages, like his metaphor of dancing and marriage, his policing Catherine's language, and his mockery of women's writing, as less forgivable (51–52, 73–74, and 14–15). I began to see him as a kind of effeminate unfeminist, someone whose effeminate qualities ultimately reinscribe his male privilege, someone who critiques the commodification of women but ultimately benefits from it.

Later, when Tilney harangues Catherine for harboring Gothic fantasies about his father (a tendency he himself fueled during their ride to Northanger Abbey, it's worth pointing out), I read the passage with fresh eyes. "Remember the country and the age in which we live," he tells her; "Remember that we are English, and that we are Christians" (136). When he implies that to be an English Christian is to be incapable of committing moral atrocities, I saw him less as a pedantic finger-wagger to Catherine and more as someone who was blindly patriotic, someone who was quick to distrust a woman's accusation. As he reminds Catherine that everyone in England is "surrounded by a neighbourhood of voluntary spies," a warning meant as a kind of perverse reassurance, I thought back to what my students had written about the Seditious Meetings Act, the Treasonable Practices Act, the Suspension of the Habeas Corpus Act, and the censorship of the press (136). I thought of General Tilney's late-night pamphlet reading, patriotic tea-set collecting, and lavish pineapple gardening, ominously suggesting his colonial ties and marking his callous privilege and muscular nationalism in a time of food shortages and political suppression (129, 119–120, and 122).[18] With my students' reading of Tilney as a patriarchal imperialist in the back of my mind, this speech made me think for the first time that Henry, not Catherine, is the one being naive in this scene. And for the first time, I read Henry Tilney as his father's son.

A few months before the #metoo movement started, my students taught me that it's not just the General Tilneys and Harvey Weinsteins and Donald Trumps of the world who disempower women through villainous abuses of power; it is also, importantly and heartbreakingly, the Al Frankens and the Henry Tilneys, with their uncouth jokes and thoughtless entitlement. The reading groups changed everyone's perspective on Austen, mine included, in ways that reflect powerfully on our own moment in history, as we witness collective silence giving way to new voices being heard and, more importantly, believed.

If our project launched in the shadow of Trump's inauguration, it concluded on a very different note. For the duration of the project, I was enormously and increasingly pregnant, and just a week after it ended, I met my daughter. I wonder if she will grow up in a world that treats her differently than what my students experienced, what the seniors in our book club experienced, what I experienced. I wonder what she will choose for herself and what will be chosen for her. I wonder if General Tilneys and John Thorpes will still be around and if she will stand up to them. I wonder if she will take as long as I did to become disillusioned with the Henry Tilneys. I wonder if she will read Austen as a vestige of another time or as one voice in an ongoing struggle. I wonder if she will feel that struggle as her own, and I worry that she will have reason to think so. I wonder whether books will be part of that struggle and part of what empowers her, nevertheless, to persist. I wonder if she will bear silence, or break it.

3: THE MUSEUM
🦋 🦋

Curating Fresh Threads of Connection

BRIDGET DRAXLER

Back in the early days of the twenty-first century, I had the privilege of majoring in something I enjoyed with nothing but a vague hope that it would somehow lead to a meaningful career. But more and more students — and their parents — ask this question: What is the use or value of an English major? A lot of the critique is not that English does any harm; courses in poetry are fine electives for a well-rounded business major. To study literature alone, though, seems a luxury.

Many critiques of the humanities in general and literary history specifically center on the issue of instrumental value: What transferable skills do students develop? What professional preparation does it offer? What kinds of internships or jobs do graduates get? What is the practical value of literary knowledge in today's competitive economic market? What is the benefit to the student-customer? They're all variations of the same question: What is the use?

I remember trying to explain to my dad why I wanted to study English. "English majors need jobs too, kid," he would joke. For me, the value of my English major wasn't something I could articulate at the time because, like so many liberal arts majors, my learning was about the long game. When he or other people would ask me things like, "Why are you studying English?" and "What are you going to do with your degree?" I wouldn't have a ready answer beyond, "I like it" and "teaching, probably." The fruits of my education are in some ways just now beginning to ripen; I couldn't justify my choice to him because the seeds planted by the books I read, the conversations I had, the papers I wrote, were only just beginning to germinate. I learned some skills along the way (critical reading and writing among them, skills that employers value), but they were secondary. The real learning for me was about developing values in a world that seemed, at twenty, less and less black-and-white.

What is the use?

This question is one, fifteen years after I chose my major, that I finally think I can answer, but as a true literary historian, I think understanding the present is tied up with the past. I might, for instance, consider ways that this question might apply just as well to a museum in eighteenth-century London as it does to a twenty-first-century major in the humanities. Bear with me. Here is where I hope to model the kind of historically contextualized learning that I practice as a teacher. Let me walk you through a story of a humanist who had to answer this question—what is the use?—not to his father, but to his government. In this case, the question was whether to preserve a vast swath of curiosities from across the globe. His answer, justifying the preservation of our cultural heritage, gives us a foothold to accomplish two things: first, to articulate the use-value writ large (political, intellectual, cultural) of humanities research in public life, and second, to reimagine current humanities research in museum spaces as a way to increase their public value.

The story of Sir Hans Sloane's life (1660-1753) is an interesting one. A prominent British physician, early member of the Royal Society, and avid collector of natural and cultural history, he was devoted to Enlightenment principles of order and classification. A plantation owner by marriage, his unabashedly colonialist impulse for collecting brought together a motley assortment of art, antiques, coins, books, and manuscripts, along with a vast array of other natural and cultural objects acquired from around the globe.[1] But while his life is a fascinating story, it's his death that's the real showstopper.

Sir Hans Sloane posthumously threw down a gauntlet to the British government, "offering" his collection to the British people in his will for a measly £20,000.[2] "What is the use?" Parliament might have asked. What is the value of preserving these trinkets? Why should such a sum be paid—and how much more, the members might have asked, would it cost to preserve and display such a collection?

Sloane's genius was in discouraging Parliament from asking this question in the first place. His will stipulated that if the British government were to refuse his donation, it would be passed not to a rival institution within the United Kingdom, but instead to royal academies in foreign cities: Paris, Saint Petersburg, Berlin, Madrid.[3] This unthinkable alternative, sending these artifacts of cultural history to rival states, made his message loud and clear: this collection is *who we are*.[4] By forcing Parliament's hand, Sloane turned his collection into a symbol of national identity, and it became the inaugural collection of what was formally established by an Act of Parliament in 1753 as the British Museum.[5]

Sloane's understanding of his collection's value was tied up in his approach to collecting, which was progressive, politically charged, and made him a source of ridicule in his lifetime. His expansive approach—not discriminating "between beautiful and ugly, useful and useless, valuable and valueless, common and unique"—erased distinctions of value in the objects themselves.[6] His empirically driven records, too, gave objects meaning through the interweaving of technical information about dates and provenance with stories, the connections among objects, and the interpretations of their value.[7] To critics, the collection seemed a mess: a random smattering of this and that catalogued with a mixture of relevant and irrelevant information and commentary. But to Sloane, this apparently indiscriminate system was part of the meaning and value of his collection. His inclusive collecting style challenged notions of what deserved preservation—and also, importantly, who deserved to see it. Sloane's will made explicit his democratic aim of "satisfying the desires of the curious, as for the improvement, knowledge, and information of all persons."[8]

Sloane's justification of the museum as having public usefulness mirrors what many aspiring humanities majors might tell mom and dad. His story can give students a vocabulary to talk about the public benefit of collecting (whether in a physical space or their own minds) and making fresh connections between cultural artifacts and texts. Appreciating old things is laudable, but it is often not enough; we also need to be able to articulate their continued value in order for them to be seen as worth preserving. Storytelling and interpretation are critical agents here in giving objects value, whether those objects are cultural relics or old books. Storytelling helps us contextualize, explain, engage, and connect with others; if done well in situations like these, it also helps us become rhetorically persuasive.

Storytelling, for instance, can make the difference between an old vase locked in an attic and one under glass with strict humidity control; the difference between the two is not necessarily in terms of intrinsic value, but rather their value as cultural artifacts. The difference between a family heirloom and a piece of cultural heritage can sometimes merely be the difference between the stories we tell about them.

The humanities are, like museums themselves, a process of collecting followed by careful classification and evaluation. What we collect says something deep about what we value. This is, of course, how I justify the hundred kitchen utensils and gadgets that clutter my drawers; they represent the value I place in preparing and sharing food. It's also how I justify the myriad books on my shelves; they represent the value I place in reading and sharing texts. What we collect is, in a sense, a representation of who we are. And what we choose to collect in our minds — the texts, the events, the relationships, the memories all intricately woven together — is the most fundamental part of who we are.

In hindsight, I see that my degree in literature contributed to my having a life of meaning, purpose, and happiness, even though — or maybe *because* — it has slowly redefined my understanding of what meaning, purpose, and happiness even mean. What is the use of an English major? Here is my answer: I learned to think. I learned to be curious. I learned to ask questions. I learned to connect with others and help others ask questions, too. This learning, this questioning, this storytelling, has become *who I am*.

And who am I? I am someone committed to using the humanities for the public good, in both the pragmatic and Platonic senses of the phrase. The humanities can help us connect with one another in ways that are meaningful and in ways that have the potential to recognize, address, and transform the problems we face locally and globally. I am someone who believes that if more people, both within higher education and more broadly in our communities, had opportunities to read and talk about historical literature, we would become more open, more inquisitive, and more capable of imagining the world from perspectives other than our own. I believe that reading and talking can make us better human beings.

Now, I recognize that this is all very grand and hopeful. In that way, I echo the idealistic accounts of the British Museum's early days, which emphasized the repeated invocations by Sloane, Parliament, and the museum's trustees of its public value. The trustees' statement, prepared for Parliament prior to its vote on whether to purchase Sloane's collections, resolved that they be kept "not only for the inspection and entertainment of the learned and the curious," but also "for the use and benefit of the publick, who may have free Access to view and peruse the same."[9] The *Statutes and Rules* for the British Museum, passed by the trustees in 1759, notes that "tho' chiefly designed for the use of learned and studious men . . . the advantages accruing from it should be rendered as general as possible."[10] Indeed, the museum's prominent display of one of its two copies of the Magna Carta—the greatest national symbol of British liberty—reinforced the narrative of the museum's egalitarian mission. The rhetoric of the museum's being a public good for both specialists and aficionados along with the variously literate general populace has a history as old as the museum itself.

From the start, however, the British Museum had critics and received complaints regarding its supposedly public purpose. The process of applying for a ticket was arduous, time-consuming, and decidedly less democratic than Sloane would have had it.[11] The museum was slow to streamline its procedures, and even as late as 1821, an anonymous fellow of the Royal Society published a letter to that body's newly elected president railing against the process:

> The conduct of our public institutions in general, and of the persons paid to superintend them, is a reproach and disgrace to the country. As yet little has been done to make the Museum really accessible. . . [You must] rebut all the assertions of those who are interested in keeping the public from our public institutions, and who say the English are not to be trusted. . . . It is true, that the public are not, in their present temper, very fit to be trusted on some occasions; but does not this arise, in some degree, from the very fact of the manner in which they are treated? Is it not proverbial, that the way to make people thieves, is to treat them as if they were thieves?[12]

Curators were accused of limiting access to the collections and only grudgingly giving tours. Admission to the reading room was notoriously restricted, open only to members of learned societies and those with a recommendation from them, with just 160 tickets to the reading room issued the year of its opening in 1759; that number actually dwindled in the decades that followed. Anne Goldgar notes that there were usually more stuffed birds on the walls of the reading room than readers.[13] It didn't help, of course, that catalogues were often published entirely in Latin.

The museum proper was not without gatekeeping either: intended primarily for educated people of the middling sort, its ideal visitor was a member of the trade or professional class with a curiosity for the wonders of the natural world and a motivation for self-improvement.[14] Principal Librarian Gowin Knight assured that the ticket application process meant "none but improper persons can be excluded," a phrase that seems to imply inclusiveness—exclusion being an exception to the rule—but nonetheless assumes interested patrons would move in circles of the intellectual elite.[15] Indeed, the grandiosity of Montagu House itself, which housed the museum in its earliest days, required some intellectual and cultural swagger to approach, and many potential visitors likely self-selected out. Despite the official rhetoric of the museum's public good, then, it was less inclusive in practice.

This debate about the public value of the museum—who it's for and how it's for them—is one that has persisted since the opening of the British Museum. The opposition between proper and improper visitors continues to haunt the museum today; in his discussion of the separation of the British Museum from the reading room, Christopher Wright notes that "the gauntlet of security checks between the museum's tourist-filled entry foyer and the library reading room has the air of an international border crossing."[16] The line between tourists and scholars, then and now, is a sharp one.

Museums more broadly continue to struggle with being truly public. Children growing up within blocks of a museum may never enter its doors if its cultural distance obscures its physical proximity. The pervasiveness of this challenge can be seen in efforts like Museums for All, an American initiative that encourages partnering institutions to explicitly train staff in good customer service for low-income patrons.[17]

In essence, museums face the same issues as the academy: they are purportedly public spaces that suffer under the stigma of the ivory tower. This shared stain and the struggle to erase it has shaped the way that civic engagement initiatives in higher education engage with museum spaces. Museums have long been a face of the public humanities. But this version of public humanities can be accused of catering to an elite audience.

If we learn anything from Sloane and the British Museum, it is to take this conundrum seriously. Museums are natural allies for the public scholar, but it is partly because the publics who occupy museum spaces, like those who occupy university spaces, are often select ones. Both spaces seek to provide democratic access, and they may be more open, interactive, and inclusive than they were during the eighteenth century, but the publics they serve tend to be privileged. The choices we make as curators, researchers, and teachers—about what objects and texts are worthy of study and exhibition, the language we use to describe them, and the way they are organized and accessed—are always in danger of re-inscribing this privilege, and risk perpetuating the early British Museum's erroneous belief that serving elite patrons would indirectly benefit all of society, a trickle-down theory of cultural capital.

Historical literature and literary scholarship might be uniquely positioned to challenge museums' reputation for being elitist. While the literary collections in the British Museum were exclusive to the space (and clientele) of the Reading Room, the museum spaces today most closely tied to literature are author house museums: small-budget operations hosting literary tourists. These boutique spaces are not of the white-columned, tall-ceilinged, laser-monitored variety; they are sites of time travel, preserved with the goal of historical accuracy. They are places where visitors can walk in the footsteps of their favorite writers—through Austen's gardens, Wordsworth's hillsides, Shakespeare's streets—or catch a glimpse or a quick brush of the hand against Keats's portrait, Johnson's books, Dickens's reading desk.

Author house museums are, in Alison Booth's words, like other forms of literary tourism, "a critical error, a digression from the real task of interpreting the text"—part snooping, part séance.[18] But, she continues, these practices also extend "immersive reading into the physical present as well as the imagined past," fundamentally changing the way we read texts.[19] Notably, she credits the rise of author house museums to "the converging eighteenth-century developments of private museums and literary biography," culminating in a shift from the religiously tinged pilgrimage to the heritage tourism industry on the fulcrum of the Grand Tour, with relics replaced by mass-produced souvenirs.[20] (Chapter 4, on archives, goes into more depth on this quest for an authentic communion with the past.) More than other museums, perhaps, a house museum is deeply tied to place and space; the objects in the collection (sometimes replicas) are subordinate to the architecture, the neighborhood, and the environment: the creaking door that warned Austen of visitors, the heavy fog of the moors, or the sublimity of the Lake District. The felt experience of a visitor is what gives a house museum meaning.

In fostering and sometimes peddling experiences and merchandise that let visitors identify with favorite authors and characters (buy an amber cross like Fanny Price's at Chawton, or Victorian-style briar rose earrings at the Brontë Parsonage! Listen to their music! Wear their bonnets!),²¹ these author house museums offer an alternative experience of museum-going, encouraging visitors to effuse readerly enthusiasm out loud, to handle replicas with willing suspension of disbelief, and to feel a sense of intimacy with the author.²² Requirement for entry is simple devotion or curiosity (and often a comparatively small fee), making these spaces welcoming to not only tourist groups but also local school trips. They are part memorial, part study, part escapism. And, of course, they become the pilgrimage sites of devoted fans.²³ The participatory, accessible quality of these museums might, in fact, make them the most public of public museums.

The British Museum has over time engaged patrons in a more participatory fashion as well. An assistant to the library at the British Museum in the nineteenth century, Robert Cowtan offers a portrayal of the museum as driven by neither democratic idealism nor damning elitism, but rather slow and steady progress in terms of public access: "Now it is open to all the world, without either fee or delay; and, if the visitor be so inclined, he may inscribe his name and address in a book kept in the entrance-hall, so that his autograph may be preserved for all generations."²⁴ By the nineteenth century, visitors to the British Museum could not only access the collections but also leave their mark. This "two-wayness" is critical, I think, to how museums justify their existence, and it can give us a dialectical model to imitate in the humanities.

To describe the public museum in its ideal form as dialectical is at the heart of both problem and solution. Museums have the remarkable potential to cultivate a sense of reciprocity between the researcher and the reader, the curator and the curious, over a shared interest in a specialized topic. Yet the issue of specialization is also the museum's Achilles' heel, and a term like "dialectical" reminds us that intentionally or not, the imagined audience of the museum has always been specialized and elite. To be dialectical is not necessarily to be dialogic or democratic.

There is a public value in the humanities, just like there is a public value in the British Museum. But to make it truly public—inclusive, open, and diverse—takes work. It is work that makes us think carefully in higher education about the objects we choose to study, the stories we choose to tell about them, the language we choose to tell these stories, and the audiences we choose to speak to. Because the museum world has been grappling with this thorny problem for centuries, museums can be a critical ally for a more public humanities; essays by Kellen Hinrichsen, Stephanie Hess, and Carol Parrish all offer insights from the perspectives of museum curators and enthusiasts.

A WIN-WIN-WIN SCENARIO

Kellen Hinrichsen

The Warren County History Museum is a small institution, with my position being the first and only paid one in the museum's history. The size and scope of our operation mean that we rely heavily on volunteers and interns from around the community, including the local college and its students. This reliance allows us the opportunity to form strong bonds between organizations as well as provide opportunities for students to gain experience in their fields of interest.

When working with students and faculty from a college or university, a museum can find myriad benefits. The level of enthusiasm that is typically found in a student intern or volunteer is very high. I have found that working with student interns and volunteers produces an environment conducive to new ideas and transformative thinking. A student or faculty member who does not come from the museum field may have the ability to look at a problem through a different lens. I have had many experiences in which an intern brought a new idea for display techniques or public outreach methods that had not come to mind before. The youthful enthusiasm and idealism that comes from the theoretical focus of the classroom can be a rejuvenating force in a field that can find itself suffering from tunnel vision and a failure to question past rationales for its work.

While I speak of these collaborative efforts with a great deal of confidence and enthusiasm, there are also other, more challenging sides of partnerships as well. The fact that students and faculty members come from another field can produce new ways of thinking, but they may also require a significant amount of supervision and oversight. It is easy for a museum professional to take for granted knowledge and skill sets that are ingrained in them due to years of education and training but that may not necessarily be common knowledge to a layperson. Though I always try to frame these situations as positive teaching experiences, they can also prove potentially hazardous to the museum or its collection. When working with students in a collection, I always make sure to make myself available for personal supervision to educate the student as well as protect the collections themselves. It is important to always remember that while public outreach and education are priorities for a museum, the preservation of its collection for future generations is paramount.

Challenges in collaborative efforts with outside academics can also come from the expected outcomes or goals of a project. Differences in expectations between museum staff and external partners can be minor or major depending on the project and the collaborating organizations. As stated previously, a paramount requirement for a museum is the preservation of its collection. This imperative goes beyond the physical well-being of the objects to include following specific guidelines that may govern access to or use of specific pieces, such as copyright restrictions, donor regulations, and privacy standards. These necessities can at times conflict with the academic goals of the free transmission of knowledge and research. I have seen collaborative efforts break down due to unforeseen problems related to the dissemination of the research, the handling of artifacts, or even the ownership of the research once completed. Many of these issues can be handled proactively by holding talks with the collaborating organizations prior to any work being done to discuss general rules, outcome goals and requirements, and any legal or ethical issues related to the research or objects used.

Collaboration, though requiring significant planning and oversight, can still provide incredible results. As museum professionals, we must try to remember that among our goals is to educate the public and ensure that research can be done on the collections when appropriate. Whether these collaborations involve research, internship programs, or even a robust volunteer program, they can truly be mutually beneficial. A good example is one of my early actions as executive director of the Warren County History Museum: the establishment of an internship program in partnership with Monmouth College. My first summer at the museum, we had a college intern who was studying public relations, marketing, and event planning, which were all activities the museum required. The intern worked for approximately twenty-four hours per week, a schedule that required approximately six to ten hours of supervision and planning from me on a weekly basis. The internship produced a new way of looking at outreach for the museum, developed largely from the experience and progressive thinking of the intern. The museum now has an active online presence in the community, reaching thousands of people each month.

Among my most enjoyable and rewarding collaborative efforts was a project that was a part of an internship program offered at an institution I worked at in the past. We had formed strong ties with local colleges and universities, providing a robust experiential internship program developed around classroom studies and hands-on supervised projects. My position involved research and content development, helping the most advanced students develop a small exhibit to be displayed for a period of six to twelve months in our galleries. This project would be the culmination of multiple semesters of internships at the museum and was designed to challenge and inspire the students, as well as test all previously acquired skills.

Among the more positive experiences of this project focused on one of our interns who aspired to become a professional curator. To begin the project, we laid out its goals and requirements along with a schedule for the semester. Working primarily on her own, though under my supervision, she determined a topic for the exhibit and pitched the idea to our departmental committee. Once the approval went through, I advised and guided her through the research, object selection, copy writing, and exhibit design phases. The project culminated with her preparing the objects for display and designing the layout of the exhibit itself.

The project in its entirety was very successful, providing what I refer to as a win-win-win scenario: one in which the student, the parent organization (in this case the local university), and the museum all benefit from it. The museum was able to display an exhibit produced by an intern, furthering our own goals of program expansion and content development. The student produced an exhibit that will be a highlight of her future work portfolio, along with gaining new skills to utilize in the future. The local university and her department had a positive educational experience, one that can be pitched to current and prospective students to show the resources available to students.

The project required a great deal of direct supervision on my part, at times up to sixteen hours per week. While this number does seem exceedingly high, the work being done happened to overlap directly with my primary roles at the museum, making the time requirements more agreeable to the administration. Along with the time, the project also raised several potential issues: devotion of prime gallery space to an intern-created exhibit, handling of valuable and extremely fragile items by an intern, and allowing someone who was not a staff member to effectively become the voice of the museum through exhibit text. These issues were all discussed prior to our approval of the project and were among the reasons that I spent so much time supervising the student. My primary supervisory tasks related to theme development, object handling and preparation, exhibit text editing, and general hands-on teaching. Projects such as this were the product of several years of development and trial and error, and I highly recommend that other institutions do not attempt them without a full understanding of the time requirements along with potential issues that may arise. That being said, the intern exhibit development projects provided a unique training opportunity, strong public relations material, new ways of developing content, and the ability to truly align the institution with its mission.

Collaboration has become a hot topic in museums and other nonprofits in recent years. We look to work with other institutions in order to broaden our reach and better utilize our limited resources. Such partnerships can be a daunting task and require a great deal of oversight, but if done properly, they are mutually beneficial. Do not shy away from working with other local groups or organizations. Make the contacts, define what all interested parties expect from the partnership, and make sure to stay organized and communicative throughout the process.

BY COMBINING OUR RESOURCES,
OUR COLLECTIVE GOAL IS MET

Stephanie Hess

The Northfield Historical Society (NHS) is a city-based historical society committed to the discovery, documentation, preservation, and interpretation of the stories of the Northfield area. Since the town is home to not one but two small liberal arts colleges, we often have student volunteers and interns who help us fulfill our mission. We also participate in collaborations with a wide variety of community partners, both academic and not.

Like many small historical institutions, our activities are limited by time, the number of staff, and funding. We are fortunate that we are based in a town with enthusiastic students who are eager for on-the-job experience in a museum or archival setting. Many projects, from high priority to long overdue, are completed with the help of student collaboration. Our student collaborators bring with them an interest in working with historic materials and learning from professionals in the field as well as a sense of community service. When they can see the wider impact of their work in the public view, they feel the collaboration is more worthwhile.

While student collaboration can be very beneficial, it also has its challenges. Students are generally very enthusiastic but have limited prior experience with museums or historical materials, so a sizeable amount of staff time is required to prepare projects, provide on-site training and oversight, and conduct after-the-fact quality control. Still, I have found that once this training is completed, many students can be let loose and become extremely reliable contributors to a project. Often they come up with ways to take the project beyond the basic goals once they understand the purpose behind the work.

The historical society also collaborates with our academic partners based in Northfield in programming, exhibitions, publications, and more. For example, 2016 marked the 150th anniversary of the founding of Carleton College. In an attempt to involve the wider community in the celebration during the 2016–2017 academic year, Carleton and the NHS collaborated on a special exhibition on the theme of college-town relations over the years. The exhibition was developed by the college's head of special collections, who knew his materials but not how to create an effective display. NHS provided the gallery space and the exhibit expertise — both in content development and design and installation. In conjunction with this exhibition, many of our spring lecture programs focused on the ways that Carleton and Northfield have been intertwined throughout their history. This exhibition and lecture series benefited both partners: the museum gained more visitors interested in the college and Carleton shared its history with the wider Northfield community.

Another way that the NHS fulfills its mission is through the Northfield History Collaborative (NHC), a community-based partnership that preserves and makes accessible digital versions of records of the history of the Northfield area. It was established in 2007 to create accessible online archives of Northfield area history, and it has grown to include partners as diverse as local libraries, archives, churches, a hospital, and a bank, as well as Northfield's two colleges, Carleton College and St. Olaf College.

Although the partners of the NHC have diverse backgrounds and different agendas, they all realize that they own items of great historical significance that are either deteriorating under less than ideal conditions, or underutilized and hidden away in a basement safe. The majority of these partners simply do not have the means, time, or knowledge to preserve or share their collection properly, but they recognize the value of what they have. In other words, our partners have the historical assets while the NHC has the digitization expertise, so by combining our resources, our collective goal is met.

While much of the digitization work is completed using grant funding, the NHC also benefits from collaborations with area students, particularly those interested in utilizing technology to increase public access to rare historical materials. In some cases, this means the students are not the history majors who most often intern with us but come from diverse courses of study like computer science, art, sociology, and more. They learn best practices for scanning, transcribing handwritten documents, and creating descriptive metadata so the digitized items can be easily found. The skills they gain, including patience, consistency, attention to detail, using concise language, and more, can be used in a variety of future settings. While these students enable the NHC to complete digitization projects, we also want them to gain usable job skills so that all of the parties involved can benefit.

Through my work with the NHC, I have become a firm believer in the power of collaboration to benefit the historical community, especially with digital projects. I believe the NHC is unique because we involve partners that go beyond traditional academic institutions, archives, or museums. We recognize that many groups in a community have a history that is relevant, significant, and valued by many. Our partners provide the raw material and receive easily usable, digitally preserved copies of their materials. Thanks to our partners, the NHC is able to grow our online database to include a variety of historical topics, ultimately benefitting the wider community beyond Northfield itself. Community partnerships work well when all parties involved bring something to the table and also stand to benefit from the result.

THOUGHTS ON INTERNSHIPS AND STUDENT VOLUNTEERISM
Carol Parrish

From 2012 to 2015, I had the opportunity to work with three different groups of Monmouth College students. The students were members of either a class or the history club, volunteers performing the thirty hours of service required by the college, or participants in an internship at the Warren County History Museum.

I would honestly have to say that I am not sure that the student volunteer programs, as a whole, worked well. At the time I was working with the students, all activity at the museum was done by local volunteers ranging in age from their mid-fifties to seventies. The volunteers worked during the day, timing that obviously conflicted with students' class schedules. Since evenings were better for them, most students were given assignments that included some type of internet research and didn't require them to be at the museum. But if they did need to be at the museum, most students had a car to get to the facility. I would personally pick up those who didn't have cars. I appreciated that they all were courteous and grateful for the rides offered to them to get their requirements completed.

With each individual or group, I tried to give them an experience that would broaden their sense of history. History becomes more alive when you can have a firsthand account of something you learned in school. My last intern assisted me in researching the local history of World War I. I did not feel confident enough to let her do research in the local newspaper archives because her grasp of history was not broad enough. I was reluctant because she might not identify topics that, although they might not work for the World War I exhibit, might be useful to me in a future exhibit. However, there was plenty of copied microfilm that needed to be typed for the exhibit, so I had her help with that. She was learning history, but typing is not the most exciting thing to do. Therefore, I took a different approach.

We made a field trip to a nearby town to visit its military museum, which focuses on the county's involvement in conflicts beginning with the Civil War. The man I wanted the student to meet is a Vietnam veteran, and I asked him to tell her about losing his leg during that conflict. I was so proud of the questions the intern asked and her desire to know him better. When we left, her comment to me was that she had believed all Vietnam veterans were angry and bitter. That is what she had learned from books or other sources. However, my friend was anything but that! He shared his love for the United States and the duty he felt to serve as a soldier for the country. The student gained a broader perspective and learned that there is always more than one side to a story. If anything, that one day made all my time with students worthwhile.

As I mentioned earlier, most students came with a limited general knowledge of US history. Since most lived outside the county, they also knew very little about its history. They don't know about places and family names that were important to our local history. However, they were very helpful when it came to moving heavy items for exhibits or creating short-term displays using the computer. Even then, I would ask them what they thought they were moving and spark a discussion. From the questions they asked, I learned that I needed to be more descriptive when interpreting an exhibit in display labels. I never felt time was wasted in discussion.

In retrospect, the student volunteer program may have been more beneficial to students than for the museum, but in the end it was important to me that these young people learned where to go when they are looking for information about their history. History is fun, entertaining, broad in scope, and beneficial to all who look for those hidden stories that make life that much more interesting!

With mentors and allies in museums like Kellen, Stephanie, Carol, and others, I learned how to use my research in the humanities for a public purpose. As a graduate student, I had the good fortune to curate an exhibit at the Old Capitol Museum[25] in Iowa City on British women writers. The educational programs coordinator read a draft of my captions for the displays, and I remember how nervous she seemed to give me feedback. When pressed, she asked if I would be willing to consider not using the word "dialectical" quite so many times in the label text for the exhibit.

I was mortified. All my efforts in graduate school to perfect the style of academic prose had so altered the way I wrote and even the way I read, that I hadn't realized my imagined audience—whether I was writing a paper, dashing off an email, or ordering a sandwich—was always other academics. My academic orientation in graduate school had manifested in an esoteric and off-putting specialization of vocabulary.

Like the debates surrounding the ambiguously public purpose of the British Museum, this moment opened a space for me to think about, in the words of Anne Goldgar, "public access and relations between elite and popular within the museum, [and it] brought debates about public culture and definitions of the public into sharp relief."[26] For me, the coordinator's criticism of my use of "dialectical" sparked a larger anxiety about my own detachment from the public, a public I so deeply wanted to reach and, more importantly, be a part of. I wanted to share the stories of eighteenth- and nineteenth-century British women writers with my Iowa community, but the language was all wrong; I was building up the very barriers I wanted to knock down.

Somehow amid these spiraling reveries on my own inadequacy, I managed to thank my colleague for pointing out the problem. "Oh," she added, once she realized I was grateful for the advice, "while we're on the subject, it might be nice if some of the sentences were a little shorter too. And, maybe with less semicolons. Maybe we could try to make the sentences less than, say, five lines?"

Now, don't get me wrong; I love precision in language as much as the next English professor who chose this line of work partly due to a deep love for the taste of beautiful words strung together. But "dialectical"? Five-line sentences? She had a point.

A few semesters earlier, I had taken a graduate seminar called the Politics of Style, in which we read examples of avant-garde scholarship: Patricia Limerick's "Dancing with Professors: The Trouble with Academic Prose" (which has given me personal comfort for my dark days in high school, hiding in the women's restroom during dances) and Susan J. Leonardi's "Recipe for Reading: Summer Pasta, Lobster a la Riseholme, and Key Lime Pie" (a copy of which is stashed, stained, above the stove in my kitchen; her summer pasta recipe is still a favorite in our house).[27] With Professor Judith Pascoe at the helm, we set out on a crusade to slash jargon and question disciplinary norms of argument and style. And here I was using "dialectical." In a museum. Multiple times.

British Museum founder Sir Hans Sloane himself was embroiled in debates about specialized vocabulary in the museum. In his case, however, he "became a prominent exponent of the empirical method as both an epistemological and a literary procedure"—in other words, his trouble was that he wrote too much like a scientist.[28] His method for meticulously recording and describing earned him the ridicule even of fellow intellectuals, who mocked his "incomprehensible language."[29] In sharing Sloane's weakness, I could count myself grateful to be only gently nudged rather than publicly satirized for my linguistic misstep.

While some poets scoffed at Sloane's style, we would be remiss to divorce the classificatory impulse from the writings of eighteenth-century literati: by the Romantic period, Judith Pascoe argues, "object narratives—tales of sofas, thimbles, old shoes, and pincushions—multiplied into a distinct genre that seems to have stemmed from a communal desire to know what physical things had to say."[30] This impulse to give voice to inanimate objects, to let them tell their own stories, is at the heart of museum writing as well. Ian R. Willison has argued that the classification of knowledge—more than the rise of encyclopedias, philosophes, public opinion, and publishing—is what most democratized learning in the eighteenth century.[31] Despite Sloane's specialized scientific vocabulary, we could also argue that his classificatory impulse made his collections meaningful for a public audience. While the artifacts may get all the glory, the curation of them through classification and description, creating "the symbiotic relationship of object and narrative," is part of what gave those artifacts public value.[32] Sloane simply struggled to express that meaning in a way the public could appreciate.

His struggle to translate specialized vocabulary to a public audience is one that haunts many curators and academics alike. However, the eighteenth century also offers us a possible solution to this tension. One of the most important ways to translate theory into practice (as Sloane learned the hard way) is to reconsider where and how we write.

After teaching freshman writing for many years and talking with students over and over about the importance of audience awareness, I have realized that's a lecture I need to give myself on occasion. "Write a paper that you'd actually want to read." "Use language that helps your reader think through your ideas." "Help your readers feel like they're discovering ideas alongside you." All of these little writing mantras suddenly took on new force as I was staring down the possibility of sharing my academic research with a public audience at the Old Capitol Museum and stumbling over my own specialized vocabulary. And, now as a teacher, exhibit curation has become one of my strategies for teaching students how to write effectively. The essays by Paul Schuytema and Jess Bybee included in this chapter offer perspectives on those collaborative assignments, and Chuck Lewis provides a model for teaching through museum curation.

SHOW THEM THE HEARTBEAT

Paul Schuytema

What was once just prairie grass is now corn and soybeans (beans planted every third year to recharge the nitrogen in the soil) as far as the eye can see. The soil is rich and dark and the land is flat—maddingly flat. In the middle is a little square town called Monmouth, the county seat and home to ten thousand people. Founded in 1831 and birthplace to the famous (and morally complicated) lawman Wyatt Earp, the town is two miles square, with Main and Broadway intersecting in the exact middle, with a roundabout called, oddly, Public Square.

I've called Monmouth home for the last twenty-five years. In that time, I've worked as a writer, teacher, computer game designer, entrepreneur, concert promoter, musician, software developer, creativity trainer, and economic development consultant. I've taught at Monmouth College. I've run my own software company (we made the games for the *Survivor* television series). Now, I serve as the director of community and economic development for the city of Monmouth, with my initial charge from the mayor being to "make downtown cool."

For much of my time living in town, Monmouth College and the larger community happily coexisted, but mostly within their own separate bubbles—the two didn't often dovetail, to mix a metaphor. There was little tension, but there was also hardly any collaboration.

Then a shift began to take place in early 2012. The administration of the college realized that a liberal arts degree was really about teaching students to be productive, creative citizens in their chosen communities. To that end, the students (and by necessity, the faculty as well) needed to get actively engaged in their community (the Monmouth community) while in college. One of the first events to sprout out of this new mission was a civic engagement symposium in late January 2012. The primary participants were faculty members, with a few community leaders sprinkled in; I was one of those sprinkles. Day two was a practical workshop to explore ways of using writing to engage students in the community—to see if writing itself could be a service the students could provide to the community. We brainstormed and discussed ideas, most coming in the form of writing to tell our community's story.

The goals were noble and the projects potentially exciting and enriching, but during the discussions, some cracks began to appear on the vase. What became painfully clear as the hours wore on is that the well-intentioned faculty knew almost nothing about the community they were trying to engage their students in. History, current and past community leaders, the form and function of civic government, business, culture outside of the campus walls—all of these were blurry concepts viewed through a kind of rich, lingering London fog.

It became clear to the attendees that day that in order to create meaningful engagements for their students, the faculty must first step up and become the first line of engagement. They needed to understand and interact with their larger community in order to bring meaningful opportunities for learning, scholarship, and service to their students. That realization was the first step toward some truly meaningful twenty-first-century dovetailing of the campus and the community here in Monmouth.

I was fortunate to be involved in a few early efforts to help tell the stories of our community for our community. The first was a solo project that grew directly out of my experience at the symposium. I was long a fan of Hirsch, Kett, and Trefil's *The Dictionary of*

Cultural Literacy, whose subtitle is *What Every American Needs to Know*. That book inspired me to create an online dictionary of civic literacy for our city website. These web pages provide concise information on our city's history, the municipal government, and how our municipal public works function.

The second came about in a flash of shared inspiration. In late 2012, the state of Illinois launched an experimental grant program called the Broadband Innovation Fund. The idea was simple: much of Illinois had at least some broadband access back then, so how were we going to use it? I attended one of the informational meetings about the grant process, and I was jotting down ideas for a grant proposal when a recent conversation popped into my head. A few weeks earlier, Bridget and I had shared a glass of wine at the local wine shop and talked about ways we could unearth and share our community's stories.

At that moment, I knew what our project would be: the Warren County Virtual Museum. Bridget and I worked to put together the proposal and brought in some key community stakeholders: the Warren County Public Library, the Buchanan Center for the Arts (which had both recently created a Journey Stories exhibit in partnership with the Smithsonian), Monmouth College, the city of Monmouth, the Warren County Historical Society, Midwest Bank of Western Illinois, and Frontier Communications (the last two for matching funds and in-kind contributions).

We *did* receive one of the inaugural awards and were proud to be the only applicant who was actually building an online application. Over the coming months, we created a custom web application that allowed us to create a virtual museum of community storytelling — based on digital artifacts and exhibits (all Dublin Core compliant, so our metadata is standard!).

In the three years since launching the virtual museum, community members and Monmouth College students have collaborated to author over forty exhibits featuring over 420 individual digital artifacts. These are the stories of our community, now available for all to share. Of specific note are dozens of exhibits that all embody the theme of local heroes, a theme borrowed from a sister project in Iowa City, in partnership with the Studio and the Virtual Writing University at the University of Iowa. Bridget created one of Monmouth College's senior capstone courses in Citizenship and Civic Engagement focusing on these local heroes. In the class, students explored and researched Monmouth and Warren County local heroes (both past and present) and learned the skills needed to tell their stories through words, images, and video as an exhibit in our virtual museum.

One form of local hero is rather unusual. In 2015, Bridget and I team-taught the course and treated historic buildings in downtown Monmouth as heroes of the community—as vessels for stories of living, working, and civic change. Through research in county records, business directories, and newspaper articles, the students explored the tales of downtown buildings and the businesses they housed. Through physical tours of those buildings, they experienced the challenges of maintaining century-old historic building stock. They toured renovated buildings with trendy loft apartments and boutique retail stores. They also toured abandoned buildings with caving-in rafters and peeling plaster that are home now only to pigeons. They learned about modern fire codes, Americans with Disabilities Act regulations, and the extremely expensive challenge of making a building erected in 1891 safe and code-compliant for the next generation.

This course and other capstone courses in citizenship at Monmouth College are a powerful step forward in engaging students in their larger community. But these courses have also revealed a challenge. I've had the opportunity to guest lecture in many of these courses, and I always ask a few standard questions of these seniors: "How many of you have been downtown to an art exhibit opening at the Buchanan Center for the Arts?" "How many of you have attended the local blues festival?" "How many of you have attended a leadership luncheon to listen to local leaders tell their story?" Sadly, maybe one or two hands (if any) pop up as answers to these questions. These wonderfully smart, gifted students who are wrapping up their four years as members of the Monmouth community have still hardly ever set foot in the events and moments that make our community alive and vibrant. And that's a shame.

Faculty members should step out of the ivory tower and do more in their community than simply shop and eat. They should seek out the history and the stories of the community (and past moments of campus and community collaboration), they should volunteer to serve on the boards of civic organizations, they should at least be a guest at a service club meeting, and they should seek out community events that have nothing to do with their institution. They should find the heartbeat of their community and embrace it—and then bring that enthusiasm back to their students.

And both the institution and its faculty members should take new students by the hand and walk them downtown—show them the community, tell them why it's important and valuable, why it matters. Say to those students: "This is *your* home, *your* community for the next four years. Be an active part of it."

HAPPY ACCIDENTS

Jess Bybee

As a senior at Monmouth College, the capstone course of my liberal arts experience and the Integrated Studies Program was called Citizenship: Local Heroes. In this course, we were asked to reflect on and challenge our understanding of the term citizenship, in order to actively engage with the community and establish our own roles as citizens in the larger world. Our professor, Dr. Bridget Draxler, took us on many field trips hoping to trigger some sort of internal response from each of us, a response that would ultimately inspire a research project that would serve as a vehicle for discovery in the realm of civic engagement. During a visit to a local history museum (on a tour with Carol Parrish, who has also contributed an essay to this volume), my classmates and I were instantly fascinated by the differences between our lives as women in the twenty-first century and the lives of women in Monmouth in the nineteenth century. We explored archives, historical documents, and old photographs to construct a narrative that simultaneously highlighted the stark contrast between the lives of female students at Monmouth College at the time of its founding in 1853 and those of the current female students in 2013, while also highlighting the immense progress that our predecessors made toward achieving the rights and privileges we had as students in the twenty-first century.

To convey this narrative, we were asked to curate a virtual

museum exhibit, an exercise that challenged us in more ways than we thought possible. As with all group projects, this curating exercise required us to meld all our individual voices and experiences into one cohesive narrative voice. After several frustrating and failed attempts at unifying our voices for exhibit labels, we found that we were most successful utilizing a filtration system that developed organically as the project progressed. Basically, each group member was responsible for researching and constructing a particular piece of our narrative timeline, which would then be filtered through the group's designated editor. Once the editor had the pieces of the timeline, she edited all of the pieces to create one cohesive voice for the exhibit.

Our success with this process fueled our interest in the topic of women even more, so for our second research project on local heroes, we focused on the life of Gracie Peterson, a lifelong pillar of community engagement for the city of Monmouth. While studying her life, we realized that we had inadvertently begun constructing a comprehensive timeline of women at Monmouth College. By starting our first project in the nineteenth century at the beginning of the college's history, we had researched the role of female students until the turn of the twentieth century. Around that time, Gracie Peterson was born, and she had become the focus of our second project. In 2006, Peterson died, and four years later, we were matriculated as freshman at Monmouth College. This discovery elevated our experience tremendously, and I believe that it compelled us all to deepen our research and personal investment—which ultimately became the key to our success.

Interesting projects facilitate these types of discoveries. At the time, realizing Peterson enabled us to tell a larger story felt like a happy accident, and I believe that's how I phrased it in my final presentation. Now, though, with a few years' separation from the project, I can safely say that discoveries like this happen when students feel excited and engaged. Momentum builds, minds come together, and before you know it, the course transcends a classroom experience, writing assignments, or group work and becomes a living, breathing experience that students will carry with them long after they graduate. The project allowed me to broaden my horizons beyond the class and ultimately college itself. It allowed me to recognize the impact that my research had on not only the community, but also my own understanding of the community and my role in it. Though at the time the project seemed slightly more taxing, both mentally and emotionally, than most of my other coursework, the amount of personal and academic growth that I experienced was well worth the time spent.

CURATING CHAOS

Chuck Lewis

A few years ago I taught a course at Beloit College entitled American Realisms: From Grit Lit to Ashcan Art, which focused on fiction and painting from the Civil War to World War I. A major part of the class entailed having the students work with me and the director and curator at the college's Wright Art Museum to put up a full-size exhibit consisting of twenty to thirty works selected from the museum's holdings, excerpts from fiction the class was reading, and both critical and creative writing by the students. The idea arose out of my own tendency to talk about literary techniques in visual terms, a campus push to integrate our two museums more into the learning experiences of our students, and a broader campus initiative we called "labs across the curriculum" that supplied funding for curricular experimentation and innovative teaching.

This was a substantial project that included opening up the museum's collection to the students, collaborating on a curatorial concept for the show (which entailed curating chaos as well), letting them select all the materials (our only theme was "realisms and representations," so we were all over the map), and giving them hands-on responsibilities for everything from labels and lighting to arranging and even hanging the work—all with the patient guidance of the curator and his assistant. The students even saw to campus marketing and the catering for the opening. It was a lot of work and a rewarding experience; now the exhibit poster on my office wall is a sort of inspiration for what can go right. One of the little highlights for me was when the students had the idea of making our show feel more like a cool installation performance. They came up with the idea of having everyone submit a paragraph of their class writing, which three of them recorded in a sort of round-robin mash-up mix to electronica. We then always had the track playing quietly when the museum was open—a sort of background babbling brook of the students' critical discourse.

What did I learn? You need a museum staff who *want* to make their resources available as a learning space. You will learn about strengths and weaknesses (and interests) that you wouldn't know your students possessed if you had stayed in the classroom. You might need to remember that making this sort of activity truly public can create additional challenges to navigate in terms of how you lead and let go (I'm a control freak, but it was their show). And you will miss it the next time you teach the course without it. Finally, I learned that even if I can't mount an exhibit every semester, there are takeaway benefits like partnering with nonfaculty staff, getting teaching and learning out of the classroom, and even stumbling onto a new line of research that has informed my scholarship and teaching ever since.

The shift in language that I was grappling with in writing the labels for the exhibit at the Old Capitol Museum was tied to a shift in audience and purpose, and most significantly to a shift in space. When I looked at my research and the work I had committed my life to as a scholar, the question, so what?—which sometimes felt like an accusation or a challenge within academe—felt like an invitation at the museum. Curating an exhibit was, for me, not just about translating my work for a public audience and putting it on display; it was a space where I rediscovered the delight I felt about my own subject area. It was a space where I felt comfortable being both the inquisitive scholar and the devoted fan, a space where I could problematize like a good graduate student but also unabashedly relish the beauty, the humor, the poignancy, and the joy of books. I studied books because I loved books, and the museum was a space where I felt both activities were valued. The words I chose, I slowly realized, needed to reflect both love and study.

I should back up and begin by saying that I didn't intend to curate museum exhibits when I started graduate school. This shift in space was one that I desperately needed but didn't expect to find. The year before I began working on the exhibit, I had participated in the Obermann

Graduate Institute on Engagement and the Academy, a crash course for University of Iowa graduate students on publicly engaged teaching and scholarship. It was an inspiring week that renewed my hope for the future of higher education—and made me instantly regret choosing to specialize in eighteenth-century British literature. It made sense, I thought, for all these urban planners, artists, and environmentalists to be doing public work. I can even see how creative writers or, say, the twentieth-century multiethnic lit camp could get excited about this. But eighteenth-century British literature? It was difficult for me to imagine how I could use my expertise in public work.

A few months later, when I was working with a group of fellow graduate students on a bid to host the 2009 British Women Writers Conference at the University of Iowa, Teresa Mangum (who had cocreated the Obermann Institute and encouraged us to host the conference, and who is coeditor of this series, Humanities and Public Life) pulled me aside and pointed out what I couldn't see. The conference would be an opportunity to assemble a small exhibit for the long weekend of the meeting, which could also be open to the public. The wheels started turning. A museum exhibit would be a way to share the research I was so passionate about with an interested academic audience *and* the wider community. It could be my entree as a public scholar.

While I had been skeptical about the public interest in, as opposed to the public value of, eighteenth-century British literature, a museum seemed to offer sacred space, a shrine for nerds like me to unite. The long eighteenth century continues to pop up in museums all the time, in both permanent and temporary exhibits, from A Woman's Wit: Jane Austen's Life and Legacy at the Morgan Library and Museum to the Jane Austen Reading Room at the Minneapolis Institute of Art to the Fame and Friendship: Pope, Roubiliac, and the Portrait Bust in Eighteenth-Century Britain at the Yale Center for British Art, not to mention the permanent Enlightenment gallery at the British Museum itself, which opened in 2003.[33] Digital exhibits like Janine Barchas's What Jane Saw have carried these conversations online.[34] While exhibits, online and offline, raise issues of access and canonical privilege, the act of careful curation, juxtaposing ideas that throw one another into relief, is familiar to any academic who has ever created a syllabus or written a literature review.[35] Making connections, explaining context, telling stories—that's what we do in the humanities.

When I first set out to curate my exhibit, I didn't realize how close to home the work would seem. Building on the conference theme of Fresh Threads of Connection, I started looking at the ways that British women writers evoke nature in their texts: scientifically, politically, or metaphorically as a representation of womanhood. I also started looking around the university's Special Collections to find early editions and illustrated copies of these texts. I put together an informal proposal. Teresa introduced me to a friend at the Old Capitol Museum who was instantly smitten with the idea of turning the Hansen Humanities Gallery into an English parlor room full of famous women writers like Jane Austen and Beatrix Potter. And suddenly, my little weekend exhibit turned into a full six-month show that opened a little over a year later.

The space of the Hansen Humanities Gallery itself epitomized the way complex negotiations of space and access figured into the exhibit. Though housed in the Old Capitol Museum, a former state building with classical architecture and tall columns, firmly planted on the top of a hill, a physical manifestation of the museum as a domineering space of privilege, the Hanson Humanities Gallery is a small basement room with low ceilings and small doorways. Tucked away half underground, it is a space within a space that embodies all the contradictions of the public museum.

Logistically, I can only describe the process as organic and serendipitous. My exhibit proposal and the conference timeline happened to coincide with an opening in the gallery's schedule, and the director happened to have a fondness for historical women writers. The museum was the only one to give formal approval; I realized in hindsight that I should have gotten consent from my graduate committee to take on a project of this magnitude, but I had no idea going into the project how much time it would take, so in the end I asked for forgiveness rather than permission.

The difficulty of fitting a major, supposedly tangential research project into a graduate student timeline turned out to be less complicated than I expected. The museum funded the project entirely, including everything from the paint on the walls to the exhibit label printing costs to refreshments at events, and even generously provided a small summer stipend for my research. It was the first time the museum staff or I had done something quite like this, and the typical hurdles in civic engagement projects (money and time) didn't trip us up, partly because we were naive enough not to worry about them.

Curating the exhibit began as an escape from traditional scholarly work, but it became an exercise in research and synthesis on a grand scale. Looking at primary and secondary texts, I was forming an argument that had a nexus but spun out to numerous variations and iterations. I was tying together textual analysis with historical and biographical context to build evidence and create persuasive case studies. I was nodding to other scholars but making a new argument. I learned the aesthetic and practical habits of intellectual work that I needed to learn as a graduate student, and this learning was deep because it was contextualized. I was, in a sense, writing a dissertation without realizing it at the time: a dissertation for a committee of diverse public readers.

Of course, I wasn't actually writing a dissertation—at the time, I was studying for comprehensive exams. The exhibit opened in March that year, and I took my exams in April. With all the pressure in graduate programs on time to degree, it might seem irresponsible to spend more than a year curating a museum exhibit that doesn't count as a course or even a publication. I did it (in the words of Darcy) against my own better judgment, and if I'm honest about why I didn't ask permission, it's that I didn't want to hear "no."

At the same time, the amount of overlap between the reading lists for the exhibit and my exams was significant. Moreover, with the exhibit in mind I read this literature and scholarship differently—closer and more carefully, but also with some distance, with some awareness of a broader historical arc. I read better, because there were real stakes to understanding and engaging these texts. And despite my stage fright, after being interviewed on the *Dottie Ray Show* on KXIC and Joan Kjaer's *World Canvass* program for Iowa Public Radio, I hardly felt intimidated by an oral defense in front of five people. Curating the exhibit helped me to do better scholarship: it helped me to succeed in my comprehensive exams, it prepared me to write a dissertation, and it helped me to think critically about language in ways that still inform my writing.

To put it another way, curating a museum exhibit developed all the skills in reading, research, and writing that any graduate program could hope to offer its students, with the added bonus of giving my work a public purpose. In addition to all the intangible qualities of self-awareness, critical thinking, and connection to a broader human consciousness, this experience gave me very concrete skills like developing a working timeline for a collaborative project, planning and hosting community events, writing grant proposals, and designing publicity materials. In addition to responding to the pragmatist's call for transferable skills, it also satisfied the idealist in me. I found inspiration in the women writers I was studying, but I also found a different kind of inspiration in the female colleagues on the museum staff with whom I collaborated; they mentored me and were supportive and interested in my work in a nonacademic, gratifying way. They also, as noted earlier, taught me a thing or two about writing.[36]

The exhibit also benefited the museum, whose own staff were strapped for time and didn't have the content expertise needed. They saw the potential for broad public appeal in the topic, in addition to the guaranteed audience of several hundred scholars who would visit the museum as part of the British Women Writers Conference that spring.

When I participated in the Obermann Graduate Institute on Engagement and the Academy, we had talked a lot about reciprocity: the need for academic and community partners to have a mutually beneficial relationship. I agreed with the concept in theory, but I didn't fully understand what reciprocity meant until I began working with staff at the Old Capitol. On one level, it was fairly utilitarian: I had expertise in the subject matter, and they had the space and resources. However, the reality was much more complicated than that.

To begin with, there were many people involved in small and large ways: museum staff, library staff, layout designers, builders, printers, framers, and not least my fellow conference planners. And although the Old Capitol Museum is affiliated with the University of Iowa, negotiating the specifics of long-term loans of the books from Special Collections was an involved process. Our original plan of borrowing portraits of the women writers from various British institutions was scaled down to finding and framing reproductions. After choosing books and images and writing label text, we then had to address logistical details like the design and layout of the room, including everything from recreating a fireplace fit for an English country parlor to choosing paint swatches for the walls. (Though the exhibit focused on women, William Morris provided the ambiance.)

In addition to preparing the exhibit itself, we also coordinated public programs, including a Jane Austen film series at a local public library; an original stage production of *Emma* by the Usher's Ferry Theatre Company; twin events on Beatrix Potter, a puppet show for children and a lecture on environmentalism for adults; and an evening of English country dance lessons. We even had a Frankenstein arts-and-crafts day, in which I got to rewrite *Frankenstein* for three- to five-year-olds (and may be guilty of waxing poetic about why they should replace neck bolts with lustrous black hair on their pictures of the Creature, who was *not* called Frankenstein).

During the year leading up to the opening and the six months of the show, the public programs coordinator and I met multiple times each week. After our meetings, we would linger to talk about the persona that Lady Mary Wortley Montagu created through her portrait and the thrilling eccentricity of Margaret Cavendish's *The Description of a New World, called the Blazing World* (1666). These conversations reinvigorated my passion for this literature by seeing it through someone else's eyes — not only the eyes of my imagined audience from the conference and the community, but also the eyes of a new colleague. These conversations reminded me why I was getting my PhD, while also making me wonder whether an academic position would be the only or even best way to share my love of historical literature.

Curating a museum exhibit became a form of alt-ac training, increasingly popular in graduate education (see the essay by the Graduate College's Dean John C. Keller included here). It helped me to write for public audiences, it introduced me to making arguments with both text and images, and it gave me an opportunity to develop public programs and events. I learned to think about budgets and loan agreements. It gave me skills and experiences that could easily transfer to a career in a cultural institution or a nonprofit agency. Maybe more significantly, when I later went on the market, I was excited by the possibility of an alt-ac career: it wasn't a backup plan, but a real possibility, and one I felt prepared to enjoy and succeed in.

PUBLIC HUMANITIES AND GRADUATE EDUCATION

John C. Keller

As associate provost for graduate and professional education and dean of the Graduate College at the University of Iowa, I seek to foster an intellectual environment conducive to exemplary research, scholarship, and creativity — ensuring our students receive the best education possible and helping them secure employment that matches their interests with their skills and experience.

To achieve this goal, in 2007 the Graduate College partnered with the University of Iowa's Obermann Center for Advanced Studies to start the Obermann Graduate Institute on Engagement and the Academy, a one-week interdisciplinary institute in which graduate students from across campus explore how civic engagement can enhance teaching, research, and creative work.

The Graduate College and the Obermann Center work together to connect graduate students with activists, scholars, community members, and many others. Graduate students use the institute to bring their vision for community engagement to their classrooms, their projects, and their community at large. Seeking a public audience for their research allows graduate students to establish partnerships that they turn to daily in their current work.

Civic engagement early in graduate school helps shape students' professional and personal trajectories, infusing their work with a dedication to local communities. We see this play out with engaged students who later become engaged, socially conscious faculty. In addition, early experience with civic engagement provides the spaces and relationships with which students can practice vital professional skills such as networking, leadership, and teamwork. These skills and this familiarity with civic engagement become essential later when students seek jobs in academe or beyond.

One recent University of Iowa PhD student in history parlayed his community engagement work, along with his well-written dissertation, into a position as a senior historian at Vantage Point Historical Services, Inc., an award-winning, full-service historical consulting firm that works across the United States and Canada. This student was an Obermann Graduate Institute scholar and senior fellow. As such, he helped develop a program that included a visit to the Office of the State Archaeologist, where graduate students learned how connections between research and public outreach are integral to working with American Indian tribes on Native American Graves Protection and Repatriation Act claims.

In addition to promoting community engagement, we have created initiatives to help students clearly articulate the importance and relevance of their work to the public. The notion of the public dissertation abstract and the Three Minute Thesis Competition enhance the relationship between graduate research and scholarship on our campus.

As Graduate College Dean, I encourage graduate students to be creators of change in their communities by establishing connections for sharing their innovative ideas with the public and advancing their careers.

Helen Small's 2013 *The Value of the Humanities* suggests that, after a "long history of anti-instrumentalism in the humanities," scholars are warming to the idea of our "social benefit."[37] Interpreting this benefit broadly as both economic and cultural value, Small subtly frames the utility of a humanities education as an interplay of applied value, personal growth, and social improvement. Citing Louis Menand's 2010 *The Marketplace of Ideas*, Small paraphrases his argument: "At a time when there are fewer and fewer jobs in academia to be trained *for*, the academics presiding over doctoral education can easily feel in bad faith with their students."[38] But she suggests that critics like Menand underestimate the value of a humanities degree and concludes that a broader understanding of use value persists despite market realities: graduate students "take pleasure in the intellectual experience despite the poverty of the economic return, because they perceive some remaining cultural value in their studies, and because they can reasonably hope that if they do not stay in academia they will nevertheless not have wasted their time there."[39]

Before collaborating with the Old Capitol Museum staff, I can't say that I would have agreed with Small on that final point. I felt there was personal and cultural value in my studies, but I wasn't quite prepared to face the possibility of not getting an academic position without feeling at least a twinge of regret at my wasted time. But while Small rejects the idea that public engagement is enough to secure the future of graduate education, it is precisely that engagement that has allowed me to endorse her optimistic conclusion. Public engagement is what made alt-ac careers feel interesting and exciting instead of like a consolation prize. In addition, public engagement is how I developed skills and experiences that I needed to be a viable candidate for nonacademic positions—and as it turned out, for academic positions, too.

By the end of my graduate studies, the binary between academic work and public work seemed spurious. I came to see the academy itself as a public good, curating courses of study for its students, and public engagement as a natural extension of the mission of higher education institutions. And as I have found, there are many meaningful, satisfying ways to use a graduate degree in the humanities. In the end, I left a tenure-track position for an alt-ac career; but even though my current position doesn't require a PhD, I wouldn't trade those years in graduate school for the world. My education isn't just a credential; it's who I am and how I think.

After the exhibit was over, the public education and outreach coordinator and I met for coffee to reflect on the experience. I was eager to get her advice on how I could be a better collaborator next time with future community partners. While I had thought of next time in an abstract sense, we quickly began scheming a new project: I was teaching a course on Gothic literature in the fall, and my students would write and perform adaptations of the assigned works for children at the Old Capitol's annual Halloween event, the Creepy Campus Crawl.[40] And just like that, we were onto the next project.

This moment, I think, marked a new awareness for me: that publicly engaged projects could arise not only from questions like "I have a great idea—what community partner can I work with?" but also from questions like "we want to continue working together—what can we do next?" True reciprocity, I think, is marked by a privileging of the relationships over the work. Find people, not projects; work *with* someone, Teresa Mangum taught me, not *for* someone. While we often hear about the value of long-term projects for public scholarship and one-off short term projects are dismissed as drive-by service, I would argue that true sustainability is about long-term collaboration that may take the form of a series of projects or a long-term project that may cycle through a series of collaborators.

I find it telling that Fresh Threads of Connection was nominated for an Iowa Cultural Corridor Alliance Excellence in Innovation Award, not for the exhibit itself but for the collaboration between the museum, public libraries, university, and local theater behind it.[41] The exhibit, in the end, was as much about the fresh threads of connection between community partners as it was between British women writers. This nomination was a testament to the fact that part of the value of the public humanities is tied up in the collaboration, the process rather than the product.

That, in my mind, was our greatest success. It was dialectical: we just didn't call it that.

Curating this exhibit also created fresh threads of connection for me. In addition to ongoing collaboration with the Old Capitol Museum, I continued to collaborate with the university and public libraries we had worked with for the exhibit. I started bringing my students into Special Collections and the Women's Archives at the university library to do research projects, and I started a series of reading groups at a local library that had hosted several of our events (see chapter 2).

At one point, I put together a genealogy of engaged scholarship to help tell my own story of how I got started sharing historical literature with community partners. Like all stories, this story has many versions. Sometimes I focus on the audience: my dissertation had five readers, and nearly ten thousand people visited the Old Capitol Museum while Fresh Threads of Connection was open. Sometimes I emphasize the importance of starting small or building relationships when doing public scholarship: each partnership or project can connect you to new people and places, leading to more partnerships and projects. Sometimes I talk about the value of collaborating with libraries and museums as natural allies for humanities scholars. Sometimes I talk about the value of public scholarship for graduate students, whether it is interdisciplinary research or the scholarship of teaching and learning, and whether they are headed toward careers in academia or alt-ac. Sometimes I talk about the many faces of continuity and how several of the community projects I started were taken over by other graduate students after I earned my degree. Sometimes I talk about how I got a tenure-track job at a liberal arts college (and finished my doctoral studies ahead of schedule for my time to degree) because of, not in spite of, what might seem like distractions. All of these stories emphasize the back and forth of collaboration and exchange, but of course, none of these stories ever uses the word "dialectical."

One of my favorite versions of this story is a metaphor for the public value of the humanities that became quite literal. On the final night of the British Women Writers Conference, I got to announce (in the Senate Chambers of the Old Capitol, which was directly above the exhibit in the Hansen Humanities Gallery) the Iowa Supreme Court's decision to legalize same-sex marriage in our state, standing, as it were, on the shoulders of these courageous women writers. That night, with Mary Wollstonecraft's portrait and the 1792 edition of her *Vindication of the Rights of Woman* just beneath my feet, I could raise my hands to celebrate a victory that felt, particularly in that space, part of a larger history. This broad historical perspective was, on that night, the greatest public value that the humanities could offer.

4: THE ARCHIVES
🦋 🦋

Place-Based Undergraduate Research in the Humanities

BRIDGET DRAXLER

If Greeks invented the lecture and discussion model of education, we can credit the eighteenth century with popularizing experiential, high-impact learning. While these ideas may be buzzwords in contemporary pedagogy, they draw on Lockean empiricism, the belief that our understanding of the world can be traced to experience, and the Rousseauian notion of an individualized, discovery-based, natural education structured through sensory experience and serving a civic good.[1] Indeed, the entire scientific method of observation and experimentation (another product of the long eighteenth century) informs much of the way we imagine active learning takes place in the modern college classroom.

The heady conversation typical of the literature classroom can make it seem an unlikely site for hands-on learning. But while reading is often framed as a passive form of learning upon which experiential learning improves,[2] we might more productively muddy the distinction between reading and experiencing or frame them as symbiotic.[3] Indeed, Natalie Phillips's interdisciplinary research in literary neuroscience has found, by taking fMRI scans of volunteers reading Jane Austen's *Mansfield Park*, that careful, close reading activates areas in the brain associated with movement and touch. National Public Radio's coverage of her research notes that "it was as though readers were physically placing themselves within the story as they analyzed it."[4]

This kind of physical placement, this imaginative journey, erases distinctions between reading and bodily experience, as so perceptively observed by Eric Calderwood in his work on study abroad (a contemporary vestige of the eighteenth-century Grand Tour):

> Many people read up on a place before traveling there. This experience can be like reading the book before seeing the movie: your perception of the country is tinged by nostalgia for the country you had already visited in your mind. For many, reading is itself the journey, and the

subsequent trip is merely a souvenir to refresh your memory of an ad-venture you've already enjoyed.[5]

The idea of literary tourism, then, is something of a redundancy: litera-ture is *always* a kind of tourism. And yet, with JASNA members world-wide taking Literary Lyme Walking Tours and tracking the various sites for film adaptations of Austen's novels ("Where Exactly Did Louisa Mus-grove Fall?" reads one blog post),[6] and teachers like Amy Weldon cre-ating off-campus programs like Frankenstein's Footsteps (see her essay included in this chapter), the desire to recreate or rediscover these imagi-native journeys in historic places is common. In some cases, as with Anne Stapleton's the Waverley Project, we even create historical markers from fictional references.

THE WAVERLEY PROJECT

Anne McKee Stapleton

The website Under the Banner of Waverley began with a question: Why is Waverly, Iowa, named Waverly? I was teaching novels by Jane Austen and Walter Scott at the time and contacted the Waverly Public Library. I learned from the reference librarian that, indeed, the town was named for Scott's 1814 global bestseller *Waverley*. Curiosity ignited, I next found a website for Waverly, Nebraska, whose streets are named after characters and settings in the series that followed that first novel! Within six months I had visited six towns dubbed Waverly between 1829 and 1878, and I soon discovered many more.

A pattern of naming across the Midwest emerged, most towns positioned at essential nodes of travel and cultural exchange during western expansion in the nineteenth century. Location clearly mattered to town founders, perhaps explaining one reason for the appeal of Scott's historical fiction. Just as Scott's twenty-seven novels narrate watershed historical moments and unforgettable places, first in eighteenth-century Scotland and then elsewhere, the constellation of American towns named Waverly map important historical moments and notable communities, each with stories to tell. My simple question introduced me to a fascinating network of collaboration with dozens of individuals and institutions, both civic and academic. Launched in 2017, my digital humanities project explores connections between Walter Scott's epic Waverley novels and the swath of American towns that bears their name.

In the course of my research, I soon learned to spread a wide net and be open to unexpected connections. While the work of scholars researching and publishing in the areas of Scottish and American studies is indispensable to my project, I soon discovered that visiting locales and meeting individuals actively involved in their communities also yielded fruitful discoveries. Thus, I began calling or emailing libraries, historical associations, newspapers, visitors bureaus, preservation societies, and other organizations to identify people who might inform my work.

I followed with visits when possible, each of which enriched my research and yielded unforeseen pleasures. Examples include access to personal archives followed by a catfish lunch with a local historian in Missouri, an introduction to the local museum and public library by the executive director of a convention and visitors bureau in Ohio, a rewarding day perusing a mid-nineteenth-century edition of the Waverley novels in Iowa, and driving tours of several towns. People everywhere have been eager to share their expertise, although they sometimes require a bit of detective work to find.

I also learned how important it is to consider timing and strengths in your community. Local academicians, librarians, historians, and community members all expressed interest in my project, which led me to a second goal: to celebrate Walter Scott's legacy in Iowa during 2014, the year of *Waverley*'s bicentennial.

Funding from university and local organizations was crucial and allowed me to arrange for lectures by Professor Alan Riach, a Scottish scholar from the University of Glasgow. He drew eager audiences to talks about the Waverley novels and the recent Scottish independence referendum and met with students, faculty, and community members. In addition, I worked with the executive director of the Iowa City UNESCO City of Literature organization to arrange a literary and musical performance of Scott's work, narrated by Professor Riach, during the town's annual book festival. Timing contributed to the success of this event, since coverage of the referendum coincided with advertisements for the Book Festival as well as the bicentennial of Scott's first novel.

To engage both community and university, I sought a mix of students and scholars interested in Scottish literature and culture, as well as local and professional performers. Highland dancers from Iowa and Kansas, a children's choir, and local musicians performed new choreographies and arrangements based upon the traditional pieces Scott features in his novels, while a professional bagpiper from Scotland and a renowned fiddler from New York City also contributed their talents, all woven together by a compelling narration of Scott's influence in the Midwest. Over four hundred people cheered on performers at Iowa City's historic Englert Theatre. The following day, a private music school hosted a workshop featuring the Scottish fiddler, as did the University of Iowa Department of Music.

This performance inspired me to make another effort to bring historical literature alive and show its relevance today. Research, archival materials, interviews, and the bicentennial celebration led to my digital humanities project, the website Under the Banner of Waverley. Here I investigate why the Waverley novels appealed to readers, map where and when the eponymous towns were founded, and illustrate how Scott's legacy continues. His novels promote communal experiences and explore themes pertinent today, and I seek to provide lively examples to elucidate these connections, as I do in my teaching. My site shares access to the histories, colorful images, and archival material I have discovered. I have relied heavily upon the expertise of individuals in the Digital Scholarship and Publishing Studio at the University of Iowa, from the initial exhibit design and ongoing collection of materials to the interactive map of nineteenth-century railroads intersecting Waverlys. Because this is largely a community project, Under the Banner of Waverley provides an ideal place to enliven Scott's fiction while welcoming suggestions and future collaborators.

GAIN EXPERIENCE!

Literature, Travel, and Life

Amy Weldon

Mary Wollstonecraft died of complications from childbirth on September 10, 1797, leaving behind a devastated husband, a brand-new baby girl, and an unfinished novel: "The Wrongs of Woman; or Maria." The narrator, locked in a madhouse and anticipating her own untimely death, addresses her lost daughter directly: "I would then, with fond anxiety . . . save you from the vain regret of having, through irresolution, let the spring-tide of experience pass away, unimproved, unenjoyed. — Gain experience — ah! gain it — while experience is worth having, and acquire sufficient fortitude to pursue your own happiness."[7]

On our January term study-abroad trip, In *Frankenstein*'s Footsteps: The Keats-Shelley Circle in London, Geneva, Venice, Florence, and Rome, students and I imagine that Wollstonecraft is speaking not only to her own infant daughter — the future Mary Shelley — but also to us. And maybe she is. Wollstonecraft believed in experience of the world as a way to stretch the self's boundaries, put the ego in check, and counteract the timidity instilled in women by those who "rende[r]" them "objects of pity, bordering on contempt."[8] As I look at my own students — awash in a sea of social-media noise and fake news, hedged about by protective parents and teaching-to-the-test rules, separated by electronic convenience from the endangered natural world, yet still searching for more life-sustaining ways of being — I see her words as a guide for all of us. My books *The Hands-On Life: How to Wake Yourself Up and Save The World* (2018) and *The Writer's Eye: Observation and Inspiration for Creative Writers* (2018) attempt to help students find the meaning they seek, with life in the living world as a bright thread to follow. Encounters with that-which-is-not-me — perhaps especially overseas — enlarge what students thought they knew and, in the process, enlarge minds, selves, and hearts.

As I prepared to lead the third (2016) and fourth (2018) incarnations of In *Frankenstein*'s Footsteps, a subtle question shimmered into view: How can I both prepare students for what they will see *and* preserve the dignity and freshness of their own first encounters? Walker Percy's essay "The Loss of the Creature" (1975) describes the existential Mobius bind of tourists, continually regarding themselves regarding a place and short-circuiting the very experience they seek. Yet do I really want to ask a first-generation college student who has never been out of the Midwest to read such an essay before she departs? No, actually, I don't. Although it's my responsibility to keep students safe, to equip them with the raw materials of texts and contexts, to emphasize intellectual curiosity, and to build a peer group in which that intellectual curiosity can flourish, it's not my responsibility — or my right — to tell them how they should feel in the moment of encounter itself.

This realization leads me into evaluating my own teaching. Always before me is the deadly dry specter of Mr. Causabon in George Eliot's *Middlemarch* (1871-1872) sucking the life out of Rome: "There is hardly any contact," Eliot writes, "more depressing to a young ardent creature than that of a mind in which years full of knowledge seem to have issued in a blank absence of interest or sympathy."[9] Accordingly, my pedagogical goal is to offer imaginative encounters with a place through the lens of historical and literary texts — the same kinds of encounters the Romantics staged and described for themselves. I try to capture the imaginations of curious but travel-weary students. Once inside the Colosseum in Rome, we head straight to an overlook point above the arena for a few minutes of pure staring. Then everyone gathers around to build a quick platform of shared knowledge. "Lord Byron imagined gladiator contests, too, when he visited here," I say, and a student reads aloud the dying gladiator passage from *Childe Harold*, canto IV (1818) to show us how.

In Byron's time, the Colosseum was even more of a ruin than now, weed-covered and open for anyone to wander through at will. Yet to the ancient Romans it epitomized the glory and spoils of empire. Spectators entering the Colosseum would have been spritzed with exotic perfumes from all the recent shipments into Rome, flaunting imperial greatness to their noses as well as their eyes and ears. And several species of animals went extinct because they were harvested so often for contests here. Yet to the average Roman — as to an average member of *any* culture — these norms must have seemed, well, normal. From here it's a short step to the sort of reflections on empire Byron also led us to as we read *Childe Harold* in Venice a week and a half earlier. In closing, I share aloud Charles Dickens's 1846 verdict: "Never, in its bloodiest prime, can the sight of the gigantic Colosseum, full and running over with the lustiest life, have moved one heart, as it must move all who look upon it now, a ruin. God be thanked: a ruin!"[10] By now, about twenty minutes have passed since we first walked onto our viewing spot, and I invite students to walk, write, and explore for the next hour. All around the arena, students wander, perch, scribble, gaze, ponder. Someone always circles back to ask me if they can copy Dickens's words (the perfume and the animals show up too). Even those who confess to not knowing much about history feel energized, propelled to reflect and seek further knowledge.

Of course, I have to foreclose some types of overseas experience, since one person's bad choices affect everyone. I teach students that the greatest danger is their own naivete: "You must always maintain a 'second sight' for how you look and sound to others," my syllabus states, "Obliviousness to context can lead others to perceive you as entitled and insensitive—which is not a positive way for *anyone* to move through the world." In on-campus orientation sessions, we model appropriate jackets, shoes, and daily wear, designed to make us comfortable and unobtrusive (no college logos, "athleisure" attire, or leggings worn as pants; sweaters, scarves, narrow dark jeans, and tall boots or hiking shoes are the norm). Students travel in small groups, not alone, during independent exploration times in each city and check in with me around nine o'clock every night. If they enjoy a glass of wine with dinner, they do so knowing we'll be on our way bright and early the next morning. Always, they tell me the course standards make them feel prepared, safe, and empowered.

Preparation starts on campus. Reading applications and conducting interviews, I build a group of students willing to "geek out" and to be active, curious learners and good colleagues. I share my syllabus (with its standards, packing list, and mobility considerations) as soon as they show interest in the course. They read our primary texts—*Frankenstein*, Daisy Hay's group biography *Young Romantics*, and poems and letters by the Romantics—in advance and bring them along. In November, students attend the Center for Global Learning's mandatory predeparture orientation and two orientations of my own: a get-acquainted lunch in the cafeteria and a show-and-tell tutorial that helps them organize logistics and feel, viscerally, the challenges of fast-paced travel. To this session, all the students, dressed in appropriate daily wear, bring their passports, coats, and carry-on-sized suitcases and backpacks— our whole luggage allowance for the trip. We review the syllabus.

Then, moving at city pace, we carry our bags down the stairs from a classroom, outside to a crosswalk, across the street, and then onto the opposite curb, all in five minutes.

Once we're overseas, the preparation pays off. Trusting that their peers and I will protect them, students flourish amid swiftly changing challenges. By the end of the second day in London, they're comfortable with the Tube (the city's subway system) and the unfamiliar mix of coins with which they buy coffee. They keep journals on paper and pen. During the day, we sit down to rest and write on Rome's Palatine Hill or the windswept meadow beside the Villa Diodati, overlooking Lake Geneva in Switzerland. During our discussions, I stand ready with texts and exercises but try to let the students lead the conversation. Sharing stories of independent small-group explorations is always great fun when we're back together again. Always, I try to trust that the point I need to make will arise from discussion and from experience—and it usually does. Brandishing Mary Wollstonecraft's words as a rallying cry— "we are gaining experience!" they joke when faced with crowded Metro trains, museum closings, or "weird" food—students grow and change in amazing ways, right under my eyes. (Of course, Wollstonecraft knew this: "It is almost as absurd," she writes in *A Vindication of the Rights of Woman*, "to attempt to make a youth wise by the experience of another, as to expect the body to grow strong by the exercise which is only talked of, or seen.")[11]

In 2018, I tried two new ways to bring text and experience together. In any teaching situation, I believe in reading texts aloud, yet I don't want my voice to dominate. So I made copies of short poetry or prose texts related to sites we visit, wrote the date and place connected with that text on each, and put it in a numbered envelope (keeping a master index). Before we boarded our departing flight, I handed out those envelopes. Students could open their envelope and discover what their text was and where they would read it aloud—but they kept it a secret from the whole group until the moment itself. The students loved the readings and the range of texts—short excerpts from our course packets and related works like Dante's *Inferno* (early 1300s), Lauren Elkin's *Flaneuse* (2016), Machiavelli's *The Prince* (1532), and Freud on Rome as a model of the mind from *Civilization and Its Discontents* (1930)—and their peers' voices seemed to animate the words in their minds very readily for discussions and writing.

Thinking about reading at Keats's grave led me to my second new idea: fragmentary gravestone rubbings, made directly on the pages of students' journals. How might carrying a piece of a famous name that let you engage with the reality we discuss together, that for the Romantics the fragment was emotionally suggestive and rich in a way the complete thing could not quite be? How does it feel to hunker down with charcoal in your fingers, scratching it across the page you press against the stone? So I tucked a packet of good ivory resume paper into my suitcase and presented it to students (with pencils and charcoal sticks) on site. Students *loved* making the rubbings, which heightened their imaginative engagement with the writers — frequently, they'd choose one portion of the stone for their (public, frameable) piece of paper and another for their (private) journal page.

I'll never forget the moment in Rome's Protestant Cemetery when a student pointed to the tiny white daisies in the grass. At the Keats-Shelley House that morning, we had learned that Keats sent his friend Joseph Severn to check out this cemetery, where Keats knew he'd soon be buried. Severn reported back that the grass was full of daisies, just like the ones that adorned Keats's bedroom. Lifting his eyes to his bedroom ceiling, Keats had smiled. *I think*, he is reported to have said, *I can feel them over me even now.* And now, as students reflected on this anecdote, their gaze was fixed on these newly blossomed flowers, modern echoes of this nineteenth-century story. "Severn was right," one student breathed. "He would have come out to this cemetery in January. And it's January now." In that moment, the student's imagination passed through past and present swift as a needle through cloth, stitching them elegantly — and permanently — together, with physical experience in a place as the key. Other students remark on this process as well. Assessing the course in her journal, one student wrote, "Dr. Weldon helps point out things to us and opens the doors to possibilities and knowledge. . . . We choose to step through the door and out into the world, and we need to grasp the knowledge and experience for ourselves, to snatch up the world around us and feel the cravings for knowledge ourselves." Of course, Keats anticipated this. "Axioms in philosophy," he wrote, "are not axioms until they are proved upon our pulses: We have read fine things but never feel them to the full until we have gone the same steps as the Author."[12]

On our last day in London, students and I walk to Mary Wollstonecraft's gravestone in Old St. Pancras Churchyard. With our feet in the mud, we review the story of her daughter Mary learning to read by tracing *Mary Wollstonecraft Godwin*. Later, of course, that engraved death date, ten days after her own birthday—September 10, 1797—must have seemed like a single reproach, endlessly renewed. *Frankenstein*'s author met her mother only in the pages of her books, the portrait that hung in her father's study—the same portrait we view at the National Portrait Gallery in Trafalgar Square—and her own imagination. We remember how she and Percy Shelley met secretly and declared their love to one another at this spot. We speak Wollstonecraft's words from *Maria* aloud, hearing how they surely would also have rung through the heart of a girl in love with a sexy married man, chafing to escape from her father's chilly house, eager, in following her mother's advice, to find her way toward the older woman, if only in the pages of books and a lifetime of travel, physical and intellectual. *Gain experience—ah! gain it.* Yes, we respond, across distance and time. We will.

As an undergraduate, I would have swooned over a course like Amy Weldon's. The desire to combine graduate studies with literary tourism, visiting all the places I had read about as an undergraduate English major, is largely what motivated me to enroll as a graduate student in England at the University of York. I went on various literary pilgrimages,[13] including one in which I memorized Keats's "To Autumn" as I walked the riverbank trail south of Winchester that inspired its composition. *How romantic!* I thought, quite pleased with myself. I went to London, Edinburgh, Bath, Nottingham, and the Lake District to stand on the soil where my favorite works were conceived or written. I even went to the Gulf of Spezzia, where Shelley drowned, on a jaunt to Italy. The power of such a pilgrimage, as George Dekker argues, lies in synecdoche: "For tourists as for pilgrims, sacred sites and relics possess their aura and talismanic power because they are perceived to have an authentic link with the person or event that lends them significance."[14]

The problem, though, is this: the symbiotic relationship between reading about a place and traveling to that place can't be fully realized when that place (eighteenth-century England, for instance) cuts across boundaries of both space and time. You can go to the Theatre Royal at Bath, where Catherine Morland (and Austen herself) was known to have enjoyed a play or two, but the Orchard Street Theatre was sold in 1805 (it's now a Masonic Hall), and the Beaufort Square Theatre burned down in 1862. The lights are electric, and there is street parking outside. We can visit these historic sites, but meaningful transport across boundaries of both space and time is something achieved only in our imaginations.

However, a text in an archives can give students that authentic link—the instant, talismanic connection to another time, like a visceral, Proustian time warp. The experience in an archives allows readers go beyond imaginative transport to engage with the physicality of a text: a first edition, a marked-up copy owned by a favorite figure, a dusty, musty, beautifully bound text from another era. If visiting historic sites is a reader's pilgrimage through space, then an archives is a reader's pilgrimage through time.

When I think back to which experiences transformed me most during my time at York, which experiences gave me a jolt of authenticity, to use Dekker's term, it was moments in the archives at the university library. I recall vividly the day I held a first edition of Wordsworth's poetry during a visit to Special Collections. The book was enormous, with thick, bleached pages, large fonts, and wide margins. It was totally unlike the *Norton Anthology of English Literature* in which I first read Wordsworth on transparent pages with miniscule fonts. Wordsworth, I thought, would not be pleased with my *Norton*. I remember my advisor, Jane Moody, talking with us about the ego of a man who would—and could—insist that his poetry be printed and bound in such a way. As I ran my hand along the binding and touched those thick, bright white pages, I felt communion with the past I hadn't experienced before.

While imaginative transports are part of the pleasure and cognitive impact of reading, an archives offers a certain authenticity: a kind of direct access to knowledge. To the untrained eye, its contents can seem like nothing but old books and papers, slowly decaying or, in the case of many nineteenth-century texts, self-digesting. But to a scholar of the past, these pages are the sacred relics of our intellectual pilgrimages.

The research possible in the archives is, in some ways, both the most tedious and the most glamorous version of what we do as literary historians. While the drama of faculty meetings somehow hasn't drawn Hollywood's attention (though they would make an ideal mock-heroic dramedy, I think), the scholar as archival researcher is worthy of the big screen. *Possession* (2002), for instance, reinforces the thrilling sense of discovery possible with archival research—albeit while fast-forwarding through the painstaking slowness of the process.[15] I myself have witnessed serious scholars in an archives squeal like children on Christmas morning. It is a complex site of work and pleasure and work as pleasure.

In the past, the archives was often not the first place educators thought to bring undergraduate students; teachers often assumed that close reading skills needed to be taught before instead of alongside archival work, or that a full class of undergraduates would overwhelm the archives' space and staffing. Bringing undergraduates into the archives would also require careful balance: a student's experience there requires at once unmediated engagement to be authentic and significant scaffolding, contextualization, and reflection to be meaningful. However, while their work as student readers is often necessarily framed with introductions, footnotes, appendices, and other scholarly apparatus, particularly when engaging with historical literature, their work (and identities) as a student researchers benefits from the authenticity and authority of direct access to primary sources.[16]

Professors' growing interest in high-impact, student-driven, inquiry-based learning has drawn more undergraduates to the archives in recent years. Silvia Vong draws on constructivist learning theory to explain how the archives can empower students to produce original research, drawing on their prior knowledge and experience.[17] Anne Bahde frames the archives in terms of object-based learning theory, in which "cognitive processing, sensory activities, and affective reactions are all combined in a meaningful, multidimensional learning experience."[18] Other scholars are simply keen to deepen information literacy instruction in our changing world, tapping into students' "reverence" and "curiosity" for the text as physical object.[19]

Pushing students beyond the drop-in, show-and-tell model of archival orientation, some schools now offer full-semester courses held in the archives, teaching students advanced skills like paleography and statistical analysis while helping them to reflect critically on the laws of copyright and permissions or the role of the archivist in the acquisition and discoverability of archival material. Through experiences like these, students discover that no decision in an archives is neutral or objective.[20]

Many of these archives-driven courses focus on the eighteenth century; printing and literacy were just ubiquitous enough then so that many handwritten manuscripts and published texts have been preserved, and the distance of time is just long enough so their long S type, custom bindings, cross-hatched letters, and yellowed pages have an air of exceptionality. Students at Haverford College, for instance, try to solve an eighteenth-century murder mystery in their library's Quaker Collection,[21] while students at the University of Houston conduct semester-long independent research projects in the archives as part of a literature course centered on the year 1771.[22] Harvard offers a year-long course in material culture that begins with an archaeological excavation in seventeenth- and eighteenth-century college buildings; students then use archival research from the college's own administrative records to contextualize their discoveries. At the University of Pennsylvania, students elbow for a spot in a course on the *Pamela* craze to explore the "small universe of responses, critiques, parodies, spurious continuations and back-stories, operas, burlesques and farces, poetry and songs, fashion, and pornography" inspired by the 1740 novel.[23]

For over fifty years, the Newberry Seminar: Research in the Humanities, a Chicago-based off-campus study program, has brought advanced undergraduate humanities majors to conduct original research in the Newberry Library, one of the world's great archives.[24] Students earn a full semester of course credit for participating in a graduate-style seminar, then researching a major independent project based on the Newberry's collections. Student projects span the fields of literature, history, religion, and philosophy and cross wide expanses of time and space. The seminar is the best of a liberal arts education and the best of graduate school wrapped into one: the interdisciplinary lens of the former combined with the rigorous individual research of the latter, bound together with close mentoring in a community of scholars.

As an off-campus study program, the Newberry Seminar combines place-based learning in Chicago with rigorous, interdisciplinary research in the Newberry's archives. The juniors and seniors who participate are often likely candidates for graduate school in the humanities; for many of them, the experience either solidifies their desire to pursue an academic career or introduces them to alternative career paths, including research librarianship, museum studies, and archival studies. As members of a research community that includes visiting scholars and independent researchers, the students develop not only research skills but also ways of working and thinking as humanists, as noted by Joan Gillespie and David Spadafora.

HUMANITIES IN THE FIELD

Joan Gillespie

When the Chicago Cubs won the World Series for the first time in 108 years on November 2, 2016, the *Chicago Tribune* printed a million extra copies of the issue that carried a front-page photo of ebullient team members tightly bound, as though sculptured, in a spontaneous and thrillingly high leap, and the headline "At last!" The pages were filled with interviews of players, coaches, and fans, not only of the Cubs but of the opposing team as well, that testified to the victory. Customers for this celebratory edition were limited to one copy each, and many newsstands in the city sold out within hours. Extra copies continued to be printed for several days and continued to sell out. This story speaks directly to the value that so many of us give to authentic materials even when the declining interest in print journalism is well documented in the United States. Authentic materials convey more than a digital copy or Word document through physical characteristics such as size, color, odor, and texture. Along with the visuals and text, these characteristics capture a historical moment, a moment that the *Tribune* customers wanted to claim.

Undergraduate students who encounter the authentic materials at Chicago's Newberry Library, a private independent research institution, during a semester-long research seminar sponsored by the library in partnership with the Associated Colleges of the Midwest (ACM) likewise can claim a piece of history. Many of them are seeing such materials for the first time, and the prospect of using primary documents such as letters, maps, texts that are long out of print, and personal memorabilia for research is at first daunting, then exciting, and finally, humbling as they bring their projects to conclusion. The Newberry and ACM celebrated the fiftieth anniversary of the seminar in September 2015 with alumni of the program, including members of the first class, visiting faculty directors from the ACM and Great Lakes Colleges Association, whose students also enroll in the program, and key Newberry Library staff members. The program has remained true to its original goal, to provide students in the humanities with a hands-on laboratory experience that would parallel the opportunities for students in the sciences.

The Newberry seminar is one of sixteen ACM off-campus study programs with a focus on site-based research as a required component in the curriculum. As we learn more about how best to engage students in their learning through such pedagogies as primary research, direct experience, and community outreach, the Newberry seminar serves as a model of site-based research that combines all three of these practices in a novel intellectual and personal challenge for most students. Students' archives of materials often extends to actual sites in Chicago and its environs if their research question develops from the literature and history of the city. Students are encouraged to explore these sites on foot and, as appropriate, talk to the people who are associated with them, an assignment that often nudges students beyond their comfort zones. Neighborhoods in transition, special-interest museums, lakefront parks, and cemeteries bring to life the documents in the collections at the Newberry and serve as case studies for research. This exercise in "humanities in the field" invites students' personal observations on the links between past and present, enriching their analysis of their topic. It also prompts their reflections on the continuum of their own learning during the research process, a metacognitive exercise that serves them going forward in their scholarly work.

Parallel to students' intellectual development is the personal development that they describe in setting an ambitious goal for themselves, in this case, a large research project, and achieving it; being welcomed into a community of scholars and trusted with archival materials, in some cases materials that are new to the archives and are being assessed for the first time when the student examines them; and building friendships with like-minded students and mentoring relationships with the faculty who lead the seminar and Newberry academic staff who may guide their research. These achievements rank as high as the credit on their transcript.

THE HUMANITIES EQUIVALENT TO A SCIENCE LABORATORY

David Spadafora

The Associated Colleges of the Midwest–Newberry Library Seminar in the Humanities originated with an idea from Professor John J. Murray of Coe College, a historian of the early modern Low Countries. Murray knew that this new consortium of liberal arts colleges, founded in 1958, had already decided to offer a science seminar to be hosted at Oak Ridge National Laboratory. He believed that a parallel program in the humanities was desirable. The humanities equivalent to a science laboratory being a research library, Murray—having done considerable research of his own at the Newberry—was persuaded that its collection and staff would provide just the right environment for the kind of seminar he had in mind. Accordingly, in 1962 he urged Stanley Pargellis, the director and librarian of the Newberry, to work with the ACM on establishing such a program. Notwithstanding his impending retirement, Pargellis was intrigued, and conversations with the ACM ensued. His successor as Newberry chief executive, Lawrence W. Towner, followed up vigorously, and by 1964 he and the ACM had explored options for the new program and settled on one. In the fall of 1965 the program commenced with a seminar on the Renaissance. It continues more than fifty years and 1,300 students later, the only course of its kind in the United States.

From the beginning, the seminar emphasized six principles. First, there would always be some topic of interdisciplinary interest, capacious enough to attract students from such humanities disciplines as history, literature, philosophy, art history, and "softer" social sciences as anthropology, and the course would always be team-taught by two faculty members from ACM institutions. Second, the program would involve seminar-style discussion sessions in which students could try out their ideas on the topic, balanced with a substantial essay featuring the exploration of primary—and wherever possible original—sources. Third, both students and instructors would draw upon not only the rich collection of the Newberry but also its staff's expertise and commitment to helping readers find relevant materials. Fourth, students could help pay for their semester's expenses by working as interns in various Newberry departments. Fifth, the experience of taking the seminar and doing the research should serve as inspiration for and a test of the students' interest in advanced graduate study. Finally, during their time living near the Newberry, students should take advantage of the resources of Chicago, especially its cultural resources.

Initially, only ACM students could participate in the seminar; later it was opened to students from the Great Lakes Colleges Association. Across the years enrollments have varied from ten to twenty students and seminar topics have ranged widely, but the basic principles of the program have endured.

In September 2015 the Newberry and the ACM hosted a celebration of the fiftieth anniversary of the program. Among the more than 100 alumni who attended, there was universal enthusiasm for the program. Participants (including several from the earliest cohort in the fall of 1965) spoke glowingly of their entire experience: the bonding with each other, intellectual excitement at having access to a wealth of collection resources and expertise, academic guidance from the faculty and Newberry staff, honing of research and writing skills, enjoyment of Chicago, and diverse career choices growing out of the semester.

My own experience confirms what these alumni said. During the fall of 2001, I served as one of the instructors in this program, teaming up with my Lake Forest College colleague, Professor Richard Mallette. We had an average size group, some of whom were thinking about pursuing PhD programs in humanities disciplines and others who just wanted to study the topic at hand, make use of the Newberry, and explore Chicago. For us it was an exceptional teaching and mentoring experience. We and our students imbibed the culture of the Newberry and benefitted from the intellectual and social hospitality of the place. In forty years of teaching, most of it at Yale and Lake Forest, never did I have more capable, engaged students in such a stimulating environment. Our students were in effect junior Newberry Fellows, doing the same kind of intellectual work as those senior scholars from around the world who as official fellows of the library that fall actually interacted with these young colleagues, making suggestions about their projects and offering research strategies to ponder.

Undergraduate research represents what is best and most important about higher education. It calls upon and cultivates the curiosity and quest for knowledge around which colleges and universities ought to be organized. It presents students with the thrill of discovery. It requires that they identify and hone the use of tools of investigation that will serve them well, not just in one individual career but in many. And it gives them confidence—particularly the confidence not to accept what they are told without performing their own skillful analysis. For half a century the ACM-Newberry Seminar in the Humanities has offered its participants these benefits and more, and it promises to do so for generations to come.

An archives like the Newberry has the mission of a public library and the unique holdings of a museum, but it is being transformed more than either of these public spaces by the possibilities of digitization. As archival materials are increasingly available as online scans, for instance, undergraduate researchers (who might not otherwise have funds or opportunities to visit an archives personally) have unprecedented access to primary materials. I mention this change to note that the Newberry seminar experience could be replicated, on a smaller scale, through digital archives alone, as Danielle's chapters on 18thConnect show.[25]

However, the experience of engaging the text as physical object still holds unique value, both scholarly and personal—whether it is the watermarks invisible to digitization, the size and thickness of the paper I felt in Wordsworth's first edition, or even the slightly musty smell of old books. We gain insight into not only texts but also their readers when we read their marginalia or see how ornately or simply they bound their books. And of course, digital archives are arguably more ephemeral than physical archives; I speak from experience, as someone whose entire undergraduate career is sealed like a time capsule in a box of floppy disks. But at an institution deeply committed to preserving and making accessible both paper and digital works, the Newberry seminar was an ideal site to think about the connections between the material archive and the digital archive.

The Newberry seminar, by the nature of the library's rich local collections, also offers a rare opportunity for undergraduates to engage in public scholarship.[26] Building this connection between undergraduate archival research, digitization, and public scholarship at the Newberry formed the backbone of the application I wrote with a colleague, Professor Hannah Schell in Religious Studies at Monmouth College, to serve as faculty fellows (visiting instructors). Traditionally, the program has included public presentations of student research to a mixed scholarly and public audience at the weekly colloquia. However, drawing on the library's rich resources in Chicago history and the growing digitization of Newberry collections, we suggested that students could also find deeper opportunities to develop as public scholars through local research and digital publishing. If the site-based archival research offers students a pilgrimage through time and place, public scholarship draws rich connections from these historical spaces with the here and now.

Hannah and I titled our 2014 Newberry seminar Knowledge and Technology: From Socrates to the Digital Age. Our syllabus described the course as follows:

> Who produces knowledge? How is it organized? Who has access to it? This seminar explores the relationship between knowledge, technology, and power and provides students with a chance to reflect on and engage in the activity of creating, organizing, and accessing knowledge in a digital age. The seminar's cross-disciplinary readings represent literary, philosophical, and historical perspectives and invite reflection on the intersection of knowledge and technology, from Bram Stoker's use of communication technology in a vampire hunt to Johnson and Bayle's careful exercise of social commentary in encyclopedia entries, from Socrates' suspicions about the written word to Robert Darnton's dream of a national digital library.
>
> Knowledge and technology inform both the content and the form of the seminar. We will trace the dominant trajectory in Western thought regarding knowledge that begins with the ancient Greeks and then, drawing upon the work of Nietzsche and Foucault, critically interrogate how our categories come to seem natural, beyond history

and human agency. At the same time, we will discuss the interplay of knowledge and technology in the twenty-first century, the value of archives in a digital age, collaborative knowledge creation online, and the ethics of digitization and digital preservation. We will consider the digital humanities not only as a way of using digital tools to conduct humanities research, but as a way of using humanities questions to address the digitization of culture. As students in this seminar, you represent a generation of future scholars and knowledge practitioners who will be thinking about the limits and possibilities of digital research and publishing, and we will think critically about the impact of digitization on the future of the humanities and the future of archives.

Our hope was, within the metatheme of the seminar, to prepare students to think critically about the public value of humanities research as they were themselves *doing* humanities research within the archives.

Among the greatest perils and opportunities of guiding undergraduate students in archival research are the larger questions about the purpose and public value of the humanities that such research inevitably invites. One of the biggest challenges we faced as instructors was finding a way to support a student who was perennially frustrated with the archives' suffocating whiteness, from the staff to the collections to the portraits in the reading room. What is the public value of the humanities, she asked, when the objects of our study don't include diverse voices and experiences?[27]

We began the semester with an assignment that would confront students with this question by immediately getting them into the city and thinking about the link between libraries and archives and the communities that surround them. Each student visited a different library or archives in Chicago, interviewed both an employee and a patron, spent time exploring the institution and its surrounding neighborhood, and wrote a reflection essay comparing their chosen institution with the Newberry Library. This assignment immediately prompted students to think about issues of race, class, and privilege and the various ways in which libraries and archives serve (or fail to serve) their local constituents.

We also arranged a neighborhood walk, led by Peter Alter, a Newberry seminar alumnus and the archivist at the Chicago History Museum, so students could learn about the history of the Newberry's Gold Coast neighborhood. They discovered that the ritzy commercial district where they were living was the former home of Bughouse Square, a radical site of free speech in the early twentieth century, a fact that would later inspire one of our students' research projects (described later in this chapter). The Newberry website notes, "Bohemians, socialists, atheists, and religionists of all persuasions mounted soapboxes, spoke to responsive, vocal crowds, and competed informally for attention and donations."[28]

Welcoming students into an academic community of scholars is, in a way, inviting them to mount their own soapbox. As students began looking ahead to their research topics, we invited them to identify not only as visiting researchers but also public scholars at the Newberry Library, asking them to identify a specific public audience for their final project. What "responsive, vocal crowd" will line up to hear them speak? As part of the scaffolding for their research process,[29] we assigned students to identify a person at a library, archives, or university in Chicago whom they could use as a secondary source in their research. We also asked them to identify a potential public audience for their work and frame their argument meaningfully, in both content and form, to reach that audience. Our goal was to add to the typical research question of "so what?" the question "for whom?" This is a question that Nikki White helps scholars, including myself, ask all the time.

THERE REALLY IS NO SINGLE PUBLIC

Nikki White

My full job title is digital humanities research and instruction librarian. I'd break down my workload as roughly equal parts project management, consultation, teaching, and development. The project management and consultation involve working with patrons (faculty, students, and occasionally community members) who range from having a very clear idea of a public digital humanities project or course assignment they'd like to do and just need the technical infrastructure to put it in motion, to having vague hopes or aspirations but no clear ideas on how to shape them into concrete plans. I work with them to help them determine what their goals are with the project, what resources they can leverage, who their audience is, a timeline and milestones to reach along the way, and specific technologies that may be useful. As those things start to take shape, I pull in appropriate people from my department, the libraries, or our extended network of collaborators whose expertise is a good fit for the project.

My first piece of advice is to not define a project audience as "the public," because there really is no single public. Assuming we're generally talking about American, English-speaking adults, there's still going to be a lot of variety in things like technological access, literacy, cultural background, and priorities. Generally when people say "the public" what they really mean is college-educated, upper-middle class, usually white people with ready access to technology and a fair amount of spare time, which is not actually that broad an audience at all in the grand scheme of things. I think it's important first off to be honest about who you want your actual audience to be and what value your project can bring to them, and work from there. Questions you need to consider include, for instance, how mobile-friendly your project is, the reading level of the text, and whether you can assume that your audience is already familiar with the basic concepts of your work. That's not to say everything should be super-duper simple, just that the content should be appropriate to those whom you actually want to see or use the project. Things like usability and accessibility should especially be the center of consideration if your target audience is not described by the characteristics just mentioned.

The second is to make your project relevant or connect it to people's lives in some way. Whether that means they can somehow compare their own routes of travel to a favorite fictional character's or make connections in the politics of a given era to those unfolding today, I think people are basically interested in stuff that relates to their lives in some way. So my question for a literary historian would be, when you first got into this field, what interested you about it? How do you see elements of your research play out in your everyday life or the lives of others? Build from that.

As liberal arts students, many of our seminar participants found this kind of thinking to be familiar territory. The liberal arts college experience lends itself to public scholarship, preparing students for civic engagement and lifelong learning and helping them to find a path to productivity but more importantly purpose.[30] The emphasis liberal arts institutions place on training students as whole persons and on thinking about the humanities as a way of life rather than just a disciplinary perspective easily translates into thinking about the public value of humanities research. The absence of graduate students on typical liberal arts campuses also means that more undergraduates are involved in mentored or independent research, and smaller departments in shared spaces can facilitate cross-disciplinary collaboration.

But while undergraduates in the sciences regularly contribute to the scholarly work of their advisors at liberal arts institutions, getting high-impact learning experiences while giving faculty a high-impact return in the form of data, I see more humanities scholars living bifurcated lives: we often teach and do research on similar topics, but undergraduate students rarely contribute directly to our research. We may teach a few courses in our areas of specialization, but our students may not even be aware of this other life we lead, researching and publishing in our field.

Historical literature may seem like a field in which it is particularly challenging to develop research opportunities for undergraduates, as they tend to find the cultural context and language alienating and we may find ourselves sufficiently busy helping them comprehend and appreciate what they're reading. To hope that undergraduate students can make meaningful contributions to humanities scholarship, while also giving that scholarship a public purpose, can feel overly ambitious.

To confront this barrier, I'd like to walk you through some texts (many of which we read in the Newberry seminar) that make a case for publicly engaged undergraduate research in the humanities, and share some student projects that have stayed with me as a reader, writer, scholar, and teacher because they worked to bend and blend those categories.

To frame our discussions of the public digital humanities during weekly "hacking sessions," we read a series of essays from *Hacking the Academy: New Approaches to Scholarship and Teaching from Digital Humanities.* Early in the semester, as students were just beginning to think about archival research and digital publishing, we talked about Gardner Campbell's claim that innovation can be rooted in history:

> Sometimes progress is linear. Sometimes progress is exponential: according to the durable Moore's Law, for instance, computing power doubles about every two years. Sometimes, however, progress means

looping back to earlier ideas whose vitality and importance were unrecognized or underexplored at the time, and bringing those ideas back into play in a new context.[31]

This link between looking backward to see forward is where public scholarship and historical literature can productively meet, and it opens productive questions for scholars and students alike. As we look at current crises in the world we live in, what can be learned from looping back to earlier time periods? How are archives rediscovered by each generation, as trappings from the past find new relevance in our present communities?

Next, students debated Kathleen Fitzpatrick's claim that humanists, like scientists, have an ethical obligation to share our work with a public, because the work we do "has potentially profound implications for popular discussions about the politics of cultural representations, about the meaning of human interactions."[32] Reaching a public is not only a worthy goal—it is a moral imperative.[33] Fitzpatrick is not alone here. Teresa Mangum has argued that it is important for humanists to go beyond "problematizing" issues to doing something about them.[34] Kathleen Woodward also calls for public scholarship that "honors commitment and concrete purpose, has a clear and present substance, reduces the distance between the university and life, and offers civic education for all involved."[35]

But of course, in order for the humanities to work in this way, we need an audience for our scholarship—or, to put it in a way that is more responsive to community-driven needs, we need scholarship that has an audience. One of the most concrete barriers is access: academic books are often not readily accessible to public audiences in terms of content, marketing, or price. And this is where the digital humanities and public scholarship can work in concert.

Returning to *Hacking the Academy*, John Unsworth's chapter conjures a Pascalian sense of probability: digital publishing causes no harm and opens up plenty of possible good.[36] We found that students assumed digital publishing as a given for their work, so we could quickly move beyond questions of whether to questions of how. Students were reticent, however, when it came to Robert Darnton's nuanced definition of open access, pushing beyond digitization: "Yes, we must digitize. But more important, we must democratize. We must open access to our cultural heritage. How? By rewriting the rules of the game, by subordinating private interests to the public good, and by taking inspiration from the early republic in order to create a Digital Republic of Learning."[37] In other words, it is not enough to make the humanities open access; we must also give them broader purpose.

Many of our students bristled at having to articulate a purpose for their research. Unpacking what it means to democratize knowledge, to rewrite the rules, to focus on the public good—these are substantial and difficult questions that will shape the future of humanities scholarship and that budding humanities scholars should be thinking about. However, our seminar left them unresolved. These questions get to the heart of our methodologies, our writing styles, and even our topics of study. What should we be looking for in the archives? What does it look like to make our cultural heritage truly open and relevant? And how can we frame the archival recovery and digital publishing process for students who may feel underserved by the traditional historical record?

It is not an overstatement to say that some class discussions became existential. Alison Byerly, in another Newberry seminar reading that provided a scaffold for our students' research experience, identifies seismic shifts in the nature of humanities scholarship created by the digital humanities. For instance, she notes the inherently collaborative, data-driven nature of the work: "At some level, this requires us to abandon the notion that meaning can be generated only through the power of the individual mind. A different kind of meaning is exposed when technology uncovers patterns or information that would otherwise remain invisible. Coming to terms with that meaning requires a different way of thinking."[38]

Students countered that this different way of thinking is possible through the technology itself, but also through the hive mind of online communities; we are mistaken if we see Byerly removing the human element from this new way of creating meaning. And while we often think of digital humanities as applying digital tools to historical texts, it is worth remembering the way that humanistic methodologies can also be used to understand our contemporary digital world. In this broader definition, the digital humanities and the public humanities are natural bedfellows, sharing a vested interest in democratizing knowledge and empowering marginalized individuals and groups.

This common ground between public humanities and digital humanities became a focus point in our seminar discussions at the Newberry. We explored sample digital humanities projects in categories like digital scholarly editions, timelines, virtual reality, data visualization, and ex-hibits. Many of our sample projects, such as the Shelley-Godwin Archive, Mapping the Republic of Letters, Commonplace Cultures, Locating London's Past, the Eighteenth-Century Common, the Electronic Enlighten-ment, and What Jane Saw, came from scholars of the long eighteenth century. Others were created by peer undergraduates: A Sentimental Journey, the Grinnell *Beowulf*, Through Time, and Crytek Off the Map. Some projects were local to Chicago or the Newberry Library itself, such as the Great Chicago Fire and Realizing the Newberry Idea.[39] In many of these cases, however, the digital nature of the projects served a larger public purpose: digital humanities were the means, public humanities the end.

As the Newberry students chose their own research topics for a semester-long project that would culminate in a research paper or a digi-tal project (or both) and a public presentation, we encouraged them to consider how their research might have public value and (drawing on our seminar readings) how their work in the archives could not only reach a real audience, but also serve a real community. We invited them to use the archives to become public scholars. The ways that public humanities manifested in student research, however, varied considerably, from en-gaging in contemporary debates through a historical lens to conducting activist research that would change academe from within. But whatever their approach, many became driven by a desire to bring the humanities to public life.

Several students took advantage of the option to build a public digital project alongside or instead of a formal research paper, including Tess Henthorne (College of Wooster). Tess's project mirrors the work that Danielle's graduate students did on *The Countess of Dellwyn* (see chap-ter 6) — in fact, it was exploring their work as part of a seminar assignment that introduced Tess to the idea of creating a digital scholarly edition of a text. For the student scholar, sometimes a shift toward a public audience is simply a matter of having a model of what public digital humanities projects can look like.

Tess's research paper, "Uncovering the Unpublished: Construction, Publication, and Exploration of Gladys Fornell's *Montel*," considered why Gladys Fornell's novel (a fascinating modernist text, with the only existing copy, as far as we know, at the Newberry Library) was never pub-lished. Tess's explanation pivoted around a controversial 1949 revision that added a postmodern-style preface, which she surmised could have been inspired by Fornell's concurrent work as the editor of Walter Kaufmann's seminal 1950 *Nietzsche: Philosopher, Psychologist, Antichrist*.[40] Her scholarly exploration of *Montel*'s history and context served as the editor's introduction to her own digital edition of Fornell's novel, published at last.

Like Tess, Lindsay Hansard (McKendree University) also focused on a mid-twentieth-century American author, exploring the marginalia of editor Malcolm Cowley and how his reading of William Faulkner's works not only recovered but has also profoundly shaped the icon's legacy in American literature. The website she developed, which she titled the Faulkner-Cowley Dynamic and targeted at new readers of Faulkner, sets up Cowley as a model reader, based on his approach to themes and symbols, his identification of key passages, and his engagement with setting. Her paper, "'Maybe Happen Is Never Once': How Malcolm Cowley's Approach to the Benjy Section of *The Sound and the Fury* Undermines Faulkner's Message about Time," which is available on the website but directed to a scholarly audience, teases out the subtle limitations of Cowley's approach to Faulkner.

On the website, Lindsay looks at margin notes that reorder the achronological narrative of *The Sound and the Fury*'s Benjy, a character who experiences life outside of time. "Almost obsessively," she writes, "Cowley wrote in the margins about chronology over fifty times in the first section of the novel alone."[41] She notes the benefit of this strategy for new readers who may be frustrated by Benjy's "eternal present." While she praised the marginalia as a model for new readers on her website, her scholarly work explored how Cowley's marginalia developed into the contentious "Compson Appendix," a timeline of events Cowley published in his 1954 *Portable Faulkner*. The appendix, Lindsay argues, can "cause readers to lose important insight into the workings of Benjy's psyche and the nature of trauma, mischaracterize an important comparison point that is designed to help readers understand the narrative of the entire novel, and overlook the importance of stasis in the work (and in Faulkner's overall canon)."[42] Because the appendix offers a shortcut to a linear narrative, she suggests, "Readers can gain a sense of genealogical history from reading the Compson Appendix, but they also lose a sense of some of the nuances of Benjy's psychological processes"—processes driven by "signifiers, patterns, and emotions rather than linearity" and valuable to readers "precisely *because* of his misunderstanding of linear time."[43] What may be useful to a new reader, then, might actually close off more sophisticated readings of the text for more advanced readers.

Grinnell student Meredith Carroll, like Lindsay, produced a scholarly research paper complemented by digital resources for popular audiences. While her paper "Punch's Apes and Darwin's Bulldog: Making Natural Knowledge at the Dawn of Darwinism" contextualized Darwin in the first decade after the publication of *Origin of the Species* (1859) by exploring the "Darwinisms" of Victorian popular culture, her website Origins carried this research forward into contemporary debates, emphasizing ways that the discourse about Darwin's cultural impact has shifted, sometimes radically, during the past 150 years. From *Punch* magazine to the *New York Times*, Darwin has always been embroiled in debates about progress, teleology, and ethics—topics, Meredith notes in her paper, that "barely appear in the original text."[44] Moreover, the public debate has been fueled, then and now, by bombastic rhetoric and blurry equivalences—and often only draws on Darwin as an entree into broader social controversies. In her blog's discussion of *Punch*, Meredith notes how Darwinism, from its earliest days, was never a "primarily scientific theory" but was "intertwined with social issues, race, gender, and empire" in the 1860s and, only more recently, religion.[45]

For each of these students, having a dual project allowed them to explore complexities of scholarly debate, nuances of audience, and, most importantly perhaps, the relevance of historically driven humanities research for contemporary audiences. Writing in two genres, in two media, for two audiences, for two purposes gave students practice translating not only their language but also their ideas to two contexts, sometimes drawing divergent conclusions. In this way, public scholarship not only opens their research to new readers but also deepens their understanding of that research, both in terms of its content and its meaning and value.

A few students, however, engaged in what we might call activist research: retelling the history of figures or movements in a way that shows how methodological trends in their field can have unintended real-world implications and seeking to remedy this impact by shifting the critical lens through which they study their source material. As public scholars, their attention was on topics of public interest, but their critique was aimed squarely at the academy itself.[46] I want to end with two such examples, both of which have left deep impressions on my own thinking about humanities research.

Emily England's "'Simply Irrepressible': The Life and Identity of Lucy Parsons" was simultaneously a biographical approach to radical labor activist Lucy Parsons and also a critique of methodological trends in history that make easy correlations between female figures in the past and the movements they have come to represent, limiting them to a narrowly definable role within history. I remember talking with Emily over an early draft of her paper, saying that her argument lacked focus—she was offering multiple and contradictory interpretations of Parsons. That, she told me, was her point: frustrated by how female figures in particular are pigeonholed (Lucy the wife or Lucy the anarchist), she sought to paint Parsons with the richness and complexity that she saw as typically reserved for male figures in history. For Emily, retelling the story of Lucy Parsons was not only a critique of historiography and revision of the historical record itself, but also an act of feminism.

Ai Miller from Knox College echoed Emily's methodological critique of zir field, in zir case queer studies, in a paper titled "Sometimes You Have to Shoot the Storyteller in the Neck: Reexamining the Role of the Dill Pickle Club in the Queer Community of the Near North Side, 1920–1935." During a neighborhood tour of the Gold Coast, our archivist guide described Bughouse Square as a bastion of free speech and the nearby Dill Pickle Club as the nexus of Chicago's queer community. Thrilled to discover that zir neighborhood held such history, Ai dove into researching this legacy—and came up short. The Newberry's vast archives and even that of the Chicago History Museum down the street had almost nothing on this queer history that zie found so fascinating. Ai's paper turned into an exploration of what zie *didn't* find in the archives and a raw and personal reflection on reconciling queer studies with archival research.

A HISTORY OF MY OWN

Ai Miller

In some ways, the misunderstanding and exaggeration of the role of the Dill Pickle Club in the queer community arises from a lack of evidence.[47] Without a solid historical record to go on, we can only speculate on the importance of the Dill Pickle Club to queer individuals, and given the sparse nature of the evidence we do have, finding enough pieces of evidence to complete a picture seems time-consuming at best and impossible at worst.

Looking at the gap in Chicago gay historian Gregory Sprague's research on the Dill Pickle Club forces historians to stop and reexamine their own practices and research methods.[48] Queer history as a field is relatively new, with much of its early historiography focused in part on the legitimization of queer identity in history. John D'Emilio, a gay historian whose work has focused on the twentieth century, notes that in many ways, early queer historiography focused on overt resistance only and the way that significant individuals fought against homophobic laws and police harassment.[49] This is a problematic concept of history, because it erases the experiences of those whose resistance manifested in surviving a lethally homophobic world. By centering historical research around visible resistors and visible resistors only, we make, however unintentionally, value judgments about the types of queer lives we find worthy of research. As historians, and specifically as historians looking to place themselves as individuals in a historical context that has been denied to them, making those judgments and potentially erasing lives seems counterintuitive.

Yet in some ways, the attempt to claim queer lives in history without focusing on visible resistance problematizes the practice of queer history even more. Perhaps the most famous, controversial, and in some ways visible practice of queer history is C. A. Tripp's 2005 *The Intimate World of Abraham Lincoln*. Tripp, a psychologist who worked under Alfred Kinsey and wrote about homosexuality, claimed that Abraham Lincoln was gay or at least had several same-sex relationships with men. The claim released a torrent of criticism against it, with several Lincoln scholars arguing that Tripp's ahistorical reading of homosocial relationships placed a contemporary understanding of sexuality on a historical situation that had little or nothing to do with same-sex sexual relationships. Tripp's claims have caused questions of Lincoln's sexuality to persist in the public mind and in some ways serve to undermine practices of queer history, painting it as a practice intent on making exaggerated claims for political reasons rather than a genuine practice of history. The controversy, however, raises many questions about the homophobia and heterosexism in the academic practices of traditional historians; many queer historians point to the fierce opposition they have received from historians of other practices as evidence of that. To have to prove a figure's homosexuality centers heterosexuality as the default without any question as to why that is or any thought about the damage that supporting such a narrative might have. Queer historians have a responsibility to respect and treat delicately claims they make about the sexualities of individuals, but they also have a responsibility to raise questions about assumptions made about historical practices that may not hold true. This is the issue that a queer historian must contend with—how to combine an opposition to heteronormativity with a desire to develop a historical practice that can be viewed by others as legitimate.

This is not to suggest that all queer history up until this point is built on bad practices or illegitimate claims. This paper stands on the shoulders of queer historians. In particular, understanding queer identity as socially constructed has greatly impacted the way this paper positions itself in queer history. By seeing identity construction and community construction as interconnected processes that happened simultaneously under specific circumstances, one can consider a queer history outside of resistance and begin to see how that movement against a homophobic culture began to coalesce.

When considering my own approach to queer history, I have the struggle I describe between finding and forming a history and the desire for a legitimate and legitimizing practice at the forefront of my mind. Through my experiences in the academy, I have been trained to trust certain types of historical practices, and without those practices in place, constructing a historical narrative becomes practically impossible. In order to trust the history I construct, I must have a framework for my approach to queer history. For this, I find it most helpful to draw upon my training in and understanding of intersectional feminist history. Over the decades as feminist history has changed and transformed, its methods for achieving its goal—centering women in history—have shifted away from the problematic women as resistors approach to one that reexamines the historical record to find where women were and what women were doing and valuing those experiences, while being conscious and inclusive of the intersections between class, race, gender, and sexual practices. I find this approach valuable in my own research because I find its methodology powerful—it makes historical actors out of those who might be viewed as victims in light of other methods of history.

But researchers cannot merely apply the historical methodology used with one group to study another group. As previously mentioned, my work rests on research about the historical development of sexual identity as a social construction—John D'Emilio's suggestion that the homosexual identity came to be in part because of the emergence of industrial capitalism and that movement's impact on the importance of the family structure in American society. These social transformations in turn explain the emergence of literature about homosexuality in the twentieth century.[50] What this argument also indicates is that, in some regards, the queer individual is part of a hidden class—the straight historical record will document only those with overtly nonnormative behavior. Those expressing more normative behavior in their day-to-day lives rarely documented the sexual part of their lives for fear of being identified. Thus to center queer people in history is a task more complex than one in which the group being studied—such as women—are ever present and more easily identifiable.

This complication brings up another important point that undermines the attempts to transpose existing historical practices onto queer history: the question of whose testimony we rely on when constructing a narrative. The limited accounts we have of queer individuals' experiences at the Dill Pickle Club makes the task of asserting it as a place of community incredibly difficult. When relying on the observations of presumably straight individuals, not only do we remove queer individuals as actors from the situation, but we encounter the stories filtered through a straight lens—and thus the lives of only visibly nonnormative individuals are recorded.

I approach historical possibility with caution; I hesitate to identify individuals as gay if they lived in an era when that identity did not exist—or when it did exist, but an individual chose not to use it. Separating romantic orientations from sexual acts allows us to see a full spectrum of behaviors without making ahistorical judgments about the identities of those we are studying.

But in making that distinction, are we left with a history merely of behaviors—and behaviors that were often identified in the past as illegal and unnatural? How does the understanding that the identities associated with a historical practice are defined by their illegitimacy shape a research practice striving for professional legitimacy? In some ways, the pursuit of queer history requires comfort with ambiguity; and when searching for a well-defined history, that ambiguity can be frustrating, enraging, or disheartening. Rather than a solid historical record from which we can draw, we have inconsistent pieces, behaviors that need to come with a historical context to be understood, and the dangerous task of walking a fine line between finding history and making claims that cannot be reliably backed up by the historical record. Without a legitimate practice, rooted deeply in evidence, I cannot make any claims to a history of my own.

Ultimately, the pursuit of queer history pushes against the boundaries of what is considered legitimate historical practice and forces a reconsideration of why those practices are deemed legitimate.[51]

Ai's paper captured the spirit of what we hoped to see in our students' experiences in the archives, echoing both the mediated, scaffolded conversations we had about the public value of the humanities and also the raw, authentic, first-hand experience of working with archival materials, digging deeply into history in a way that is also deeply relevant today. By examining the limits of both the archives and historical methodologies, zie challenged fellow scholars to rethink our practices and our assumptions, promoting a more inclusive and nuanced model of historical scholarship, while acknowledging the problematic exclusions that are systemic in academe.

Will the students who participated in our seminar become humanities professors? Some of them may. But even if not, they will be the ones who volunteer on local library boards, encourage their kids to study the humanities in college, and attend academic talks at the Newberry in their retirement. They will be patrons of local archives, promote broader access to those archives, and might even use their training at the Newberry to participate in civic discourse about what they find, or don't find, in those archives. In short, they will be the ones who shape the future of the humanities—whether in higher education, libraries, archives, or other cultural institutions. Discovering and articulating the public value of humanities research is a valuable lesson for future academics, but perhaps even more so for the future advocates of the humanities.

5: THE DIGITAL ARCHIVES AND THE DATABASE

愛愛

Digital Service Learning and Networked Reading
in the Undergraduate Classroom

DANIELLE SPRATT

When you want to find out details about a breaking news story—from the potential for a winter storm or hurricane to affect your commute, to election coverage or tantalizing celebrity gossip—what sources do you use? If you looked down at the phone that's in your hand or flipped open your laptop, you're not alone. While past generations sought out information about current events using their radio or television or awaited columns from respected print journalists (or perused the pages of tabloids while waiting in line at the grocery store), people today are more likely to check their social media accounts on their smartphones or other electronic devices than they are to seek out one of these older media sources. In fact, a 2017 Pew Research Center poll proclaimed that 67 percent of US adults get some of their news from social media sites; nearly half—45 percent—of all US adults use Facebook for this purpose (other sources, like YouTube, Twitter, Snapchat, and Instagram, were also used but the overall audience size was far smaller).[1] Information, especially electronic information, is seemingly available to us at all times, in both reliable and unreliable forms, and while this democratization of access is liberating, it is also daunting. As Laura Mandell and Liz Grumbach note in their essay in the next section, fake news can be just as—if not more—powerful than factual news, and discerning between the sensational and the reliable proves challenging for the most savvy media consumer.

While this inundation of information can seem positively postmodern—a dilemma specifically encountered in the twenty-first century—we can look back to another moment of media revolution in the eighteenth century to see striking and important parallels that might help us address some unanswered questions about our own time. Allow me to explain this comparison by way of two literary anecdotes. Toward the end of *The Battel of the Books* (written around 1697; published in 1704), Jonathan Swift portrayed the dizzying experience of consuming media through a tumultuous allegorical battle between books authored by classical writers, or the "ancients," and those penned by Swift's seventeenth- and eighteenth-century contemporaries, or the "moderns." He describes the battle as "a confused Multitude, . . . infinite Swarms of *Calones* [unbound pamphlets], a disorderly Rout led by *Lestrange*; Rogues and Raggamuffins, that follow the Camp for nothing but the Plunder; All without *Coats* to cover them."[2] By associating the seventeenth-century publication of unbound pamphlets with those written by the likes of Roger L'Estrange (1616–1704), a prolific pro-government Royalist pamphleteer, journalist, and censor of the press after the Restoration of Charles II to England's throne in 1660, Swift characterizes the literary marketplace as a riotous bedlam whose bottom line is "plunder," or profit.[3]

At the same time that Swift expresses his concerns over the inundation of the marketplace by such disordered materials, his repeated reference to the uncovered nature of these texts — "all without *Coats* to cover them" — satirically confirms Peter Stallybrass's observation that "printers do not print books. It is the process of gathering, folding, stitching, and sometimes binding that transforms printed sheets into a pamphlet or book. Certainly, some printers may have undertaken or paid for all of the latter processes. But that is not what printing is about. It never was."[4] Unlike modern printing practices dating to the later nineteenth century, whereby publishers would bind and cover all documents to create the object that, for modern readers, is legible as a published book, the eighteenth-century convention was to publish the bound pages without a cover, which purchasers could add later at their discretion. These uncovered eighteenth-century texts were all the more potentially transient for their initial lack of binding.

To put all of this another way: the explosion of media technologies that made cheaper, unbound books possible in the eighteenth century mirrors recent innovations that have made smartphones, laptops, and social media platforms reasonably accessible for people from many backgrounds. This access has also made news and information equal parts accessible and ephemeral, a concern that Swift also articulated. *A Tale of a Tub*, published concurrently with *The Battel*, also envisions the literary marketplace of the early eighteenth century as saturated to the point of dizzying (if ultimately forgettable) madness. In dedicating the *Tale* to the Prince of Posterity, Swift's deranged Grub-Street Hack writer opines,

To affirm that our age is altogether Unlearned, and devoid of Writers in any kind, seems to be an Assertion so bold and so false, that I have been sometime thinking, the contrary may almost be proved by un-controulable demonstration. 'Tis true indeed, that altho' their Num-bers be vast, and their Productions numerous in proportion, yet are they hurryed so hastily off the Scene, that they escape our memory and delude our Sight. When I first thought of this Address, I had prepared a copious List of *Titles* to present *Your Highness* as an undisputed argument for what I affirm. The Originals were posted fresh upon all Gates and Corners of Streets; but returning in a very few Hours to take a Review, they were all torn down and fresh ones in their Places.⁵

As the Hack wanders around Grub Street, a London neighborhood that housed impoverished, struggling writers and myriad printing houses and booksellers, he notes how the ever-changing book advertisements register the ephemerality of these printed works. Their fleeting existence makes laughable any pretensions these works might have of achieving recog-nition in their own time, let alone in posterity. Blaming the explosion in the number of publications on mass production and booksellers' and printers' obsessive attempts at marketing, Swift regards the supposedly brilliant productions as substantial only inasmuch as they demonstrate their aftermarket uses as supplies for "a *Jakes*, or an *Oven*; to the Win-dows of a *Bawdy-house*, or to a sordid *Lanthorn*" (Swift, "A Tale," 17). Through the Hack's defense of his brethren, Swift figures the majority of published texts as waste, made valuable only as cheap utilitarian tools for wiping asses and obscuring disreputable acts in brothels.

Both of these satires thus underscore the perpetual state of obsoles-cence that characterized the early eighteenth-century literary market-place. The Hack laments, "Books, like Men their Authors, have no more than one Way of coming into the World, but there are ten Thousand to go out of it, and return no more" (17). If many eighteenth-century printed books served as waste products to help contain other forms of (bodily) waste, e-texts from the twenty-first century offer other forms of waste: they help distract us while we are in line at the supermarket, waiting for a train, passing the day at work, or avoiding a stack of grading. But they accumulate into the recesses of the internet rather than ending up as wrapping for fish or toilet paper.

Although we tend to think of media technologies as intimately tied to objects with USB ports and screens, the book—as lo-fi and low-tech as it seems—is itself a significant and durable media technology. In the eighteenth century, the increased ability to mass-produce books was intensified by a radical shift in the political landscape, another parallel to our twenty-first-century context. Swift's description of the generally chaotic state of the literary marketplace and the shabby quality of those works being produced emerged, in large part, as a direct response to the recent lapsing of Britain's Licensing Act in 1695.[6] The licensing system—"the regime under which Stationers [royally sanctioned printers and members of the book trade] had to submit any text they wished to publish to be read and approved beforehand by one of a small number of authorized officials"—is often viewed as a system that encouraged the rigorous control over, and ultimately the censorship of, all print material.[7] The lapsing of this system of censorship effected a proliferation of works by largely unknown and unlauded writers (and here, we might think about how Twitter and blogs have had a similar effect, allowing unknown writers to find audiences that would have been unthinkable twenty years ago). Adrian Johns has observed that during the nearly hundred-year period between 1586 and 1695, "some form of licensing was in force for all but nine years, and that whenever it lapsed pamphlets and piracies seemed to flourish."[8] Many critics have noted the explosion of print materials after 1695 caused a kind of chaos in the book trade that threatened not simply the quality of literary production and intellectual life in the eighteenth century. To observers like Swift, this inundation of information promised to transform from a metaphorical literary battle occurring in university libraries to a state of true civil war on British soil.[9] Swift's satire thus anxiously asserts that there was an important relationship between literary production and the stability of British society itself.

Analyzing just these few brief passages from Swift's early satires demonstrates how a cursory grasp of print culture and book history not only elucidates the multifaceted critiques that his works expressed, but also underscores the striking similarity between eighteenth- and twenty-first-century readers and media consumers. In both moments, there was a pervasive anxiety about who was writing what we read, how we access those authors and texts, and how we judge their reliability. Rather than seeing book history as the antiquarian interest of the academic few, we might consider explorations of book history and print technology as studies that recover the past while clarifying the present and future of our col-

lective media consumption. To this end, I suggest that engaged pedagogical strategies that underscore such connections can help students
understand the continuity between eighteenth-century works and those
of our contemporary setting, allowing them to become more critically
savvy readers of both eighteenth-century and contemporary media forms.

This chapter suggests that the excess of information to which Swift reacted is easily legible to students who experience a similar sense of information overload from screens of all sizes and media sources of all kinds.
Whenever I teach these works, I find it remarkable how readily students
compare the Hack's words to the twenty-four-hour news cycle on cable
television and the internet, a comparison that then develops into a conversation about ways in which this news cycle, rather than informing the
populace into a politically aware entity, often functions to distract and
dissimulate.[10] How then can educators use engaged pedagogical strategies to help students tease out the tensions in the eighteenth century and
our own time between access to reliable information and an inundation of
media sources? How can studying the mechanisms of print culture produce a deeper understanding of eighteenth-century literature, a greater
competency in analytical reading, and a more holistic understanding of
eighteenth- and twenty-first-century social issues?

I argue that by encouraging student work in traditional and digital archives and by framing digital humanities as service—a term that I interrogated in chapter 1 and use explicitly here to express the ongoing and often
laborious character of digital work—we can address these conceptual
questions while also infusing practical experience into acts of learning
inside and outside of the classroom. In so doing, I suggest that we rethink
the very nature of service work in literary studies by proposing that work
in the digital humanities is fundamentally a form of engaged pedagogical
and scholarly praxis. Focusing on how my students performed service
work by correcting the OCR of scanned eighteenth-century ephemeral
texts through the website 18thConnect, I explain that such activity serves
important intellectual and social functions. Indeed, such service work
helps us expand upon the value of the digital humanities by reimagining
the commonly bifurcated practices of close and distant reading into what
I call "networked reading."[11]

Networked reading allows students to attend to the nuances of Robert
Darnton's influential communications circuit, and as textual editors
themselves, they become players within this circuit—now broadly de-

fined and expanded to include digitizing and digital editions. Students can practice detailed, precise analyses of how meaning is made from the structure of printed letters and words (such as the use of the long S or the decision to format text and type in a certain way), while their digital editing, particularly of ephemeral texts, allows them to consider these works alongside and beyond the limits of the traditional literary canon. Correcting OCR also allows them to rethink the very medium in which they read these texts (including, for instance, plain text and XML documents they create through their OCR editing). If Gérard Genette's theory of hypertext creates a network of relations among texts that reveals their continuities, innovations, and deviations, I suggest that networked reading allows readers to perform traditional close reading practices (attending to details of word choice, repetition, and other precise details of the text), while also allowing them to connect to the network of agents involved in the production of a book and its related literary systems during the early modern period.[12]

At the same time, this work has important local and global social effects. Correcting the OCR on these eighteenth-century documents provides crucial avenues of access for myriad readers. For example, it allows the visually impaired to use computer programs to read—accurately and often for the first time—transcribed eighteenth-century works. As we discussed in the introduction, this transcription process also makes texts that are legal for audiences to use freely; while long out of copyright, the texts are typically housed behind expensive paywalls in databases that only the most well-funded universities can afford. At its core, this sort of engaged digital humanities work offers new kinds of access to multiple audiences, as Jessica Stewart discusses in her essay in this chapter.

Ultimately, the strategies I offer allow students to learn about the value of various forms of historical preservation and access by identifying how issues pervasive in the eighteenth century—in my classes, we have focused on education, access to educational texts, and other matters of social justice—remain so today. These methods enable students to develop innovative technological competencies that will serve them during their studies and well into their post-college lives, while they also respond in significant ways to Elizabeth Eisenstein's call for the continued relevance of historical studies of eighteenth-century print culture, particularly the ephemeral media from the period. She writes that we "might also take into consideration the formation of new groups engaged in the production and distribution of printed materials. . . . The early-modern Grub Street itself awaits its historian. . . . Glimpses of a distinctive sub-culture associated with literary hackwork are offered in scattered studies . . . but the full picture . . . has not yet been sketched."[13] By enlisting student scholarship *as* service, our classrooms can become sites for collective historical knowledge-making that underscores the significance of access and preservation not just for canonical works, but also for the largely unknown ephemeral texts, the "infinite swarms of *Calones*," precisely *because* they contribute to a radical reimagining of the landscape of the literature and culture of the period as a whole. In these ways, an analysis of ephemeral historical literature can also help students become more literate consumers of media more broadly; they can become more skeptical in their consumption of and their response to the constant influx of information that they receive via social media.

Rethinking the Digital Humanities as an Engaged Pedagogical Practice

If, as we have discussed in previous chapters, the link between eighteenth-century studies and experiential learning practices is less immediately intuitive than it is for other, more modern literary genres and fields, then framing the digital humanities as service work for the eighteenth-century literature classroom is perhaps, at least initially, even more perplexing. Part of the problem comes from the very definitional instability of the term "digital humanities," which is also often referred to as humanities computing or the digital liberal arts, among other phrases.[14] As countless critics have discussed in the last decade, the core identity of the digital humanities has continued to shift in response to various camps. Alan Liu has argued, for example, that "the field is vigorously forming an identity" despite also experiencing a "dialectics of inclusion and exclusion not unlike that of past emergent fields. An ethnographer of the field, indeed, might take a page from Claude Lévi-Strauss and chart the current digital humanities as something like a grid of affiliations and differences between neighboring tribes."[15] In addition to the field's emerging and ever-changing identity, the methods informing the digital humanities provide a foundational skill to include in pedagogical best practices: "digital literacy is going to be as essential as information literacy and critical thinking" for our students.[16]

One of the most exciting elements of this methodology is the way it encourages collaborative and innovative practices. Matthew Kirschenbaum has noted that work in the digital humanities is fundamentally "a social undertaking" with "an unusually strong sense of community and common purpose."[17] Even more crucially, this kind of work has increasingly come to represent a form of resistance against attacks on the very existence of the humanities in college-level curricula:

> Digital humanities has also. . . lately been galvanized by a group of younger (or not so young) graduate students, faculty members (both tenure line and contingent), and other academic professionals who now wield the label "digital humanities" instrumentally amid an increasingly monstrous institutional terrain defined by declining public support for higher education, rising tuitions, shrinking endowments, the proliferation of distance education and the for-profit university, and, underlying it all, the conversion of full-time, tenure-track academic labor to a part-time adjunct workforce.[18]

In crucial ways, digital humanities methodologies offer an egalitarian platform that is more inclusive of a wide range of academics and academic practices from across the spectrum of the academy, from students—and here, I would suggest that we actively include undergraduates in this category—to faculty and staff at universities.

We might even push the boundaries of the relevance of digital humanities activities if we consider how this work has the potential to inform and affect communities outside of the intellectual and spatial boundaries of university campuses. For instance, Laurie Grobman and Roberta Rosenberg's recent study of service-learning practices in the English literature classroom has acknowledged the importance of continuing to develop best practices informed by the digital humanities in service-learning pedagogy precisely because both fields are "reciprocal and collaborative."[19] Yet their call to incorporate the digital humanities with service-integrated practices is still nevertheless framed as a call to action, rather than an explanation of methods, because despite these significantly collaborative elements, digital humanities work is often divested of a broader sociopolitical agenda. As Amanda Phillips notes, "we're reaching a critical mass of people who are ready to see the 'Digital Humanities' (used here in the most expansive sense possible) begin to diversify itself in terms of inclusion, approaches, theorization, and application to social justice issues."[20] In other words, while the field of the digital humanities is structured essentially to require elements of collaboration, often those practices are separated, at least ideologically, from basic issues of access, equitability, and other aspects of social justice, particularly for those beyond the academy.

I am interested in redefining our understanding of the digital humanities as service work precisely in order to show that these collaborative techniques can enhance access to and preservation of important texts and contexts while deepening the learning outcomes and critical and technological skill sets of our students. It is also crucial, as we discuss in this and the next chapter, to understand that most digital humanities work is an ongoing process, a kind of "continuous publishing."[21] Put this way, students better understand that their digital humanities work is inherently collaborative and typically involves long-term planning and execution. Every project takes multiple stages, phases, and iterations, and thus such enterprises require time and commitment on the part of many in much the same way that service does. Along this line, we might also think of the very term "service" as suggesting a public utility: just as it's a public service to have paved roads and facilities like parks and libraries, so too is it important to have digital resources freely and readily available to those who wish to use them.

Another benefit of such digital humanities service work is that it can make the value of access and preservation more relevant for audiences outside of the walls of our classrooms and campuses. As Liu notes, one of the most exciting elements of the digital humanities is that the field often seamlessly incorporates new technologies with "older humanities disciplines such as literature, history, classics, and the languages," as well as with fields, objects, and spaces that often seem antiquated or irrelevant to pedagogical (if not scholarly) practices. Digital humanities projects involve "the remediation of older media such as books and libraries" and ultimately underscore "the value of the old itself (history, archives, curatorial mission)."[22]

At my own public university, students and faculty alike often believe that our campus does not have the resources available to study these often costly or seemingly antiquated areas (course offerings in my and many other universities often reflect this apparent or actual dearth). While on my campus we are, in fact, lucky to have a robust set of resources in our archives and special collections (as the essay in chapter 6 by CSUN librarians Ellen Jarosz and Stephen Kutay will show), even campuses with few or no such resources can use digitized archives to help students visualize in vivid detail the importance of the published text as material object. By expanding our understanding of archives and archival research to include digital texts and spaces, we can therefore envision an ever-expanding community of texts that reach audiences well beyond the bounds of our classrooms and libraries.

Networked Reading: Envisioning the Digital Eighteenth Century
As mentioned earlier, one of the most appealing aspects of incorporating digital humanities service work into the undergraduate classroom is the way that it simultaneously encourages collaborative, networked reading practices. Over the past two decades, many critics have theorized the field, at least in part, by teasing out the differences between close and distant reading practices. According to many scholars, one of the benefits of the digital humanities, particularly the capacity to perform quantitative analyses of a vast number of literary works, is that such work decentralizes the process of close reading, which, they claim, relies on a highly selective and elitist canon. In this line of thinking, close reading is diminished in favor of distant reading, which favors a democratic, egalitarian, and somehow even scientifically objective means of performing literary analysis.[23]

Rather than viewing close and distant reading as bifurcated methods, I endorse Katherine Bode's point that these practices are actually far more closely aligned than many have recently acknowledged, largely because both processes ultimately rely on the same works found in university libraries and other sites of canon formation. Bode reminds us that "these approaches share a disregard for textual scholarship and an assumption that literary works are stable and singular entities."[24] Following her call for a move beyond this false binary to a method that emphasizes bibliographic and textual editing as models for guiding literary analysis and articulating literary history, I suggest that we promote acts of what I call networked reading. Allowing students the opportunity to read and edit ephemeral texts alongside traditional canonical texts reveals the varied network of agents involved in producing literary history, up to and including their own reading and textual editing as part of this networked process. Networked reading practices can be encouraged through the kind of digital humanities practices that combine OCR correction with an analysis of the data and documents collected through this and other digital humanities processes, as well as other data-mining techniques, including clustering, a process that groups conceptually related topics together visually. Clustering helps demonstrate the similarity among texts that might otherwise seem disparate or disconnected.[25] At the same time that students perform these networked reading practices, by correcting the OCR of ephemeral texts, they are also both preserving these works and expanding the network of readers able to consume them. Put another way, networked reading allows students to *become* agents of change, alongside the editors, publishers, reviewers, and the newly increased group of readers who can access these texts and ultimately give them meaning.

In order to have my students engage in networked reading practices, I have them become members of the free online project 18thConnect and join a digital classroom space hosted via the website. (18thConnect's founder, Laura Mandell, as well as one of its former project managers, Liz Grumbach, explain more about the public value of the project in the next section.) In the spirit of digital humanities practices, 18thConnect serves as an online community for the range of scholarly practices associated with eighteenth-century literature and culture. It is a site that gathers digital scholarly sources and resources from libraries, publishers, and scholars in one place.[26] As we mentioned in the introduction, while most libraries make documents freely available to the public, publishers make available vast repositories of academic and archival material, although they do so for an often prohibitive fee, which means these resources are available only to those whose institutions have the money to pay for such products. In addition to data gathering, 18thConnect generates metadata, aggregates links to various sites and collections, and makes the corrected OCR plain-text versions of digital items available for full text searching. The global scale of the community that the site as a whole creates is complemented by the aforementioned classroom space, which creates a microcommunity. Among its many uses, this online space allows members to post messages to one another and access collected 18thConnect documents that will be edited through the system.

One of the most valuable resources provided by 18thConnect is a tool called TypeWright, which the site describes as follows:

> TypeWright is a tool for correcting the text-version of a document made up of page images. These text-versions are crucially necessary: they are what enables full-text searching, datamining, preserving, and curating texts of historical importance. Right now, the text running behind the

page images of these texts has been mechanically typed, leaving behind errors that need to be corrected by human eyes and hands.[27]

This OCR correction—emending the errors left behind by mechanical typing—in some respects helps put the human back in the digital humanities, as the site's description suggests. As I will discuss in a moment, the attention to detail required in this editorial process encourages students to read in a new way that facilitates both close and distant reading practices.

The sheer magnitude of scanned eighteenth-century documents available on 18thConnect would facilitate a range of fascinating classroom assignments that involved data-mining. For the purposes of my undergraduate classes, however, I want to guide the students through the process of reading and editing these ephemeral works alongside canonical texts. I encourage students to focus on particular thematic elements that can, broadly speaking, help them discover points of connection between these works. Since I teach this material in service-learning designated classes, the overall themes relate in some way to issues of social justice. For instance, one iteration of my eighteenth-century survey course, with the long-standing catalogue title of the Age of Enlightenment, focused on the question of how literature from the eighteenth century instigated awareness of various types of reform and the need for them during the period. In particular, we discussed literary portrayals of science, gender, race, and education to understand how particular people and populations were marginalized. We also considered various secondary and theoretical works on space and spatial theory to help make more vivid the physical and cultural surroundings in which these works take place and were produced. To consider these topics, we read primary, canonical works like Jonathan Swift's *Gulliver's Travels*, Mary Wollstonecraft Shelley's *Frankenstein*, and Jane Austen's *Mansfield Park*.

To complement these canonical texts, I searched 18thConnect's TypeWright-enabled holdings to find a selection of ephemeral publications from the period. Given titles ranging from *A Present for a Servant Maid* and *The Housewife* to *Gulliver Decypher'd* and *The Flying Island*, students were able to decide which broad topics they were interested in and participate in a scholarly exploration of them via both largely forgotten and canonical texts. Once students chose a text that they were interested in working with, they each selected a section of twenty to thirty pages to edit; since the class had thirty-four students, the available documents had between three to six editors. Because my campus has access to Eighteenth-Century Collections Online (ECCO), a Gale database that partners with 18thConnect, the next step of this assignment asked students to download and read the particular text that they were going to edit. Then, with their document coeditors, they also did some basic bibliographic research using the English Short Title Catalogue, available for free via the British Library.[28] For the first segment of this assignment, students then collaborated on a brief textual description that summarized the scope of the document, its relationship to a given primary, canonical text that we had read during the semester, and information on the author, publisher, and extant print copies of the scanned text. With just this small prompt, students gained a sense of the need for preservation and digital access, as many of these documents were housed in just a few libraries across the world.

Once students had a sense of the document as a whole, they then embarked on their individual editorial mission. Before students worked with TypeWright on their own, we visited a computer lab where they had the opportunity to experiment with the program's interface. We also met with Ellen Jarosz, CSUN's head of Special Collections and Archives, to allow students to see, handle, and read actual eighteenth-century printed texts; during this session, students also did a brief bookmaking exercise to see how printing, gathering, and binding worked during this period, which enabled them to understand the necessity of signatures (the letters and numbers that appeared at the bottom of gatherings to help with the compilation and assembly of early modern printed works), and catchwords (the word at the bottom of each page that helped printers and assemblers understand how to assemble pages in sequence) in constructing the final product of a bound codex. We also had the opportunity to consider how certain eighteenth-century typographical characters, like the long *S*, are typically misread by the computer programs that people (particularly those students who are visually impaired) use to read and interpret texts.

So that students had a set of standards and guidelines for best practices in OCR editing, the class collaborated to create a style guide that included rules such as not modernizing spelling or capitalization and not correcting typographical errors in the original document. In general, students decided that they wanted their editorial interventions to be subtle and critically noninterpretive in order to allow the text to speak to multiple audiences in many ways. As a result, the students concluded that they wished to maintain the authenticity of the printed details of these eighteenth-century texts as loyally as possible, to emulate the experience of reading the archival text itself in its original printed form or a digital image of that form; as Bridget discussed earlier, the students recognized that there is a kind of aura and energy that these texts convey in their original form, whether we see it in print or on a screen. We also discussed how maintaining the appearance of the texts required sustained attention: it is very easy for any modern reader to transcribe faulty text and not even realize that they have modernized the spelling or capitalization. Even more perplexing for many new readers to eighteenth-century documents is the long S, which appears, on first glance, like an italicized lowercase f. Students are often curious about the very existence of this letter during the period, so we also spend some time discussing the transition from manuscript and scribal culture to mechanized print culture, because the long S was a holdover from the Roman cursive and then the calligraphic scribal tradition.[29]

As students worked on correcting the errors in the mechanically typed OCR text, they had the opportunity to read their selected document at a hyperclose level, attending to individual lines and characters. The illustrated figure demonstrates how TypeWright's layout allows students to see a thumbnail of the complete page of the original document to the left of the screen, but draws an editor's attention to issues at a microlevel. The tool accomplishes this focused editing by zeroing in on a single line from the original scanned document and then placing a rectangular text box showing the OCR text in the center of the screen, enabling the editor to compare the transcription to the original and edit as necessary. In this example, from Eliza Fowler Haywood's *Present for a Servant-maid* (1785), the majority of the OCR text was read correctly, but the long S followed by a faded "h" that appears in the word "should" was interpreted as "fhoud" by the mechanical reader. The student thus made a small edit to emend the text and make the text-searchable version accurate and readable. While this example demonstrates the relative accuracy of mechanical readers for certain texts, others indicate quite the inverse: often, lines or even whole pages offer garbled characters that require editors to entirely retype them. Far from serving as just busywork, this kind of activity requires students to read slowly, carefully, and diligently — while their edits, whether minor or major, all work toward the broader goal of

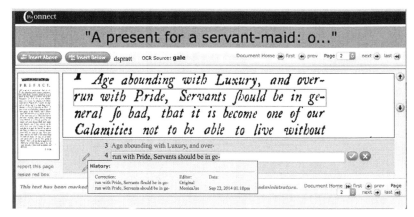

Screenshot of the TypeWright tool on 18thConnect.

making these texts readable, searchable, and more meaningfully accessible to a larger audience.

Once students completed their edits, the project manager for each editorial team paired up students to check each other's editorial work. This step is often crucial to ensuring that editors have not accidentally introduced errors into the OCR version of the text. Once this process was complete, students then received a plain text file that contained the corrected OCR. If students have used basic HTML (Hypertext Markup Language) and XML (Extensible Markup Language) coding to edit the documents, they also receive an XML file. Students are then free to use this document as they wish: as a primary document for their own essay writing, as a project that creates a website or blog to disseminate this text, or even as the basis for a creative project in which they print it out, cut it up, and rearrange it. In the next chapter, I discuss how a group of my graduate students took these files and constructed an online edited edition of an eighteenth-century novel. In my large undergraduate class, however, there is typically not enough time in the semester to help students learn coding languages beyond the basic HTML that they can use to edit the documents themselves (I discuss the key differences between HTML and XML in the next chapter).

Yet even when time constraints disallow students from learning more advanced digital humanities techniques, I encourage them to perform basic distant reading tasks like creating a word cloud of their documents through sites like Wordle (a process that students simply cannot do with the image scans). Students can see visually that certain words appear most frequently; this repetition reveals how certain word usage might be suggestive and important for the interpretation of a given text. This quantitative analysis helps train students to attend to elements like repetition and frequency and encourages them to linger over word choice. Through this method alone, students gain a sense of how basic statistical analyses of literature can help them identify important linguistic or imagistic trends in these documents. These OCR corrections have multiple other generative possibilities, too. They make these documents accessible for future students, particularly for those whose visual impairments would have made it difficult or impossible for them to read the uncorrected texts. The emended files also offer the ability to create an ongoing project involving future students and classes who can engage in practices like annotating these works and creating websites to make the annotated editions available for audiences across the internet (this is a strategy to which I will return in chapter 6).

After student editorial teams have completed their tasks, I encourage them to turn to comparative close reading strategies in order to analyze the relationship between the ephemeral documents and the primary texts we have read in class. Since at this point I am interested in helping students revisit the idea of different forms of textual and sociocultural spaces, I introduce key readings from the likes of Jürgen Habermas, Michael McKeon, Simon Varey, and Cynthia Wall, among others.[30] Focusing on Habermas allows students to gain a critical vocabulary for thinking about the separation of public from private space during the eighteenth century, whereas works by McKeon, Vary, and Wall provide important details relevant to the representation of public and private and urban and rural spaces in eighteenth-century literature. To bring the landscape of London closer to home for my students, we also read excerpts from Edward Soja's *Seeking Spatial Justice*, which theorizes the vast urban spaces of Los Angeles in ways that allow students to think critically about their access to resources in public and private spaces alike.[31]

Once students gain this critical vocabulary, I ask them to write essays that respond to the following questions:

How did reading and editing this eighteenth-century text help you better understand one of the texts that we have read this semester (Swift's *Gulliver's Travels*, Shelley's *Frankenstein*, or Edgeworth's *Castle Rackrent* in particular)?

What was it like to read the 18thConnect text so closely? What were the challenges (the long *S*, old type, bad scans, ink blots)?

How did reading and editing your 18thConnect text help you better understand issues of space (domestic or scientific, city or country, natural or cultural) in a new or different way? Did opening up the space of the text help you better understand or envision the use of different spatial images in the work(s)?

Student responses demonstrated a wonderful array of creative, networked associations and constructive inferences made thanks to reading and editing these ephemeral texts alongside more well-known canonical works. One, from Nora Chatchoomsai, offers an exciting reading of an understudied facet of *Gulliver's Travels*: the vegetarian diet encouraged by Gulliver in Houyhnhnmland. Another, from Alyssa Dominguez, reads issues of domesticity alongside the tension between Victor and Elizabeth in *Frankenstein*.

CONNECTING CARBS IN THE CLASSROOM

Finding Vegetarianism in *Gulliver's Travels*

Nora Chatchoomsai

In the process of editing a portion of Laetitia Montague's *The Housewife* on 18thConnect, I found interesting facts regarding eighteenth-century cuisines that helped illuminate my reading of Jonathan Swift's *Gulliver's Travels*. On this user-friendly website, I can apply, free of charge, the historical contexts of my research on eighteenth-century diets, connecting factual accounts of how dishes were made in the upper middle-class English household to the fictional milieu of the Houyhnhnms, the rational horses who reign over Gulliver and his distant relatives, the irrational yahoos, in Book 4 of *Gulliver's Travels*. After having finished editing Montague's digitized document, I was able to copy the corrected texts more easily and use them in my essay, in which I contrast Montague's English recipes to Gulliver's favorite vegetarian recipes made by the Houyhnhnms. From the historical context provided by 18thConnect, I argue that Swift uses Gulliver's praise for the Houyhnhnms' diet to criticize the eighteenth-century English diet.

The Housewife guided me to understand how an English person in the upper middle class ate in the eighteenth century. In a recipe for summer pottage, Montague writes, "Take a shin of beef, crags of muttons or veal, chop the meat in pieces, and boil them. . . . Dish up your pottage with roasted pigeons or ducks in the middle of it, and small slices of bacon fried . . . , sausages cut into little bits, and fried balls; you may also add gravy and palates, and cox combs boiled in water tender."[32] Here, seven different kinds of meat (beef, mutton, veal, pigeon, duck, pork, and chicken) are used in making one dish, which might include a large amount of fat and uric acids, contributing to a prognosis of gout and heart attack. Moreover, a review of several recipes in the book shows that each dish is accompanied with few or no vegetables. However, the subtitle, "Being a most useful assistant in all domestic concerns," suggests Montague, a self-proclaimed expert, considered these recipes adequate for a good housewife to serve to her family.

18thConnect allowed me to contextualize Swift's satire on the issue of diet. Having learned from the kind of food a normal English middle-class household served, I found it easier to discern how Swift might be addressing the idea of vegetarianism, which, although somewhat foreign to the eighteenth-century British, was nevertheless a fairly well-known practice during the period. Having lived with the Houyhnhnms, Swift's Gulliver comments that his diet there consisted of "honey out of hallow trees," bread, oats, grains, and milk, which contribute to, he concludes, "perfect health of body, and tranquility of mind."[33] To summarize Gulliver's standpoint on the issue, the simplicity and inherent healthfulness of vegetarian food and the hard labor that comes along with it induce him to conclude that "nature is very easily satisfied," though he also considers it "a insipid diet" for the common people.[34] He then criticizes the English diet, which would have included dishes similar to the recipes mentioned in *The Housewife*, for being made of "a thousand things which operated contrary to each other. . . [and which] inflamed our bodies, and precipitated or prevented digestion."[35]

It might be anachronistic to simply identify the recipes in *The Housewife* as unhealthy or to conclude that Swift's Gulliver is advocating vegetarianism, as the word did not exist in the eighteenth century. Having 18thConnect as a tool enables me to argue that, though not yet coined as a term, vegetarianism can be found in *Gulliver's Travels* as an alternative to the regular recipes made predominantly of meat that Swift argued were unhealthy. *The Housewife* contextualizes Gulliver's advice to start eating a diet of strictly vegetables and grains, a practice that has become prevalent in today's society.

Nora's topic allows her to delve into aspects of quotidian eighteenth-century culture and connect them to our own cultural moment. In addition, since vegetarianism also raises important social concerns about the ethical treatment of animals and sustainability, this topic also allowed her to connect with her own contemporary moment—as well as some ethical concerns inherent in Swift's portrayal of human-animal relations in the novel—in innovative ways. What is perhaps most exciting here is that Nora was able to perceive what was *thinkable* for early modern audiences by reading these different texts together.[36] By focusing closely on a small passage of the cookbook, she was able to read across texts and genres to perform an irreverent analysis of Swift's well-studied text.

In Alyssa's essay, we can see how reading an ephemeral text alongside a deeply canonical novel helped her reconsider cultural notions of gender and agency.

DOMESTIC CONSTRAINTS IN *FRANKENSTEIN*

Alyssa Dominguez

At times, eighteenth-century literature presents the consequences of separation of the genders. The social construction of gender portrayed throughout this literature values men over women. Society at this time separated the sexes into two spheres; the man inhabited the public sphere, while the woman was automatically restricted to the private or domestic sphere. The men were able to engage in public life, which included duties and pleasures outside of the home, while it was inappropriate for the women to leave the home and partake in public life. The women, it seems, were confined to the home and all the duties it entailed.

The domestic duties of a housewife of this time are exemplified in the 18thConnect piece appropriately titled, *The Housewife, Being a most Useful Assistant in all Domestic Concerns, Whether in a Town or Country Situation.* In this instructional manual for the housewife, Laetitia Montague gives expert advice from "setting out dinners," to "general rules in cookery." The piece connects to novels of the eighteenth century through the enactment of the domestic sphere. For instance, in Mary Shelley's *Frankenstein*, the men and women belong to the socially constructed spheres. The protagonist, Victor Frankenstein, being a part of the male sphere, is able to leave the home for his education and any endeavor he desires, while his love interest, Elizabeth, being a woman, was expected to stay home. Reading and editing *The Housewife* allowed me to grasp the reality of the emphasis society placed on the spheres. Editing material line by line enabled me to conduct a closer reading that aided me in analyzing *Frankenstein* and the socially constructed notions it portrays.

The significance of the spheres is presented when Shelley writes, "Elizabeth approved of the reasons of [Victor's] departure, and only regretted that she had not the same opportunities of enlarging her experience, and cultivating her understanding."[37] Shelley herself emphasizes the scant opportunity women had in her generation. In the passage, Elizabeth is acknowledging her place in society and accepting it. Studying *The Housewife* alongside a work of the British canon helped me see how Shelley responds to issues and concerns that were at stake in multiple literary and cultural texts from the period.

Like Nora's, Alyssa's reading of Shelley's canonical work became richer and more intellectually sophisticated through her detailed reading of this noncanonical, didactic domestic manual. These interpretations of canonical works offer innovative readings in large part because the students' editorial practices made them deeply aware of particular rhetorical or topical issues that connected often seemingly disparate texts. Indeed, students began this project wondering how they would connect a domestic manual and cookery book with literary texts that seemed divested of such concerns, but instead they discovered the important way that these thematic concerns resonate with readers from the eighteenth century and today. In other words, students were able to see that all texts, whether literary or not, can be read and analyzed rigorously and carefully and that historical research often requires that we explore little-known texts and archives as a series of networked systems.

At the same time, students were able to see the importance of preserving and making accessible seemingly inconsequential, ephemeral eighteenth-century texts. By correcting the OCR of these documents, students make them accessible for those who are on the outside of expensive paywalls or who have visual impairments. Yet this specific benefit of service-learning activity is rendered at least somewhat ironic if one of your students happens *not* to be sighted. As Jessica Stewart writes, however, making texts accessible can take myriad forms, and she offers another kind of networked reading experience.

THE AUDIBLE EIGHTEENTH CENTURY

Jessica Stewart

For students enrolled in courses in which service-learning activities account for a significant portion of students' final grades, making audio recordings is a great way to create accessible texts. This is especially true for those who rely on screen reading programs that may be incompatible with sites such as 18thConnect. In the fall of 2015, I was such a student. Tasked with editing an obscure eighteenth-century text for service-learning credit, I was faced with one of the many objective realities of visual impairment: inaccessibility.

I use a computer screen reader called JAWS (Job Access with Speech). The program is described as "the world's most popular screen reader, developed for computer users whose vision loss prevents them from seeing screen content or navigating with a mouse. JAWS provides speech and Braille output for the most popular computer applications on your PC."[38] Like many JAWS users, I often encounter the message "empty document" when attempting to access PDF files. This is especially true if pages of a hard-copy book have been manually scanned. These types of PDF files are images that contain no text, which JAWS does not recognize and therefore cannot read aloud. This shortcoming is very problematic for students taking literature courses wherein many of the assigned readings are scanned and uploaded to a learning management system. Such files can be converted from image to text using OCR, but this process can be slow, arduous, and, even with modern textual sources, often produces incorrect or illegible texts (as discussed earlier).

It is for this reason that some students may elect to acquire free online versions of texts. Websites such as Project Gutenberg, the Academy of American Poets, and the Poetry Foundation are excellent sources for accessible material. However, as is sometimes the case, students may not have the advantage of twenty-four-hour computer or internet access. Also, screen reading programs such as JAWS are incompatible with certain sites. Whether a JAWS user will be able to access a webpage largely depends on the amount of graphics and the way the page has been formatted (multiple columns, for instance, frequently cause problems in which the program attempts to read linearly across separate columns).

Moreover, undertaking to comprehend and explicate eighteenth-century literature through JAWS can be a daunting task. This is especially true of the poetry, with its eighteenth-century cadences, rhythms, and pronunciations. This task is even more difficult for persons with print disabilities, a group that includes those who struggle with dyslexia and those who are visually impaired and blind, who must rely on one or more forms of assistive technology. JAWS offers awkward or improper pronunciations of unfamiliar or antiquated words. An example would be words containing the long S. The long S occurs again and again in the opening section of the Project Gutenberg e-book of Jonathan Swift's *Tale of a Tub*. Rather than the words "speedily published," a JAWS reader might hear "feedily publifhed." This is because JAWS recognizes this letter as an f rather than an s. These issues and others can make the task of reading and editing difficult if not impossible for many JAWS users, most especially for those individuals who are majoring in disciplines wherein the relationship between form and content often forms the basis of critical interpretation.

As an English major with a serious visual impairment, I have often encountered accessibility issues that have impeded my learning process. Such was the case in my Age of Enlightenment literature course. Students were asked to edit portions of obscure eighteenth-century works and manifestos as part of a service-learning project, ironically in part to make them accessible for the visually impaired. I was unable to complete the same assignment as my sighted classmates because my screen reading program did not interact with the 18thConnect site. Dr. Spratt and I developed an alternative assignment that allowed me to serve the disabled community in much the same way I had been served.

I began this project with two main objectives in mind. The first was to present urgent and relevant research, research that would ground and inform my interpretations of two of the most controversial units of eighteenth-century discourse. The second and more important objective was to provide students, most especially those enrolled in eighteenth-century literature courses, with accessible versions of these texts. I was primarily interested in students who, like myself, would have to contend with difficulties stemming from a print disability. It is only recently that I have had the idea to expand my project to accommodate a wider audience, in particular those readers who may be neither English majors nor literature students but may be interested in eighteenth-century literature.

I was particularly concerned with eighteenth-century gender norms. This interest led to my performing a feminist interrogation of "The Lady's Dressing Room," one of Jonathan Swift's more infamous poems. This analysis led to the discovery of a poem entitled "The Reasons that Induced Dr. S to Write a Poem Called the Lady's Dressing Room," a poem that the satirist Lady Mary Wortley Montagu wrote in response to Swift. The incendiary nature of these works notwithstanding, I had never heard of either of them, nor had I ever heard or read anything describing Swift as a hater of women.

These poems are at the center of a literary war, one that survives the centuries and pits scholar against scholar and student against student. I had questions. I needed to get into conversation with both poets before sending my own intellectual dog into the fight. I acquired half a dozen blank disks and an advanced recording device from the university's Disability Resources and Educational Services Office, went home, and pulled up online versions of both poems. I recorded myself reading Swift's poem in two parts. This process took approximately ten to twelve hours. Reciting the poem from memory proved not to be an option: even the smallest mistakes meant deleting sixty perfect lines of poetry at a time. Carefully feeding each line into the recorder was a more effective strategy. I went through each line, repeating after JAWS and inserting stresses, inflections, and pauses where appropriate. I repeated this process with Montague's poem and had the MP3 files burned onto a disk, which I then donated to our Disability Resources and Educational Services Office, so that other students in the future could use my own accessible research to aid their own. Rereading and rerecording various portions of the poems allowed me to approach the images and metaphors from different angles. Out of these readings emerged an argument about Swift's misogyny—despite, or perhaps even enhanced by its Juvenalian satire—that allowed me to pursue my own research interest in feminist interpretation.

This project and the required research have taught me to understand the necessity of raising and answering difficult questions, even when your first impulse is to latch onto the surface level aspect of a text; making these texts accessible through the recording process disallowed any quick, shallow reading on my own part. Moving beyond superficial and quick reading is an essential component of the reading, analytical, and writing process, one that now, as a current first-year college writing teacher, I strive to impart in my own classroom. As an instructor of composition, I advocate for the employment of these critical reading and writing skills as the first and most important step in formulating a balanced, logical, and rhetorically powerful argument.

Still more important is a respect for text in all its forms. Making audio recordings of literary works allows but also requires students to engage with popular texts, obscure texts, contemporary texts, and classical texts in a concentrated, meaningful way. Expanding this project of making documents accessible to multiple kinds of reading experiences affords sighted and visually impaired students with the opportunity to do rewarding work in the disabled and literary communities.

As Jessica's account highlights, while programs like text-to-audio converters are important, we still need more technology *and* more human agency to overcome the obstacles that many would-be readers face.[39] Importantly, her project allowed her to discover "a respect for text in all of its forms," an insight that underscores how networked reading and its related service work open up possibilities for literary and textual analysis together. I am proud to say that Jessica's brilliant alternative accessibility service activity garnered her first prize at our campuswide Research and Service Symposium, hosted annually by the Office of Community Engagement. Judges, other nominees, and audience members marveled at Jessica's project—not just for her talents as a voice actor (which are impressive on their own), but especially because she so adeptly conceived of a project that at once enhanced her mastery of the class subject matter *and* had a deliverable. Her series of audio recordings are now available, free of charge, for any future students who want to experience these poems in ways that would likely mirror how most eighteenth-century audiences would have encountered them: read aloud. In this way, Jessica's twenty-first-century project, aided by JAWS and digital recorders, enhanced an element of the historical reading experience for her future listeners.

While Swift's Hack ironically dedicates *A Tale of a Tub* to "the Prince of Posterity" to mock the idea of anyone remembering or caring for long about most eighteenth-century printed works, the dynamic digital service work that Nora, Alyssa, Jessica, and their classmates performed reveals the enduring value of works that even at their inception seemed positioned to be forgotten. Laura Mandell and Liz Grumbach, who have together been instrumental in developing and expanding the scope of 18thConnect—the site that allows these digital ephemeral documents to circulate unbounded again—remind us at this chapter's end about how the digital humanities contribute to the public good in myriad ways.

18THCONNECT AND TYPEWRIGHT

Public Engagement through Crowd-Sourced Transcription

Laura Mandell and Liz Grumbach

The trend in public humanities has been for humanities researchers to collaborate with local communities on issues relevant to them.[40] These projects typically require that the humanistic research conducted with the public *serve* that public by addressing a local problem or concern or, if a global issue, that the project be concerned with social justice. In the case of crowd-sourced transcriptions of cultural heritage material, the Australian Newspaper Project was so successful (three million news items transcribed over two years, without advertising for volunteers!) because it engaged citizen genealogists, people (mainly the elderly) who were interested in finding out about the history of their family. But does crowd-sourced correction of past texts necessarily engage only those people who have something personal to gain from the work or who are explicitly concerned with social justice? And what public good might be served by such transcriptions or the process of transcribing? Our work in engaging the public to correct the transcriptions of 296,257 documents published in the United Kingdom and the United States between 1473 and 1800 has provided one answer to the public good served by corrected transcriptions: preventing the spread of what we call "inadvertent fake news."

18thConnect.org was developed early in the 2000s as a companion site to NINES, or the Networked Infrastructure for Nineteenth-Century Electronic Scholarship.[41] NINES and 18thConnect, along with others that followed, are field-specific online scholarly communities and finding aids.[42] When Jerome McGann and Bethany Nowviskie first launched NINES in 2005, the goal was to peer review digital projects, catalogue metadata and keywords about their contents, and then make it possible to search simultaneously through all nineteenth-century digital projects (such as the Blake Archive, the Whitman Archive, the Poetess Archive, and the Rossetti Archive). Journals from the JSTOR and Project MUSE databases were added to make NINES into a complete research environment.

When we started 18thConnect, a complete research environment for eighteenth-century scholars, we realized it would definitely have to include Gale's Eighteenth-Century Collections Online (ECCO) and ideally ProQuest's Early English Books Online (EEBO). However, in the ECCO catalogue, as well as in Artemis, which houses the data from both ECCO and Nineteenth-Century Collections Online (NCCO), the textual data running searches was far from perfect, and only a third of the texts in EEBO had been transcribed. Both EEBO and ECCO are comprised of digital images that had been made from microfilm images, so they were very low quality. The Text Creation Partnership, which paid typists to transcribe EEBO documents and some from ECCO, tried to use mechanical typing, that is, OCR. The software was so poor at the time they started their paid transcription project that the mechanically typed texts were worthless. OCR has improved, and the 18thConnect team launched the Early Modern OCR Project in order to create OCR text documents from EEBO and ECCO images to load into 18thConnect's signature tool, TypeWright.[43]

TypeWright allows the public to correct OCR transcriptions of EEBO and ECCO documents.[44] All anyone has to do in order to be able to click on the "edit" button of a document retrieved when searching 18thConnect is to create an account: a real email address, a fictional or real name, and a password are all that is required to participate in the correction project. Any person or group who corrects an EEBO or ECCO text is then *given* that text—not the page images, but the transcribed copy of it, and they can publish that copy online as a digital edition, listing themselves as the editors. (Gale and ProQuest graciously allowed us to make this possible.)[45] Many scholars who want early modern texts but whose institutions do not subscribe to these costly databases are thus able to access these documents for themselves and their students. For database users, there is an added benefit: 18thConnect also sends the corrected transcriptions back to ProQuest and Gale for use in EEBO and ECCO. There has been much debate among Renaissance scholars about helping for-profit companies with sentiment running against it, but the truth is that corrected texts in EEBO and ECCO do not increase company profits, only scholars' experience in using the text databases. Moreover, digital scholarly editions peer reviewed by 18thConnect—with an editorial board as illustrious as that of Cambridge University Press—can be counted toward promotion and tenure.

But does crowd-sourced correcting of the 296,257 documents do anything else? How does it serve the *public* good? In an article forthcoming in *Digital Humanities Quarterly*, Laura Mandell explores the use of search engines on uncorrected OCR. ECCO's OCR captures on average 50 percent of the results in searching for a phrase made up of two words; the Early Modern OCR Project (EMOP) OCR garners 60 percent of the results;[46] the Google N-gram viewer's OCR finds only 46 percent. Currently, the results returned by tools designed to find word usage over time, such as the Google N-gram viewer, the Artemis word frequency tool, and HathiTrust's Bookworm are deeply misleading—they even contradict each other, as Mandell shows—simply because the texts are too flawed to work well in the tools. The Google N-gram viewer solved this problem by removing most early modern texts from its database. Insofar as both scholars and citizens make arguments based upon using digital tools and search engines to sort through cultural heritage materials, the fact that 50 percent or more of the texts are not yet findable because of dirty OCR means that public knowledge of the past will be flawed and historical arguments misleading. Those who make these arguments are guilty of inadvertently spreading fake news. Correcting the mistyped transcriptions of early modern texts serves the public by directly improving their accuracy and consequently the accuracy of public knowledge about them.

But the process of correcting transcriptions may serve the public even more than the results. The participatory engagement in preserving cultural heritage materials undertaken by Transcribe Bentham at University College, London, and the Letters of 1916 at Maynooth University in Dublin, Ireland, as well as 18thConnect's TypeWright, introduces users to the touch and feel of historical research as much as to the methods involved. To complement the Transcribe Bentham project, the British Library blog *Untold Lives* recruited 19,000 users to transcribe Bentham's letters and papers; citizens are interested in the past and in participating in its retrieval and survival. Our students at Texas A&M University created a Facebook game called Anachronaut (their own name!) for correcting OCR and are fascinated by what they can find in TypeWright, some of them blogging on 18thConnect to describe their findings.

The Early Modern OCR project and TypeWright continue to develop: we are working to adopt new OCR technologies developed by Google that can make transcription easier and faster. But ideally the software will never become perfect so that TypeWright can continue to give the crowd of professors, students, and citizens the opportunity to participate in sustaining our past.

6: THE EIGHTEENTH-CENTURY NOVEL, ONLINE

꽃꽃

Scholar-Activists and the Creation of Digital Editions in the Graduate Classroom

DANIELLE SPRATT

If you've ever searched the internet for the title of a book that is in the public domain, chances are, you've encountered a digital edition of that book produced by Project Gutenberg.[1] Begun in 1971, the initiative — the oldest of its kind — uses thousands of volunteers to create free, digital versions of texts that have gone out of copyright. So if you're searching for an accessible copy of Henry Fielding's *Tom Jones* (1749) or Jane Austen's *Northanger Abbey* (1817) for your e-reader, you can easily navigate to the Gutenberg website and download an edition for free. Because this open-access format is available, my students often select these texts in order to save money on book purchases at the start of the semester. Since they are immediately available online, these works also offer a kind of instant gratification: readers don't need to wait days for shipping, and they are flexible enough to read across e-reader platforms. And as Jessica Stewart notes in her contribution to chapter 5, sites like Project Gutenberg also offer text that is readable by software used by print-disabled audiences.

Sometimes these editions are perfectly wonderful options; other times, they have myriad errors, lack explanatory paratextual material like footnotes or endnotes, or are not the same edition as the text that I have ordered for the class, all situations that cause various kinds of confusion when we try to discuss passages in class. Using different editions, students can't find the same passages or they find textual variations; this situation slows down discussion, but it also increases student awareness of textual variants that are important to acknowledge. In other words, digital reading can be another occasion to engage in networked reading practices that help students consider how various agents — including anonymous or scholarly textual editors from the eighteenth century to today — make texts and textual meaning.

As discussed in the previous chapter, what I am calling "networked reading" is inspired by the work of digital humanists like Katherine Bode, whose influential argument about close versus distant reading practices ultimately posits that a more accurate methodology for digital reading practices must accommodate what she calls "a new object of scholarly analysis, modeled on the foundational technology of textual scholarship: the scholarly edition."[2] In this chapter, I explain how both a consideration of digital editions and, ultimately, the process of creating student-driven digital scholarly editions intensify learning outcomes for participants while the latter also provides the crucial public service of making literature available for larger audiences. Digital initiatives like Project Gutenberg or the annotated eighteenth-century novel that I discuss in this chapter provide a necessary service by opening up free, equitable access to these texts to all curious researchers and readers.

This is not to say that the act of networked reading in the service of creating a digital edition is without problems. Crowd-sourced digital editions amplify the potential for inaccuracy, from a typo in transcription to a fuzzy or inaccurate explanatory note. But these issues can present themselves as productive problems if we simply ask ourselves about their theoretical and practical ramifications. On the one hand, generations of educators have relied on rigorously edited and annotated scholarly editions of texts because they make historical and contextual information easily available for new readers and guide students as they create their own written and verbal analyses of these works. That's why Bridget opted to provide Norton Critical Editions to all of her community readers in her *Pride and Prejudice* book club, as discussed in chapter 2. On the other hand, as scholars of bibliography and textual editing and as teachers who care about the archives, we must continually ask the question: What constitutes textual reliability, anyway?

For some teachers, the easiest choice is to recommend that students refrain from using open-access formats in favor of one standard print edition. Yet even this strategy is far from foolproof: often out of necessity, many students choose the cheapest print text available, which is not always the text ordered for the class. With the persistence of these open-access e-texts in our classrooms, particularly in courses whose texts have gone out of copyright, we must be mindful of the collision between print and digital text. Indeed, Yin Liu reminds us that "debates about the meaning and nature of text persist and have been sharpened by the anxieties, challenges, and opportunities of realizing textuality in digital forms."[3] In other words, crowdsourced digital texts remind us of the inherently unstable nature of text across platforms, whether analog or digital; they also invite exciting opportunities for scholarship related to data analysis, topic modeling, and other metrical analyses of digitized texts. Such digital humanities work has allowed recent scholars to conclude, for instance, that there are distinctive qualities of "literariness" across canonical publications.[4] These questions, as Bridget and I have discussed in the earlier chapters and as I continue to examine here, are central to the exploration of print ephemera and noncanonical texts as well.

We hope that by this point in the book, we (along with so many other scholars) have made a convincing case for the importance of uniting digital humanities techniques with traditional bibliographic approaches to textual analysis in the service of offering historical literature to broad public audiences. Even more, we hope you agree that, as Jessie Daniels and Polly Thiselthwaite's recent work on digital humanities scholarship contends, "Being a scholar in the digital era means connection to the larger social world."[5] They continue, "The architecture of participation in the digital era has opened up new possibilities of being a scholar-activist."[6] But what does being a "scholar-activist" look like when students are nascent practitioners of both sides of this hyphenate?

Building on our previous chapters and much of the recent scholarship on the activist potential of digital humanities—all of which, we think, offer important theoretical frameworks for uniting scholarship, activism, and digital humanities techniques—I will focus in this chapter on the methodology of using the graduate classroom to create a scholarly digital edition, in this case of the understudied 1759 novel *The History of the Countess of Dellwyn*, written by Sarah Fielding. My class called their edition the *Countess of Dellwyn* Digitization Project.[7] The broad theme of the class was Defiant Women of the Long Eighteenth Century, and this project encouraged students to assume active scholarly editorial roles; rather than being passive, individual readers, they experienced and created an environment of collective debate and discussion that allowed them to engage with a presumed audience of new readers of Fielding's novel. In so doing, these students became experts in the novel and gained valuable skills in editorial and digital humanities practices. Unlike Project Gutenberg texts, this free online edition also offers a scholarly apparatus that offers important literary and contextual information for audience members and encourages further transhistorical inquiry.

This is not to say that what the class produced is a perfect edition. In fact, there are *many* errors that still exist, particularly small typos and misspellings (I will say more about this matter in a moment). For instance, I just randomly pulled up a page from the edition and found some typographical errors in a note about Swift's Houyhnhmns, the rational horses of *Gulliver's Travels*, which Fielding references in chapter 7 of her novel: "Houybnbnms: reference to Jonathan Swift's work *Gulliver's Travels*. Houybnbnms are a race of horses that base their beliefs off reason and have a peaceful society." But projects like the *Countess of Dellwyn* Digitization Project are in what Mark Carrigan calls a process of "continuous publishing"—an ongoing effort that produces various iterations via readers external to the project, as well as new students and editor-participants who engage with the text after its original editors have finished their work.[8] Reading online allows the performance of what Gérard Genette and Julia Kristeva have called intertextual and hypertextual reading; this ongoing editorial process goes one step further, allowing Genette's concept of transtextuality to function as both networked reading and as an engaged practice for the public good.[9]

By increasing access—both to the primary text and to relevant historical, literary, and contextual details (even if they sometimes need another revision before they are fully correct, as in the example just mentioned)—the student-editors have given more readers from diverse backgrounds and with diverse skill sets the opportunity to offer new readings of works like Fielding's. Such a process is perhaps even more exhilarating and necessary for texts that are not yet canonical but not entirely ephemeral (this latter category is discussed more fully in chapter 5). In producing a scholarly edition of a noncanonical text, participants in this project were "broadening scholarship itself through fostering extensive cross-disciplinary, public ties and rewarding connection, collaboration, and curation between individual scholars, rather than through their institutions or professional roles. . . . [In these ways] participants were performing the scholarship of engagement."[10] And nowhere is this process more important than for the very nascent scholar-activists that I aforementioned: they are all looking to carve out their own space in the academy, and many of them are looking to find points of relevance beyond the academy to help them communicate their work to nonacademic friends, family members, and outside readers.

For generations, Sarah Fielding's authorial legacy was largely contingent on her relationship with her brother, the aforementioned Henry Fielding, or her mentor, Samuel Richardson (author of the 1740 novel *Pamela; or Virtue Rewarded* and his 1748 tragedy, *Clarissa*, two of the most popular novels of the mid-1700s and two of the most studied eighteenth-century works today). But recent scholarship by critics like Sara Gadaken, Susan Carlile, Kate Rumbold, and Betty Schellenberg has suggested the importance of Sarah Fielding's prose work, particularly her 1759 novel.[11] Nevertheless, her most popular work was then—and currently remains—the 1744 sentimental novel *The Adventures of David Simple*, as the title page of *The History of the Countess of Dellwyn* itself suggests by proclaiming it to be written "by the author of *David Simple*."

Yet in *Dellwyn*, her penultimate published novel, we see elements of formal and literary allusion and experimentation that make it ripe for critical attention. These experiments in character, psychic interiority, and narrative suggest the novel is worthy of study and recognition in its own right. Indeed, even the competing plots of the novel indicate Fielding's interest in experimentation: she subordinates the sentimental story of the typical heroine, Mrs. Bilson, a devout, hardworking, and supremely ethical wife and mother, to that of Charlotte Lucum, later the Countess of Dellwyn. The daughter of an exiled politician whose only interest is using his daughter to barter for his own political power, Charlotte experiences a persistent, if gradual, downward spiral from the start of the novel. Her first fall comes early, when her lust for material objects (a pair of diamond earrings and a diamond necklace) combines with her unbridled jealousy of her friend, the aptly named Fanny Fashion (later Fanny Chlegen), to coerce Charlotte into marrying a feeble and elderly rake, Lord Dellwyn. From there, Charlotte soon grows tired of her marriage and ultimately commits adultery, only to be divorced publicly and exiled to France.

To put it simply, this is the story of a heroine who is very unlike the prim and proper figures in Richardson's novels or in those of many of Fielding's contemporaries. Exploring this extremely flawed heroine is thus important in helping students understand not only the state of the prose novel in the middle of the eighteenth century (a long-standing concern of scholars in the field), but also the way that other women—beyond Pamela Andrews, Clarissa Harlowe, and Sophia Western (the love interest in *Tom Jones*)—were portrayed in popular media during the long eighteenth century. Indeed, considering Fielding's protagonist is perhaps even more important, as she is an example of a defiant woman written by a female author. As my students read and understood these plot points, they became more excited about making accessible the story of Sarah Fielding's version of the "defiant woman," a figure who has been relegated to the wings of the public stage of eighteenth-century characters we know about and study. Revealing this alternative history not only improves our understanding of gender in the long eighteenth century, but also offers meaningful insight into the ways in which women writers were actively resisting gender norms centuries before the modern feminist movement took hold.

But if most students in the class agreed that the novel was of interest from a disciplinary and a readerly perspective, there was still the matter of transferring this information to the digital scholarly edition. Before we began the project of annotating the novel, I divided it into sections and asked students to sign up for a specific section; each student would be the lead editor for the chosen section, although it would receive attention from other members of the class as well. Our first task was to read the novel as a whole while correcting the OCR of these individual sections through 18thConnect (see chapter 5 on how this process works).

During the time that students were reading the full text of *Dellwyn*, they also visited CSUN's Special Collections and Archives to view and handle works printed from the period. Ellen Jarosz, head of Special Collections, brought out a range of works, from the visually and canonically significant (Samuel Johnson's 1755 *A Dictionary of the English Language*) to small children's books bound only by a single thread. Among the documents, students were particularly fascinated by the 1812 didactic manual by Henry Thomas Kitchener, *Letters on Marriage*, a work that attempts to prevent women from being seduced or engaging in other disreputable behavior.[12] Since Fielding's novel confronts similar themes, this form of networked reading allowed students to compare social norms from the mid-eighteenth century to those of the early nineteenth century. To help make this one text accessible to the whole group of students (and any other readers who were interested), Ellen and her colleague Stephen Kutay, a digital services librarian, created a tool to make the students' first major foray into networked reading as comprehensive as possible. In their essay they describe this project.

Ellen Jarosz and Stephen Kutay

Many academic libraries have been amassing unique primary source collections for decades. These materials are extraordinarily rich for studying a host of national and local events, trends, and concepts. As a special collections librarian and a digital services librarian, we often collaborate with teaching faculty members in developing instructional tools and platforms that incorporate primary and archival sources in the Oviatt Library at California State University, Northridge. After securing funding from an on-campus program, we embarked on a yearlong project in which we designed one such platform, the Guided Resource Inquiries (GRI) tool. As part of the project we further developed customizable templates faculty members could use to create assignments requiring the use of primary sources from a variety of physical and virtual locations. The GRI tool is unique in that it presents assignments, archival materials, and contextualizing information in a single environment that also allows librarians and faculty to provide information literacy tutorials and support for students as they embark on their projects.

We reached out to several teaching colleagues interested in collaborating on the project. One who participated was Danielle Spratt. She was teaching a graduate-level course on representations of women in eighteenth-century literature. After reviewing several items in Special Collections, she identified several excerpts in a single text for students to read in the GRI tool. They would identify an issue the text claimed was a primary cause of women's "impurity" and conduct further independent research on that cause, ultimately writing short essays comparing and contrasting the contents of the primary source, *Letters on Marriage*, to the assigned texts the class read that semester, particularly Sarah Fielding's *The History of the Countess of Dellwyn*.[13] The instructor hoped that in completing the assignment, students would reflect on the didactic and rhetorical aims of each work and how various characteristics of the primary sources, especially intended audience, publication format, and genre, helped determine the similarities and differences between all works they considered. As librarians we further hoped students would learn to evaluate and critically engage with primary sources, and develop skills to help them intellectually connect related sources, whether primary or secondary.

To achieve these objectives, we set out to design and implement a new tool. We first developed the GRI tool as a conceptual model to inform the design of complex, document-based course assignments using online content from multiple sources combined into a single, integrative platform. The tool mediates all aspects of the assignment, such as the prompt, digitized primary sources, relevant tutorials, supplementary online resources, and overall learning objectives. It therefore facilitates the progressive inquiries inherent to the synthesis of knowledge. These inquiries are realized as layers of analysis applied to each step of the assignment that together build and advance students' arguments within a scaffolded research process.

We designed the GRI tool as a digital interface providing a flexible template of structural placeholders within a webpage (or course website) to be populated with essential assignment content. These placeholders can be filled or removed as needed, depending on the goals of the assignment. We designed the tool to provide ample screen space for the selected digitized works from Special Collections and Archives, as well as for contextual information critical to understanding the documents' origin, use, and meaning. This context is accessed through resource descriptions in the tool, as well as through added links to archival databases where students can read information relating to biographical or organizational histories, dates of inclusion, and content inventories of the collections from which the assigned sources are derived.

One of our objectives was to use numerous online resources for supporting primary and secondary source literacies. We therefore added links to tutorials on the use of primary sources for research in addition to links to databases for locating related online primary and secondary sources. Instructors could supply supplementary content in a variety of ways. For example, links to resources and tutorials regarding the use of computational analysis tools for digital humanities could be placed in the supplementary location of the GRI assignment. For those interested in creating or investigating the tool, a more comprehensive assessment with examples is available in our article on the project.[14]

Once we created it, we wanted to assess how well GRI worked. Danielle's students, along with other student groups who used customized versions of the tool, completed pre- and post-tests to help us evaluate the tool's effectiveness and also responded to open-ended questions about their experiences after completing the assignment.[15] One student felt like "a *real history detective*" (emphasis in the original), while another commented the assignment "enhanced . . . critical analysis of the eighteenth century for me." Many remarked on the impact exposure to original eighteenth-century materials had on them, especially one student who said the assignment "became the conversation piece . . . with my friends. I actually showed them the letters, and they too were amazed."

The GRI project was a success in many respects. Student and instructor feedback indicates the assignments were challenging but rewarding. The tool was effective in helping students to understand what primary sources are and how to analyze them critically in their coursework. Students who used the tool also showed improvement in understanding the research process and were more likely to come back to Special Collections and Archives to use materials, even in print, for future assignments.

As we began the first phase of networked reading by connecting ephemeral works from Special Collections with various kinds of digital reading, the logistics of the project began to come together. Students divided up the OCR correction in 18thConnect and then discussed the matters that seemed most salient to the participants. Nearly all of the students noted the proliferation of references to Shakespeare in *Dellwyn*, an interesting detail in itself because the publication date of the novel roughly anticipated (by a decade) Shakespeare's Jubilee, a 1769 event that was promoted by famous eighteenth-century actors like David Garrick and that cemented Shakespeare's status as perhaps the preeminent literary figure of England (a point that Kate Rumbold makes in her article). With this and other issues in mind, we began the process of annotating the text, focusing on two core questions: what literary, historical, and cultural details and references would Fielding have assumed her readers would have known? What details do our contemporary readers need to know in order to understand the text?

With these questions articulated, participants set out to offer provisional answers. While most students were comfortable performing traditional literary analysis in our classroom, some were fairly nervous about assuming the role of scholarly editor. Yet in our discussion, we noted that crowd-sourced information has been an increasingly important mode of making information accessible for those who use the internet as a reference tool. Take, for instance, Wikipedia. When I was an undergraduate and then when I first began teaching as a graduate student in the mid-2000s, students were encouraged to avoid Wikipedia because of its seeming lack of authority. Now most educators agree on the value of using Wikipedia (with appropriate evaluation of a given entry's credibility); some even see the value in using it and so-called Wiki edit-a-thons as a platform for student research and contributions to public discourse, as my colleague Colleen Tripp discusses in her essay.

WIKI-EDITING AND THE DIGITAL CLASSROOM

Colleen Tripp

Educators interested in public humanities often struggle with conveying to and teaching students the expansive practices of public engagement, including writing and editing public conversations.[16] While teaching writing is difficult enough, teaching the art of editing, such as scholarly editing, can seem insurmountable, particularly because of students' lack of confidence. In my spring 2017 English course, I announced that we would be editing Wikipedia as an inside and outside class assignment and would participate in a Wiki edit-a-thon at our university. Not surprisingly, my students reacted with a mix of horror and concern. "But, Colleen, we can't edit Wikipedia. We are not experts!"

However, the success and confidence gained from editing Wikipedia in the classroom offer a potentially life-changing experience for students. There are already a number of teaching and learning research studies that reveal how students' attitudes influence their learning and which pedagogical techniques effectively boost student morale.[17] Like many of the recommended student-centered activities, editing Wikipedia can help bolster student confidence and serve as a hands-on tool that shows students writing and editing as both social acts and facets of public conversations.[18] The instantaneous, collaborative nature of editing the world's largest public encyclopedia also allows students to identify themselves as active producers of knowledge and transcends the paradigm of the classroom.

Like many ideas, the seeds of the Wiki edit-a-thon came from a serendipitous accident, as well as from my desire to include community engagement in the literary classroom. How could I show my students that our preferred literary analytic tool — close reading — is useful as both a pragmatic skill and a potential force of social good? At the time, I also happened to be reading the Wikipedia entry on American literary regionalism, because — as a specialist in nineteenth-century American realist and regionalist literatures — I knew, statistically, my students would be reading it, too.[19] As I read the entry, I noted the vagueness of the description; even worse, I realized the absolute dearth of women and minorities on the list of authors. Knowing that my classroom is often multiethnic, multicultural, and multiracial, this article presented to me the perfect opportunity to show students how they might effect social change in a very visible way. How many students can leave a classroom saying they edited an encyclopedia and revised a rendition of our cultural history?

My wiki assignments took shape as both an outside class assignment and as attendance at a formal Wiki edit-a-thon event that was open to the everyone at the university (it was held during my class period). Because the event would take place shortly after the 2016 presidential election and during a tumultuous political period, I gave the Wiki edit-a-thon the theme of Art and Social Justice @ CSUN and used Wikipedia's open, online format to encourage participants to edit Wikipedia entries on the arts, broadly speaking, with a focus on social justice.[20] Because large university events like these often take a village, I contacted my university's digital humanities librarian, Mary Wahl, for resources. Mary graciously volunteered to help host the event, bring pizza, and give periodic introductory lectures on editing Wikipedia throughout the three-hour edit-a-thon. To orient my own students to the craft of editing, I lectured and assigned readings on scholarly editing and the politics of Wikipedia, such as the encyclopedia's male bias and its strict peer review process.[21] I also created an outside classroom assignment, asking my students a week in advance of the edit-a-thon to choose two Wikipedia entries that they wanted to create or add to, supplement, and critique, and then to discuss their editing plans in a Moodle forum post and during class. This preparatory assignment not only helped boost students' confidence during the edit-a-thon, but also contextualized the impact of their work and allowed them to pursue their own interests.

The Wiki edit-a-thon produced fruitful student research and absolutely became a favorite classroom activity involving public engagement, particularly because of its effectiveness in teaching literary research and methods. One student, for example, edited the Wikipedia entry about the themes of her favorite Jewish American author's major works, while another added an entry for a Native American author. Many students marveled at the politics and rhetoric of the Wikipedia entries after the exercise, noting for the first time, for example, the overall brevity or complete absence of entries on women and minority artists.[22] My favorite student summary of the event was, "I can't believe I just edited Wikipedia! And my friends can read my work!" While editing Wikipedia can be a minor activity (an in-class exercise) or a major event (an edit-a-thon) in the classroom, both assignments foster confidence and an active learning environment. More importantly, editing Wikipedia as a collaborative community (with pizza) can be fun.

As Colleen shows, activist events connected with the construction of public sources of knowledge have important pedagogical and social functions.[23] But even if most students are aware of the value of crowd-sourced materials that have been vetted in some way, they themselves don't presume to be able to create their own authoritative editions. To help encourage students' confidence, we began slowly, by having classmates read and revise each other's work, validating clear annotations and supporting this process by recommending revisions and additions where necessary. What the students were doing was, in fact, a version of peer review. To embark on this process, individual students noted any words or phrases in Fielding's novel that seemed to require definition or explanation. We used Classroom Salon, an online learning community that allows for collaborative annotating and also creates a variety of data analytics.[24] Since students were interested in the content of their annotations along with the different kinds of annotations that they were providing across the volumes of the novel, we created a set of categories for annotations. We had tags for categories like "allusion" for general literary allusions, "Shakespeare allusion" to track the number of references Fielding made specifically to this important literary figure, as well as others ranging from "historical reference" to "typo" and "textual typo" to help correct or distinguish between those errors introduced by readers on this project and those that existed in the source text.

There are, of course, many different platforms for crowd-sourced annotations, including genius.com and plain old Google Docs (Bridget and I have gratefully relied upon the latter for years for this collaborative project, and I used it in a fall 2016 class that had a similar editorial focus). And at least when we used the site in 2014, some elements of Classroom Salon were less than ideal; even with just sixteen users in my class, the system was sometimes overburdened, and it would freeze or disallow access for certain users. But some of its tools were crucial. For instance, the tagging feature allowed our editors to say with assurance that Fielding makes at least 160 allusions to other literary and cultural texts. Kate Rumbold's study has persuasively demonstrated Fielding's interest in Shakespeare specifically, and by our count she alludes to the playwright at least sixty times across both volumes. Intriguingly, however, with her more than one hundred other allusions, we see Fielding demonstrating the true range of her literary knowledge, as she references texts from Proverbs to Pope, from epic poems to recent hit plays of the eighteenth century. By annotating the text, we saw Fielding using myriad references both to demonstrate the range of her heroine Charlotte's reading (or misreading) and simultaneously to establish herself as a true, learned virtuoso among her peers.

Once students identified these elements of information through tagging and annotating, they worked with peer partners to check their work for errors. As we began this painstaking process, we also read secondary scholarship on the theoretical and methodological concerns of annotating literature for a public audience. One of the many challenges that face any editor—and particularly a group of editors—is to avoid providing notes that delimit and prescribe too narrowly a reader's interpretation of the text. Before annotating, students discussed best practices in textual editing and annotating and were especially inspired by Claire Lamont's essay "Annotating a Text: Literary Theory and Electronic Hypertext," which considers the particular challenges and freedoms of editing a text for a digital edition. One of the potential benefits of our editorial process, which focused on a digitized text and used variants of hypertext, is that readers will have more freedom to read both text and notes nonlinearly. As Lamont puts it, "What are the freedoms to which the electronic medium invites us? They are usually proposed as freedom from the print medium, freedom from the organizational conventions and the space and time limitations of the book, and, particularly claimed for literary hypertext, freedom from 'linearity' and freedom to 'decentre' a text."[25] Readers can click on one link and then another to read outward from the text, a process that may help them gain more control over their own reading; multimedia and interactive hypertext links may make the reading process even more liberated.

We also consulted several seminal essays on bibliographic scholarship to guide our editorial practices. Following Alice Walker, we sought to create notes that help to "bridge the gap" between the language of the present day and the language of the author's time period.[26] Likewise, we referred to Martin Battestin's guidelines for annotating the works of Sarah Fielding's brother Henry. In this article, Battestin suggests that "an effective note" ought to follow, among others, these guidelines:

> It may define obscure terms or provide translations of words and passages in a foreign language.
> It may identify persons, places, events, and literary allusions, supplying the reader, when appropriate, with such additional contextual information as he needs to appreciate how the reference "works" in the text.
> It may illuminate the author's ideas or expressions either by citing specific sources for them or by adducing parallel passages from contemporary writings.
> It will record parallel or contradictory passages from the author's other works, whenever they seem significant, as well as indicating such passages with cross-references as they occur elsewhere in the text itself.[27]

The editors attempted to follow these guidelines in order to illuminate meaning without coercing a distinctive reading of Fielding's work. While the process was not seamless and still resulted in typographical errors and omissions in the resulting product, the students' edition offers important and helpful details that make it useful for people who are encountering Fielding, the eighteenth-century novel, or both for the first time.

Once the annotations were completed, students corrected and formatted their sections for the *Dellwyn* website and imported their annotations, learning basic code to provide anchors for their notes. As Bridget and I discuss in chapters 4 and 5, in addition to the ability to analyze literature, the process of digitizing texts requires another set of skills and another set of languages. HTML and XML are crucial for following Text Encoding Initiative (TEI) standards, which are guidelines that humanities scholars use to provide salient, relevant, and flexible data that will be valuable across web-based platforms and that will, ultimately, stand the test of time regardless of technological shifts.[28] If HTML and XML sound like foreign languages to you — well, really, they are. But the essential difference between the languages is this: HTML dictates *how* we see things on the internet (what text is italicized, how paragraphs are formatted, how the background looks, its colors, and so on), while XML describes data. To put this another way: if you see the name "Sarah Fielding" on a website, the HTML coding will determine the name's shape, size, font, and general appearance, whereas XML coding would include biographical information about Sarah Fielding herself.

While CSUN has relatively long, sixteen- to seventeen-week semesters, even this expansive (by academic standards) time frame would not allow the class to read *Dellwyn* and many other eighteenth-century texts, correct the OCR, provide annotations, and learn both coding languages. As a solution, students learned basic HTML coding language to help them shape the appearance of the text and provide basic anchors that would allow for the hypertextual reading of the notes that they provided for readers. One of the class's standout digital humanists, Naz Keynejad, volunteered to take the XML files that 18thConnect provided to us to make the daunting initial first pass through the document, as she recounts in the essay included here. As of 2018 the XML portion of the site was still under construction — in the future, as a combined effort of student groups, classes, and interested community partners, we will undertake the task of adding the XML language and correcting the appearance of any typos in the edition that most people will access and read when they search for Fielding or her novel.

THE *COUNTESS OF DELLWYN* PROJECT

Digital Futures, Future Work

Naz Keynejad

I have been involved in digital humanities work since the fall of 2013, when I was part of a group project looking to determine the authorship of several anonymously written texts from the Cheap Repository Tracts, a series of conduct pamphlets printed between 1795 and 1811 and largely attributed to Hannah More, one of the founders of the Bluestocking group and a formidable figure for female advocacy in the eighteenth century. The Hannah More Project was a comprehensive analysis of the tracts using 18thConnect, manual transcription of texts, text scrubbing (using Lexos, a text analysis tool developed by the Wheaton College Lexomics Group as a means to identify patterns in digitized corpora), and stylometric analysis tools (like Stylo R and the Mallet graphical user interface) to pinpoint the possible authorship of the anonymous texts.[29] Having worked as a project manager for that team, I was especially well equipped to tackle the extensive corrective and coding work needed to move the *Countess of Dellwyn* project into its next phase.

Once the class group work on the *Countess of Dellwyn* project was completed, I was tasked with cleaning up the XML-coded texts forwarded to the group by 18thConnect. One of the advantages of working with 18thConnect is that at the culmination of the project, an editable text and a separate XML-coded file are forwarded to the participants. As with any group project, human error had created some challenges with the text that I set out to correct. The errors were made during the OCR cleanup stage, where group members had either missed a long *S* replacement or had instinctively converted spellings of certain words to their modern equivalents. Considering the scope of the project, errors were relatively minimal. Once I corrected the mistakes, I began adding XML coding to the text. While 18thConnect allows for inserting coding for certain attributes (italics, underlining, bold, drop-cap, and so on) during the cleanup process, it had been decided early on not to burden the entire group with learning and applying those codes during the initial phase of the project. Coding the text necessitated a line-by-line review of the OCR (retrieved from ECCO) and the manual addition of XML to the text using the digital tool TextMate.

In addition to the coding, in order to provide better textual flow for the final product, Professor Spratt and I decided to create another XML version from which we corrected what seems like the arbitrary truncation of words in the original text. The truncated words at the end of sentences may seem arbitrary to modern readers but are in fact a function of the limitations of printing (pertaining to paper size) in eighteenth-century texts, and we felt that for the final version to be completely accessible, these would have to be fixed. We now have two versions of the text in XML: one that mirrors the original text faithfully, including where each page, sentence, line, and catchword begins and ends in the eighteenth-century edition, and one that has been fixed to read seamlessly, as if the book had been laid out and produced specifically for a digital format. What remains to be done is to add the annotations to these XML files, which will require more extensive coding. Once that is finalized and the XML versions uploaded to the site, the next steps might include some textual analysis or a review and perhaps augmentation of the annotations, providing even more contextual information for anyone who is new to Sarah Fielding and her works.

Since Sarah Fielding's writing is not widely recognized and/or read (and is not, in fact, part of any particular canon), textual analysis might provide clues to contextualize her work within the eighteenth-century literary canon. By making one of her works easily accessible, this project allows the opportunity to study an author whose works are rarely considered, creating a new space for feminist, eighteenth-century, and digital humanities scholars. Ultimately, I am looking forward to working with Danielle — and possibly a new group of her students — to extend the project's scope and provide a deeper analysis of the text.

Although our edition itself remains in a state of arrested development, this digital edition of Fielding's novel functions as a (relatively) successful experiential service-learning project because the work conducted in this course has made a digitized edition accessible for students who are visually impaired: readers can access this OCR-corrected text. Our critically annotated edition also provides explanatory notes to help make Fielding's language and references more accessible to the student who is new to her writing and the eighteenth-century novel. Throughout the process, students were able to perform networked reading practices that allowed them to assume the role of scholars-activists as well.

As the contributions by Ellen Jarosz and Steve Kutay, Colleen Tripp, and Naz Keynejad have all demonstrated, this type of digital project is an ongoing one. The logistics and infrastructure involved in creating such an edition are challenging but rewarding, and we hope that the last few chapters of this book have provided some helpful resources and suggestions for surmounting pragmatic obstacles in starting your own digital initiative. But beyond the value to potential readers (who will hopefully be patient about the lacunae in the digital text-in-progress), there is the historical value such initiatives offer. In 2015, there was no Wikipedia entry for *The History of the Countess of Dellwyn* itself, although it was referenced on Fielding's main Wikipedia page. Some of my CSUN students noted this absence during their participation at the first annual American Society for Eighteenth-Century Studies Wikipedia edit-a-thon, held in memory of Adrianne Wadewitz, which took place at the society's annual meeting in Los Angeles. During that session, students created an entry for the novel that offered basic information about its publication and critical reception.[30] Others have since begun to fill in more information, but it's still a work in progress.

The Wikipedia entry, like so many other digital humanities projects that we and our colleagues (and hopefully you) have begun or will begin, are always in a state of flux and transition. While elements of that open-endedness can be frustrating, they also mark ongoing participation. Such initiatives invite new audiences, new voices, new contributors, and new perspectives, making open-access documents fulfill the promise of the name in myriad ways. This process is, at its core, a fundamental principle of networked reading: the network expands outward and onward over time. Importantly, these historical literary projects, usually begun in (or around) the classroom, have exciting afterlives that transcend their original time and space. In these ways, digital historical literary projects mirror their printed source texts, always changing, shifting, and echoing in different ways for new audiences, if only the audiences have the chance to listen. We believe that public humanities projects like the ones that we have described, and like the ones that you are very likely formulating as you read, are the key to creating this ongoing, dynamic, and collaborative dialogue between past and present, student and teacher, and university and community.

CONCLUSION
﷽

When we teach writing classes, we often tell our students that the concluding section of any essay should answer a big (and nebulous) question: So what? If we were to make this question more specific to our project, we might ask something like, how is eighteenth-century literature relevant to today's issues? How is eighteenth-century literature relevant to our day-to-day lives, and how does a sustained encounter with eighteenth-century literature make our lives better?

Rather than a simple series of questions to answer in the conclusion, these concerns have inspired, informed, and guided this entire project; as we hope our chapters have made clear, these questions have myriad answers that are at once deeply personal and, we think, fundamentally universal. In fact, we need only look to the diverse voices included in this volume to see a sampling of the potential responses. Rachel Lynne Witzig was able to understand American culture in a new light after researching the reception of Austen's novels in the early nation. Tiffany Ouellette, a student and future educator, came to more fully understand how readers bring their background, age, and gender into their interpretation of historical texts. Elizabeth K. Goodhue brought the study of historical publishing and reading practices into her classroom to think about literacy today and the cultivation of culturally responsive learning environments. And as Joan Gillespie and David Spadafora remind us, programs like the Newberry seminar only exist because of a pervasive belief in the value of preserving and rediscovering our cultural heritage. We see our colleagues' narratives as the most exciting, vivid, and enduring evidence that our lives are richer when we make connections between our twenty-first-century selves and the often unnoticed ghosts of the eighteenth century that inform our lives. Sometimes these encounters happen in subtle ways—as Anne Stapleton notes in her essay, when we drive through a town named Waverley, invoking our memory of reading Sir Walter Scott's novel of that name—while other times they occur in radical confrontations with a past that we thought had long ceased to exist. At other times, as we find in Gabriela Almendarez's essay, these intersections of past and present happen sometimes in the classroom and sometimes in the broader political arena.

In the early twenty-first century, this radical confrontation between past and present does not just seem intellectually relevant; it feels visceral. Across the United States and in many parts of the world, political movements that seek to reject notions like universal suffrage and to deny groups of people equal access to liberty and happiness, have garnered widespread support. These movements reject concepts that were first theorized as fundamental political and civil rights in eighteenth-century philosophy and literature, while simultaneously exhuming eighteenth-century restrictions on such rights to property-owning white men. The legacy of these origins thus reinforces the same kind of exclusion that some groups look to implement today. In the eighteenth and early nineteenth centuries, matters like abolition, emancipation, and women's rights were hotly debated; then as today, citizens live in a divisive political moment in which media cater to and often promote political polarization over and against open dialogue and bipartisan collaboration.

In response to this political and cultural climate, we ask our foundational questions again, and we find even more paths to explore and possible answers to discuss. Whitney Mannies, a specialist in eighteenth-century Enlightenment political theory, responded to the wake of the US presidential election in November 2016 with an erudite and informative essay published on the *Washington Post*'s blog that demonstrates the ways in which contemporary political issues are grounded in eighteenth-century thought (she tells us more about her experience of writing about this connection in a public venue shortly). In her blog post Whitney reminds us that our nation's founders were influenced by John Locke's concept of popular sovereignty, which he articulated in his *Second Treatise on Government* (1690).

Reading Locke, Jefferson, and others, Whitney reminds us that the people do not transfer their sovereignty to governments unconditionally. If an elected official becomes systematically tyrannical, it is within the people's rights to overthrow this tyrant.[1] But what exactly constitutes tyranny? Some people view the Obama administration's Affordable Care Act as tyrannical legislation; others see the Trump administration's promise to create a registry for Muslims in the United States as one of many despotic, despicable acts against the sovereignty of the people. To be sure, the parameters of tyrannical behavior are themselves historically determined. Yet active political engagement and resistance — let alone over-throwing a tyrant — are, in spirit and in practice, far more complex pro-cesses than tweeting #notmypresident. By revisiting and carefully reading the eighteenth-century political doctrine that established the foundation of all modern-day law, Whitney helps us uncover the important distinc-tions between disagreeing with legislation and overthrowing an illegiti-mate government.

WRITING FOR THE GENERAL PUBLIC

A Defense

Whitney Mannies

The other day I made the mistake of suggesting to a young professor that he write up his important research findings and publish them on the *Washington Post*'s politics blog. "Why?" he asked, his face contorting as if I had presented him with a bowl of feces as opposed to a flattering question. He arched his eyebrows as his mind searched for any conceivable reason. One finally occurred to him: "I guess if someone wanted to get their name out there . . ." I countered, totally insanely, that his findings seemed important and relevant to our public debate. He, with the self-assurance of a cartoon villain, declared such an idea "a waste of time" — logic that he no doubt extended to his fifteen minutes chatting with me, since I, like the *Washington Post*, am not in the business of granting tenure.

Why do some scholars avoid writing for the general public as if it were a highly contagious venereal disease? Perhaps they'd like to avoid the dilettante-ish reputation (sometimes deserved, sometimes not) of the "public intellectual" — someone who is generally informed and comments frequently on matters of broad public concern. But a scholar who writes for the general public is not a public intellectual in this sense. Rather, she is a figure who works within her area of expertise, translating her research into language accessible for those without an advanced (or any) degree, and publishing it as an accessible book or in venues such as the local newspaper, the *Atlantic*, or — gasp! — *Slate*.

Is such an enterprise really so destructive of scholars' more esoteric ends? Surely informing the general public of important research or interesting perspectives is a self-evident good that requires no further defense?

But what of the (quite likely) scenario wherein the publicly minded scholar, for all her accessible overtures, fails to persuade or edify? Even if all her efforts are for naught, writing for the general public is not a waste of time. It makes us better scholars because, I argue in a moment, it provides us with the occasion to critically reflect on our presentism. More importantly, and I mean this with only slight hyperbole, it is one way to oppose the specter of nihilism, which advances like a blob through academic departments, slowly but irresistibly incorporating entire careers into its prodigious mass.

First: presentism. Presentism occurs when we interpret historical phenomena according to the concepts, vocabulary, values, problems, or opinions endemic to our own time period, leading us to misapprehend the actual nature of our historical object of inquiry. Presentism interprets things as we are, not as they are. When we feel as if liberal democracy is on an upswing, we see the past half century as a gradual march of progress. When we feel as if democracy is on the verge of collapse, suddenly we interpret the events of the past few decades as a steady erosion of liberty. Writing for a general audience is sometimes thought to exacerbate these presentist tendencies, since it motivates the scholar to describe history in a way that will resonate broadly. Writing for the masses, scholars sacrifice accuracy for popularity. Kowtowing to the general public can thus diminish the quality and validity of our scholarship when it is motivated by the desire for relevance.

But current concerns do inform our research questions, intellectual orientations, and interpretations, whether we admit it or not. Proceeding on the assumption that our scholarship is pure and insulated from contemporary events only exacerbates presentism. The more honest course is to acknowledge that our orientation is inevitably informed by our present historical context and to reflect on, and hopefully identify, the presentist prejudices in our own work. Writing for the general public, then, far from exacerbating presentist prejudices, can be an exercise in thinking critically about how our contemporary context informs our thinking.

More importantly, however, public engagement helps us to stave off a creeping nihilism, which gains purchase in our intellectual life by way of empty elitism. The scholar enthralled by elitism restricts the relevance of his work to a small circle, but this can empty scholarship — intentionally or not — of its greater social value. Shall we be satisfied with a solipsistic career that consists of speaking only to a handful of others who study what we study?

Ultimately, elitism signals not status, but a lack of confidence — a timid reluctance to assert the great social importance of our ideas. When protests erupted after Donald Trump's election in 2016 and groups called for the electoral college to reject his presidency, it was urgent that we seriously re-examine the philosophical roots of political legitimacy. My own area of study — Enlightenment political thought — not only has much to say on the topic, it is also the most proximate source of the American founders' ideas on the subject. So why not bring it to bear on the debate? I drafted an examination of the Lockean perspective on popular sovereignty — it was, after all, John Locke whom the founders paraphrased in the Declaration of Independence when they referred to a "long train of abuses" by the British government and men's right to "Life, Liberty, and the pursuit of Happiness." The analysis was not less valid for its being written for a general audience, and it was invigorating to know that my own expertise could — and should — inform a debate of national importance.

We are not scholastics debating about how many angels can dance on the head of a pin. We needn't limit ourselves to the lame suggestion to our students on the first day of class that "these ideas still matter today." Rather, we can show them this is so through our own public engagement.

At a time when academics are more and more often forced into an instrumental, capitalist logic, the urgency of making our scholarship into a marketable product so often edges out nonmarketable intellectual activity, such as writing for the general public. Every hour that a scholar spends writing for a general audience is time *not* spent writing a book for a university press or an article for a peer-reviewed journal. The increasing privatization of higher education causes scholars — and especially young, untenured scholars — to feel more keenly their status as commodities. Writing for the general public has become a professional risk. To perceive this risk and to do so anyway is admirable. It is an insistence that our work be meaningful.

It is a radical stance against the privatization that threatens to turn scholarship into an instrumental activity.

It is not, then, a waste of time to write for a broad, nonacademic audience. It is a rejection of the instrumental logic that threatens to overwhelm higher education. It is an affirmation of the importance of our work.

Whitney is not the only contemporary writer to see significant connections between this political moment and that of the eighteenth century. At the end of chapter 2, for instance, Bridget energetically suggests her own newly reinvigorated commitment to politicizing Austen, drawing parallels between the novelist's revolutionary impulses (especially in her posthumously published Gothic satire, *Northanger Abbey*) and a political moment in which women's marches throughout the world beget other movements: protests against immigration policy changes at airports across the nation and marches in major cities to support science on Earth Day, just to name a few. But lest you think we are alone in our excitement about the intellectual and cultural possibilities of politicizing Austen and her contemporaries, rest assured that others are drawing similar connections. In response to the dozens of women's marches throughout the world, Jess Zimmerman drew an overt parallel between these international demonstrations and those that fomented the French Revolution.[2]

In both the eighteenth- and twenty-first-century instances, officials treated women's protests as inherently unthreatening: Louis XVI told his army to stand down against eighteenth-century French women marchers, and twenty-first-century police at American women's demonstrations appeared in ordinary uniforms, without donning the riot gear that they often wear at protests for the Black Lives Matter movement, for instance. What do these disparities tell us about the histories of gender, race, and protest? How can what happened before help us better understand what is unfolding before us in real time? Whitney's blog post and essay in this chapter and Zimmerman's article remind us that our political and cultural present is always already informed and clarified by voices from the eighteenth century. This transhistorical methodology also invites other ways of engaging our friends, family, colleagues, students — in short, our communities — in meaningful debates about issues that are important to us today. Thoughtful pieces like those by Whitney and Zimmerman provide a framework for discussion and the opportunity to reflect on our own participation in (or rejection of) demonstrations like the 2017 women's march.

Likewise, classroom spaces devoted to eighteenth-century literature and culture offer opportunities to engage in issues that are important to our students. After the 2016 election, many people experienced diametrically opposed reactions: while some felt that Donald Trump's election signaled a moment where their voices were finally recognized, others felt fear and anger for themselves, their families, or their friends. Danielle was advising graduate students the night of the election and the following morning, and most students with whom she met were in tears. At CSUN, a Hispanic-serving institution in Southern California, feelings of panic and despair were pervasive among the students, faculty, and staff, many of whom are themselves or have family members or friends who are undocumented citizens. Along with taking time out of class to discuss these concerns about the radical shift in administrations, faculty conferred about ways that they could bring people together to talk about their confusing, perhaps oppositional feelings and worries.

Danielle collaborated with her colleague in the English department, Chris Higgs, to organize a two-day teach-in that would take place on the steps of their campus library, a public space that would invite students from multiple classes, along with passersby, to engage in discussions by connecting coursework from their classes with postelection thoughts and concerns. Chris had the brilliant idea to connect the teach-in with a dialogue begun just days before by Colson Whitehead's acceptance speech at the National Book Awards: in it, he encouraged readers everywhere to "be kind to everybody, make art, and fight the power."[3] Since most classes in English and the humanities — and beyond — touch on these broad thematic issues, Chris and Danielle hoped that these phrases would encourage dialogue across disciplines while inviting diverse perspectives into a rigorous debate.

That semester, Danielle was teaching a graduate class on the eighteenth-century experimental novel. She asked her students if they wanted to participate in the teach-in, and after a unanimous vote to participate, she asked them to identify a set of issues or themes that they had discussed in class that seemed to overlap with concerns they felt in response to the election. The class pinpointed ideas about autonomy and agency, and with that theme in mind, students revisited their own research and essay writing from the semester to discover relevant textual passages from their readings that reflected these concerns. Gabriela Almendarez, one of the class participants who also served as a teaching associate in CSUN's two-semester long "stretch composition" program, which is designed to help students who struggle with writing succeed at the college level, reflects on her experience as both a student and a teacher in her essay.

TEACH-IN/TEACH OUT

Conversations about Art, Kindness, and Power

Gabriela Almendarez

At the 2016 National Book Awards, Colson Whitehead advised the audience to "be kind to everybody, make art, and fight the power."[4] In wake of the election in November 2016 and keeping Whitehead's call in mind, the English Department at California State University, Northridge, decided to host a two-day event with the goal to foster solidarity, openness, and support for students, staff, and faculty. The Teach-In/Teach Out: Conversations About Art, Kindness, and Power event offered a series of joint readings across class sessions and across disciplines. Faculty brought their students and met with other professors to take turns reading passages from their coursework that offered sentiments of kindness. In addition to the readings, there were also art supplies to encourage students to express their own thoughts regarding kindness and offering similar solidarity sentiments to the campus community. My participation in the teach-in was twofold: I participated in the event as a student in Dr. Danielle Spratt's English 630: Experiment and the Experimental Novel in the Long Eighteenth Century, and I also participated in the event as an instructor by bringing my freshmen students in English 114A: Approaches to University Writing.

When I decided to take the English 630 course, I was a little apprehensive because of my unfamiliarity with eighteenth-century literature. However, through the readings and class discussions, we found ways to relate the texts to current societal issues. As a result, when we began discussing what we wanted to read at the event, it was a bit easier for us to develop strategies. As a class, we decided on particular social and ethical issues that worried us about the political rhetoric used in the 2016 election and connected those same issues to the eighteenth-century readings we had done. Some of the major concerns we discussed about both realms were issues of control, bodily agency, and autonomy. With those issues in mind, we got into groups and each group selected an eighteenth-century text. Some of the readings we chose were from Mary Shelley's *Frankenstein*, Maria Edgeworth's *Castle Rackrent*, Daniel Defoe's *A Journal of the Plague Year*, and Jane Austen's earlier works.

On the day of the event, members of each group read a passage from their selected text and discussed why they thought this passage exemplified the concerns we had already determined. As a participant, I had to work together with my group to choose which passage of our chosen novel we wanted to discuss. We communicated over email and discussed how different passages within the book showcased issues of identity, fear, and control. I believe that having the teach-in in mind and a clear idea of the issues we wanted to discuss allowed us to approach the literature in a different manner. We were made aware of how different passages could be read in different ways. More importantly, we decided that although the book we chose was written with the eighteenth-century audience in mind, in 2016 we were able to read the same book and generate new meanings that were relevant to our society.

As an instructor, I was excited about the teach-in. Throughout the semester, I had been engaging my class in conversations regarding issues relevant to their generation. Although the class I teach is an introduction to college writing, I feel that students should learn a wide range of skills they will utilize beyond university writing. As a result, we had already discussed how gender, culture, and identity relate to the literature we read (no matter when it was written) and how the literature exemplifies real-world issues that are worthy of discussion. My goal as a student and an instructor has always been to participate and create a classroom where conversations are happening. I have sat in many courses in which the instructor is the only one speaking. Though I do find value in formal, academic instruction, I also believe students should be active participants in their education and the conversations they choose to join. Specifically, I agree with the conclusion Wayne Au, Bill Bigelow, and Stan Karp offer in *Rethinking Our Classrooms*: "Classrooms can be places of hope, where students and teachers gain glimpses of the kind of society we could live in and where students learn the academic and critical skills needed to make it a reality."[5] Furthermore, the authors also argue that certain concepts need to be a part of students' course of study in order to create the social justice classroom. Particularly, they contend that curricula should be grounded in the lives of the students; critical; multicultural, anti-racist, and pro-justice; participatory and experiential; and hopeful.

I prepared my students for the teach-in with a freewrite. At the beginning of one of our classes, I had them write a reflection on the questions, how is prejudice created? How do we overcome it? Do you think literature can serve as a vehicle for change? The responses I received were mixed. A common theme that emerged focused on the last question, with students uncertain if the literature they deemed "boring, not fun, and just words" was enough to prompt change. In our discussion, we spoke about how ideas are important when it comes to reading literature and how such ideas become a call to action. On the actual day of the teach-in, we discussed some parts of Claudia Rankine's *Citizen* (2015) and interrogated the very title: What does it mean to be a citizen?[6] My students noted that being a citizen is synonymous to voting and owning property, and one of them even compared citizenship to tenure — the feeling that an individual will not be turned away.

Events such as teach-ins prompt us to think critically and meet together in a space where all of our ideas are heard, valued, and respected. Whether the instruction is occurring in or out of the classroom, it is important for educators to see the rhetorical value of addressing the social justice issues that are common in our society today. More important, the discussions regarding race, ethnicity, and other heterogeneous topics that events such as csun's teach-in foster are invaluable since they allow students and faculty to see each other as learners instead of seeing instructors only as authority figures. Such conversations allow students and faculty to create connections between the assigned coursework and the real-world issues we all experience. Students and faculty are able to reflect on the messages and themes their course content offers and create connections with other readings or related materials. Ultimately, issues regarding society and social justice cannot be discussed or resolved in one day.

In addition to collaborating, participating, advocating for the campus community, and providing spaces where students and faculty can interact, it is important for students and instructors to keep integrating and facilitating these conversations inside and outside of classroom walls.

Gabby's reflection nicely demonstrates how interdisciplinary opportunities for discussion like the teach-in significantly restructure the classroom space into one of equity—where all voices are important, relevant, and heard—as well as rigorous discussion and debate. Opening up the space of the classroom for such conversations seemed second nature to Danielle. She was an undergraduate in New York City when the attacks on the World Trade Center happened on September 11, 2001. Everyone on campus lost someone or knew someone who had lost parents, siblings, or friends. In the days following, the classroom became a space for intellectual and emotional processing.

Danielle remembers vividly the conversation that she and her colleagues had in a class on the eighteenth-century novel taught by Susan Celia Greenfield. Just the week before, they had read excerpts from György Lukács's *The Theory of the Novel* (1920), and Susan had asked them to discuss Lukács's infamous phrase: "The novel is the epic of a world that has been abandoned by God. . . . The objectivity of the novel is the mature man's knowledge that meaning can never quite penetrate reality, but that, without meaning, reality would disintegrate into the nothingness of inessentiality."[7] With Susan careful to balance the emotion of the day with the intellectual grounding of the course, these words guided the class through the trauma of the present while also helping them consider why narrative—its ability to construct meaning even in the face of tragedy, even in the face of moments of terror and nihilism—is so important to human experience. The novel as we know it today, a media product of the eighteenth century, has provided one of the most critical ways of understanding how narrative works.

Just over fifteen years later, in another moment of radical disruption and uncertainty, Danielle's course on the eighteenth-century experimental novel provided a much-needed point of access to emotional, intellectual, and social issues. In broader terms, the projects that this book has outlined also created innovative points of communication, interaction, and access to new audiences, ideas, and conversations. But as we mentioned in the introduction, studying the eighteenth century is not only crucial to the present because of the ways it informs our contemporary political context, but also because new digital technologies have allowed new points of access to the literary and cultural documents of the period. By the time we were in graduate school, databases like EEBO and ECCO made it possible for scholars to read archival materials once exclusively available in research libraries that would require time and money to visit—two things many graduate students, independent scholars, and faculty members never seem to have. The result of this opening up of the archives has expanded what we teach, what we research, and really what the entire field can do: we can read novels by authors now unknown alongside canonical writers and better understand the contexts for the formal, aesthetic, and sociopolitical dimensions of each work. We can recover voices that have been unnoticed for centuries, voices that might speak in sonorous conversation with thinkers and writers from our current moment.

As the preceding chapters have demonstrated, other initiatives in public and digital spaces make the period both more accessible and more meaningful. Libraries and museums, themselves products of eighteenth-century culture, complement digital initiatives like 18thConnect and the free digitized texts that such platforms make possible. In all cases, they democratize access to these texts and expand our knowledge of the period. If the eighteenth century provided new, revolutionary ways of understanding human rights and suffrage, twenty-first-century interventions in texts from this period only further such intellectual possibilities. And it is exactly these possibilities for innovation that we hope to leave you with—we hope that you embrace the energy and insight that our collaborators have provided throughout these pages and that you add to them in your own setting and context. Engaging the eighteenth century is an active, dynamic, ongoing process.

We thus see this conclusion as equal parts reflection and invitation. We consider here not specific projects but the overarching methodology of our work—and by *our work*, we mean that of all our collaborators here—in order to gesture toward future work that you can perform. Throughout the previous chapters, we have discussed a range of ways that the eighteenth century embeds itself in our everyday lives and how a conscious and overt study of eighteenth-century literature in twenty-first-century contexts can offer intellectual, artistic, and social benefits to our communities, broadly defined, whether in our local libraries, our university classrooms, or seemingly boundless digital spaces. An underlying claim of this book—and of the public humanities work that we have performed in general, whether in or outside of the classroom—is that the study of literature is itself an act of civic participation. While we ground our work in the eighteenth century and while we find particularities of the period that remain salient in twenty-first-century contexts, we actively encourage specialists and hobbyists of other historical periods to discover and recover such points of access in their own areas of interest. This is all to say that public engagement with literature need not be constrained by the boundaries of time periods: medieval devotional poems and classical Greek satires have important resonance with our everyday lives as well, if only we take the time to listen.

Just as we advocate breaking down the temporal and geographic barriers to engaged literary public humanities activities, we also encourage a radical reimagining of the public spaces that allow for such engaged work. College classrooms, libraries, and museums have for too long seemed like exclusive spaces. At CSUN, for instance, the library is a public resource open to all community members. But parking is expensive and public transportation is often challenging. Some people can't access the library even if they know it's a space that is open and welcoming to them; others don't know that such a resource exists for them. As technological innovations continue to make internet resources more readily available to diverse audiences, combining these physical places with digital spaces is a necessary and complementary step. Online exhibits, texts, and websites can function as standalone engaged projects or they can disseminate information that helps attract new participants to visit local sites. This synergy can create a more cohesive and inclusive sense of community.

One concrete way that we believe temporal and physical divides can be addressed and overcome is by offering a free, public space on campus for sharing engaged public humanities work with colleagues, staff, students, and community members. When Danielle began her role as director of Faculty Engagement and Service Learning in the Office of Community Engagement at CSUN, she knew that she wanted to spearhead a public symposium, a forum for students, staff, faculty, and community partners and members to discuss projects that connected the campus to the broader public. While there are myriad ways to organize these events,

Danielle and her colleagues began small, asking faculty members who taught engaged service-learning courses to nominate students or student groups whose projects exemplified the mission and goals of their experiential activities. Students offered presentations or posters in a round-robin format, which allowed continual conversation among participants and observers; community partners were invited to join in the presentation or to help evaluate student work.

Amid the palpable and infectious enthusiasm from those involved, what was most fascinating to Danielle was the energetic conversation across student groups. Students in journalism classes had no idea that their peers in engineering, education, or fashion design also participated in civically engaged projects. Community partners met one another for the first time and met new faculty members with whom they might collaborate. All participants learned more about community projects and course content through this interdisciplinary experience. They also learned how to ask each other better questions about their subject matter, because their own experiential, engaged learning activities had fostered dialogue and developed a collective intersectional consciousness, skills that we think are important in many different forums. The experience of these students is just one of many strategies for encouraging lifelong learning among participants in civically engaged projects. In 2018, Danielle and her colleagues were excited to add other California State University campuses into the mix, inviting other engaged students, faculty, and community members to extend and connect their networks and share their engaged knowledge.

Bridget cohosted similar symposia at Monmouth College with Professor of Communication Studies Lee McGaan. In January 2012, Bridget and Lee offered a Saturday event called Writing as Civic Engagement, which focused on developing projects that would engage students with the community through writing. The morning included a crash course for twelve faculty from across the campus in best practices for publicly engaged pedagogy, and the afternoon was a hands-on project development workshop that included faculty, community members, and students who worked collaboratively to brainstorm new or extend existing community projects. The Writing as Civic Engagement symposium also hosted two guest speakers for a linked public presentation titled Civic Engagement 2.0, which focused on civically engaged, digital writing projects and drew forty students, faculty, and community members.

In November 2013, Bridget, Lee, and Communication Studies faculty member Lori Walters-Kramer offered a second symposium with support from a Bringing Theory to Practice grant, which supports civic development for students in liberal education.[8] The initiative, titled Fostering Civic Skills: Expanding the Role of Fundamentals of Communication in Monmouth College's Education of the Student/Citizen, focused on reorienting the required first-year communication course to develop students' civic literacy skills, making it a kind of capacity-building effort that could prepare students to be thoughtful and effective civic participants in later coursework. In addition to supporting department-level action, the three organizers hosted a campuswide event with faculty and students from various majors to get feedback (and buy-in) for the new first-year curriculum.

Bridget found that setting the stage for community-engaged learning for first-year students, even without including a direct civic engagement project in the course, gave them an essential framework for ethical engagement in later classes. This collaboration is one example of how we can build incrementally developed, publicly engaged experiences for students that stretch across multiple courses. Likewise, Danielle's experiences highlight not only how important it is to allow students and faculty to collaborate in designing civically engaged pedagogy, but also how meaningful engagement must *begin* by including community partners in the planning process, and not simply presume that pedagogical strategies or effective learning outcomes can be created without their sustained input. We have both found that hosting broad conversations on our campuses and in our communities about publicly engaged teaching and research, along with offering faculty development opportunities to support our colleagues, are equally essential components of our ongoing work as public scholars and teachers.

So in the spirit of the quest for lifelong learning, we leave you with a series of questions: How do you see the literature and culture of the eighteenth century — or of any other period — in conversation with the people, places, and things that matter most to you? If you love Jane Austen or Daniel Defoe, how can you uncover what it is about their works that resonates with you? If you are a college faculty member or instructor, who are people who should, would, or could talk to you about such points of resonance? Or, if you're a community member or organizer, how could linking with college campuses help you reach more of your fellow community members in meaningful ways? We intentionally end the narrative of this book with questions rather than answers to encourage you to contribute your own thoughts, comments, and experiences. Such questions, pursued collaboratively in open community places and spaces, lead to civic discourse that, even when opinions differ, remains respectful, productive, and enlightened.

AUTHOR AND CONTRIBUTOR
BIOGRAPHIES
🐾🐾

Author Biographies

BRIDGET DRAXLER is a writing and speaking specialist and adjunct assistant professor of writing at St. Olaf College, in Northfield, MN. Her teaching and research interests include the scholarship of teaching and learning, writing pedagogy, writing center studies, British women writers of the long eighteenth century, and public digital humanities. Bridget is an alumna of the University of Iowa's Obermann Center Graduate Institute on Engagement and the Academy, and she has been honored as an Imagining America PAGE Fellow, HASTAC Scholar, Chawton House Library Fellow, Fulbright Specialist, and ACM Newberry Seminar Faculty Fellow.

DANIELLE SPRATT is an associate professor of English at California State University, Northridge. Her areas of interest include the literature of the seventeenth, eighteenth, and early nineteenth centuries (specifically 1620–1830), the history of science and medicine, the rise of the novel, feminist and gender theory, digital humanities, experiential and service learning pedagogies, and theories of social justice. She is the current adviser for the English MA program, as well as the director of Faculty Engagement and Service Learning in the Office of Community Engagement at CSUN. Danielle is a former AmeriCorps VISTA (Volunteers in Service to America) volunteer.

Contributor Biographies

GABRIELA ALMENDAREZ is a doctoral student of English at the University of California, Riverside, and holds an MA in rhetoric and composition from California State University, Northridge. Gabriela's interests are many and include gender, sexuality, geography, and multiethnic American literature.

JESS BYBEE is a graduate of the professional writing program at the Second City Training Center. Before her work was staged in various

Chicago comedy shows and revues, she studied English at Monmouth College.

NORA CHATCHOOMSAI is a 2014 graduate of California State University, Northridge, where she majored in English literature. She currently resides in her hometown in Thailand and is pursuing an MA in English language teaching.

ALYSSA DOMINGUEZ received her BA and MA in English and creative writing and playwriting from California State University, Northridge. She is currently attending the University of Southern California's Rossier School of Education.

GILLIAN DOW is an associate professor in English at the University of Southampton and executive director of the library at Chawton House. She researches and teaches Jane Austen and her contemporaries in Britain and France.

JOAN GILLESPIE is the vice president and director of off-campus study programs at the Associated Colleges of the Midwest and an instructor in the graduate program in Higher Education Administration and Policy at Northwestern University.

LARISA GOOD has an MLS from the University of North Carolina at Chapel Hill and has been the director at the Warren County Public Library District in Monmouth, Illinois, since 2007.

ELIZABETH K. GOODHUE is associate director for engaged teaching at the UCLA Center for Community Learning, where she leads the center's instructional development initiatives, cultivates community partnerships, and teaches community-engaged courses. She earned her PhD in English from UCLA with an emphasis on eighteenth-century British literature and earned a BA in English and creative writing from the University of Arizona.

SUSAN CELIA GREENFIELD, professor of English at Fordham University, is the author of *Mothering Daughters: Novels and the Politics of Family Romance* and the editor of *Sacred Shelter: 13 Journeys of Homelessness and Healing.* Her scholarly essays have appeared in many journals, including *Eighteenth-Century Studies*, *ELH*, and *PMLA*. She has also published op-eds and short fiction.

LIZ GRUMBACH is the project manager for the Nexus Digital Research Co-op in the Institute for Humanities Research at Arizona State University and director of digital content and special programs for HASTAC. An alt-ac professional since 2012, she has served as project manager for the Mellon-funded Early Modern OCR Project and the Advanced Research Consortium. Her current projects consider ethical and critical methodologies for producing and sharing data and data technologies involving public engagement.

STEPHANIE HESS received her MA in museum studies while focusing on exhibition development and public history. As curator of Special Collections and Digitization at the Northfield Historical Society, she catalogues and interprets its collections; digitizes images, documents, objects, and multimedia; and shares them online with the Northfield History Collaborative.

KELLEN HINRICHSEN is the Pattee Executive Director at the Warren County History Museum, located in Monmouth, Illinois. He received his MA in anthropology and museum studies from the University of Denver and has held positions at the Durham Museum, the Dallas Holocaust Museum, and the Amache Historical Society Museum prior to moving to Illinois.

ELLEN JAROSZ is head of Special Collections and Archives at CSUN and a past president of the Society of California Archivists. She holds a BA in history and an MA in library and information studies with an archives concentration from the University of Wisconsin–Madison. Ellen was formerly Special Collections and University Archives Librarian at San Diego State University and a project archivist at the Wisconsin Historical Society.

HANNAH JORGENSON is a doctoral candidate in English at the University of Minnesota, Twin Cities, where she studies literature of the seventeenth and eighteenth centuries, British women writers, Revolutionary writing (specifically of the 1640s and 1780s), feminist and gender theory, and the rise of the novel. She holds an MA in English from CSUN.

JOHN C. KELLER is the dean of the Graduate College, associate provost for graduate and professional education, and interim vice president for research at the University of Iowa. A passionate advocate for graduate education, Keller promotes publicly accessible research, holistic career preparation, diversity and inclusion initiatives, and institutional research support to advance the success of Iowa's graduate students.

NAZ KEYNEJAD received her MA in English literature (with distinction) from CSUN. She is currently a PhD candidate in comparative literature at the University of California, Santa Barbara, where she explores Eastern and Western religions, faith, and their ties to acts of literary and cultural rebellion.

MARIESA ARRAÑAGA KUBASEK, the volunteer manager at 826LA, trains, supports, and manages hundreds of volunteers each year. Previously, she led outreach efforts and coordinated media campaigns for an arts education program in Southern California. Mariesa attended Santa Clara University, where she majored in philosophy and political science.

STEPHEN KUTAY is a digital services librarian at CSUN. He holds a BA degree in music and an MA in library and information science with a specialization in archival studies. Steve previously worked at the Southern Regional Library Facility at the University of California, Los Angeles, and the Los Angeles Philharmonic Association Archives.

CHUCK LEWIS is professor of English and director of the writing program at Beloit College, where he teaches courses in literary studies and writing. His publications focus on nineteenth- and twentieth-century American fiction.

NICOLE LINTON has worked at CSUN since 2013 to develop its S4 database, which captures the impact of students on their communities. A committed volunteer at organizations throughout the San Fernando Valley, she has served as a board member since 2014 at MEND (Meet Each Need with Dignity). Nicole studied marketing and product development at the Fashion Institute of Design and Merchandising.

DEVONEY LOOSER is professor of English at Arizona State University and the author or editor of seven books on literature by women. Her most recent is *The Making of Jane Austen*, a *Publishers Weekly* Best Summer Book (Nonfiction) and winner of the IHE Reader's Choice Award. Her writing on Austen has appeared in the *Atlantic*, the *New York Times*, *Salon*, *TLS*, and *Entertainment Weekly*, and she's also had the pleasure of talking about Austen on CNN. She writes occasional essays on professional issues for the *Chronicle of Higher Education* and has played roller derby as Stone Cold Jane Austen.

LAURA MANDELL, Director of the Initiative for Digital Humanities, Media, and Culture (IDHMC) at Texas A&M University, is the author of *Breaking the Book: Print Humanities in the Digital Age*, *Misogynous Economies: The Business of Literature in Eighteenth-Century Britain*, and numerous articles about digital literary history and eighteenth-century women writers. She founded the Early Modern

OCR Project, created the Big Data Infrastructure Visualization Application, and serves as director of the Advanced Research Consortium, 18thConnect.org, and general editor of the Poetess Archive.

WHITNEY MANNIES received her PhD in political science from the University of California, Riverside. Her most recent publication, "Towards a Radical Feminist Historiography," appears in *The Invention of Female Biography*, edited by Gina Luria Walker. She teaches political theory at Cal Poly Pomona.

AI MILLER is a graduate student in the history department at the University of Minnesota, where zie studies political uses of queer and trans death and twentieth-century transgender history more broadly.

TIFFANY OUELLETTE is a secondary-school English teacher from western Illinois. She is a graduate of Monmouth College ('14) who is in her fifth year of teaching.

CAROL PARRISH has been a member of the Warren County Historical Society for over thirty years. During that time, she served as vice president, president, and chair of the exhibition committee. As president, she initiated an alliance of small budget museums within a five county area in western Illinois.

PAUL SCHUYTEMA currently serves as the executive director of the Iron County Economic Chamber Alliance in Michigan's Upper Peninsula. Prior to that, he was the director of Community and Economic Development for Monmouth, Illinois. Paul has worked as a writer, teacher, computer game designer, entrepreneur, concert promoter, musician, software developer, creativity trainer, and economic developer.

DAVID SPADAFORA, President of the Newberry Library since 2005, is a historian. He previously served as dean of the faculty and then president of Lake Forest College, teaching history there for many years, as well as at Yale University in the 1980s.

ANNE MCKEE STAPLETON is an associate professor of instruction in the Department of English at the University of Iowa, where she researches and teaches the literature and culture of late eighteenth- and nineteenth-century Great Britain, with a focus on Scotland. The 2014 bicentennial celebration of Walter Scott's *Waverley; Or, 'Tis Sixty Years Since* coincided with the publication of her book *Pointed Encounters: Scottish Dance in Post-Culloden Literature*.

JESSICA STEWART is an MA student and teaching associate in the English Department at CSUN. Her areas of interest are Native American literature, feminist and queer theory, and images of women in contemporary American literature. Influenced by Judith Butler and bell hooks, she is currently researching third-wave feminism's influence on contemporary literature and current sociopolitical debates.

COLLEEN TRIPP is an assistant professor of English and the honors in English faculty advisor at CSUN, as well as affiliate faculty at the Center for Digital Humanities. She holds a PhD in American Studies from Brown University and specializes in nineteenth-century American print culture, popular culture, diversity and equity, and transnationalism.

SUSAN TWOMEY is the retired executive director of the Buchanan Center for the Arts in Monmouth, Illinois. She currently serves as a member of the board of directors for the Galesburg Community Foundation and the Arts Alliance Illinois, as well as serving as an alderwoman for the city of Monmouth.

AMY WELDON, professor of English at Luther College, is the author of *The Hands-On Life: How to Wake Yourself Up and Save The World* and *The Writer's Eye: Observation and Inspiration for Creative Writers*.

NIKKI WHITE is a digital humanities librarian at the University of Iowa. She collaborates with faculty and students developing public-facing digital scholarship.

RACHEL LYNNE WITZIG is an alumna of Monmouth College and works as a caregiver at a children's home in Magdalena de Kino, Sonora, Mexico, where she assists teenagers with their daily lives and their English studies.

NOTES

INTRODUCTION

1. See Lynn Hunt, *Inventing Human Rights: A History* (New York: Norton, 2007).

2. Neil Postman, *Building a Bridge to the 18th Century: How the Past Can Improve Our Future* (New York: Vintage Books, 1999), 19.

3. "*Pride and Prejudice and Zombies* by Seth Grahame-Smith," Goodreads.com, accessed January 16, 2018, https://www.goodreads.com/book/show/5899779-pride-and-prejudice-and-zombies.

4. "*Pride and Prejudice and Zombies*," Rottentomatoes.com, accessed January 16, 2018, https://www.rottentomatoes.com/m/pride_and_prejudice_and_zombies/.

5. Jane Austen, *Pride and Prejudice*, ed. Donald Gray and Mary A. Favret (New York: Norton, 2001), 233-234.

6. For an overview, see Mike Mariani, "The Tragic, Forgotten History of Zombies," *The Atlantic*, October 28, 2015, https://www.theatlantic.com/entertainment/archive/2015/10/how-america-erased-the-tragic-history-of-the-zombie/412264/.

7. Robert Clark, ed., *Jane Austen's Geographies* (New York: Routledge, 2018), 12. In the passage in *Mansfield Park* (vol. I, chap. 16, pp. 109-110), Fanny is likely reading one of the lengthier accounts of Macartney's failed attempt.

8. George Macartney, *An Account of Ireland in 1773 by a Late Chief Secretary of that Kingdom* (London, 1773), 55.

9. On Austen's family connections with India, see John C. Leffel, " 'Where Woman, Lovely Woman, for Wealth and Grandeur Comes from Far': Representations of the Colonial Marriage Market in Gillray, Topham, Starke, and Austen," in *Transnational England: Home and Abroad, 1780–1860*, ed. Monika Class and Terry F. Robinson (Newcastle upon Tyne: Cambridge Scholars Publishing, 2009), 208-232.

10. Peter Brooks, introduction to *The Humanities and Public Life*, ed. Peter Brooks and Hilary Jewett (New York: Fordham University Press, 2014), 14.

11. What Jane Saw, http://www.whatjanesaw.org/, accessed February 15, 2018; 18thConnect, www.18thconnect.org, accessed February 13, 2018.

12. The phrase "principled action" is borrowed from David D. Cooper, *Learning in the Plural: Essays on the Humanities in Public Life* (East Lansing: Michigan State University Press, 2014), 12.

13. Carole Fabricant, "Swift in His Own Time and Ours," in *The Profession of Eighteenth-Century Literature: Reflections on an Institution*, ed. Leo Damrosch (Madison: University of Wisconsin Press, 1992), 116.

14. Fabricant, "Swift in His Own Time," 117.

15. Fabricant, "Swift in His Own Time," 119.

16. Ellen Condliffe Lagemann and Harry Lewis, "Renewing the Civic Mission of American Higher Education," in *What Is College For? The Public Purpose of Higher Education*, ed. Ellen Condliffe Lagemann and Harry Lewis (New York: Teachers College Press, 2012), 32.

17. Condliffe and Lewis, "Renewing the Civic Mission," 40.

18. Raymond Williams, *Keywords: A Vocabulary of Culture and Society* (New York: Oxford University Press, 1983), 291–292.

19. Laurie Grobman, "Is There a Place for Service Learning in Literary Studies?" *Profession* (2005): 130.

20. Jürgen Habermas, *The Structural Transformation of the Public Sphere: An Inquiry into a Category of Bourgeois Society*, trans. Thomas Burger (Cambridge, MA: MIT Press, 1991), 31–42, 57–66.

21. See, for example, the 18th-Century Common, www.18thcenturycommon.org, or Aphra Behn Online Public, http://www.aphrabehn.org/ABO/, which are committed to making eighteenth-century scholarship more public. The shared etymology of "public" and "publish" is all the more relevant given the move toward open access, an important counterpoint to the increasing cost of journals and databases that restrict access to vital research resources.

22. Caryn McTighe Musil, "Educating for Citizenship," *Peer Review* 5, no. 3 (2003): 4–8.

23. Andrew Burstein and Catherine Mowbray have documented Jefferson's voracious consumption of and intellectual preoccupation with Sterne's writing, and they trace the phrase "the pursuit of happiness" to Sterne's first published sermon; see their "Jefferson and Sterne," *Early American Literature* 29, no. 1 (1994): 22.

24. For more on the explosion of printed materials in the seventeenth century, particularly after the Restoration, see Elizabeth Eisenstein, *The Printing Press as an Agent of Change* (New York: Cambridge University Press, 1980), 43–53, and Adrian Johns, *The Nature of the Book: Print and Knowledge in the Making* (Chicago: University of Chicago Press, 1998), 3. See also Joseph Frank, *The Beginnings of the English Newspaper, 1620–1660* (Cambridge, MA: Harvard University Press, 1961), and Joad Raymond, *The Invention of the Newspaper: English Newsbooks 1641–1660* (Oxford: Oxford University Press, 1996).

25. Victoria Gardner, "Reading All about It: Eighteenth-Century News Culture," *History Workshop Journal* 77 (2014): 294.

26. Robert Darnton, Alan Liu, and Cathy Davidson, respectively. We might also look to Adrianne Wadewitz, an eighteenth centuryist committed to increasing women's role in Wikipedia who sadly passed away but whose work continues through edit-a-thons at ASECS and elsewhere, or Laura Mandell, who coauthored a contribution to

this volume and created 18thConnect and many sister websites. As Cathy Davidson writes, "I wouldn't be a historian of the Internet had I not been trained as a historian of the book. Or I certainly would not have had the long historical perspective on this new tool and been able to see its possibilities, its dangers, and our responsibilities for teaching our students how to use it well." See Cathy Davidson, "What Would Thomas Jefferson Say about the Internet?" *HASTAC* (blog), August 8, 2014, https://www.hastac.org/blogs/cathy-davidson/2014/08/08/what-would-thomas-jefferson-say-about-internet.

27. Although ironically, as we will discuss in chapters 4–6, these texts, while themselves copyright free, often are only available through pricey databases that are difficult for those without premium library subscriptions to access.

28. Martyn Lyons, *Books: A Living History* (London: Thames and Hudson, 2013), 116.

29. See, for instance, Helen Small, *The Value of the Humanities* (New York: Oxford University Press, 2013), or Peter Brooks, introduction to *The Humanities and Public Life*.

30. Grobman, "A Place for Service Learning," 130.

CHAPTER 1

1. Olivera Jokic, "Teaching to the Resistance: What to Do When Students Dislike Austen," *Persuasions On-Line* 34, no. 2 (Spring 2014), http://www.jasna.org/persuasions/on-line/vol34no2/jokic.html. The *Oxford Dictionaries* defines the term "first world problem" as referring to "a relatively trivial or minor problem or frustration (implying a contrast with serious problems such as those that may be experienced in the developing world)," https://en.oxforddictionaries.com/definition/first_world_problem. The concept has become popular as a series of internet memes; one notable example shows two juxtaposed Venn diagrams in which one of the first world problems is not being able to view a television show in high definition; the real problems include hunger, rape, and cholera; see http://knowyourmeme.com/photos/142422-first-world-problems, last accessed May 25, 2018.

2. For excellent accounts of Janeite culture, see the introduction to Claudia Johnson, *Jane Austen's Cults and Cultures* (Chicago: University of Chicago Press, 2012); Deidre Lynch, *Loving Literature: A Cultural History* (Chicago: University of Chicago Press, 2016), 33–41, 155; and Devoney Looser, *The Making of Jane Austen* (Baltimore: Johns Hopkins University Press, 2017).

3. Marcia McClintock Folsom, "The Privilege of My Own Profession: The Living Legacy of Austen," *Persuasions On-Line* 29, no. 1 (Winter 2008), http://jasna.org/persuasions/on-line/vol29no1/folsom.html.

4. Devoney Looser, " 'A Very Kind Undertaking': *Emma* and Eighteenth-Century Feminism," in *Approaches to Teaching Austen's* Emma, ed. Marcia McClintock Folsom (New York: MLA, 2004), 101.

5. Laura Mooneyham White, "The Experience of Class, *Emma*, and the American College Student," in *Approaches to Teaching Austen's* Emma, ed. Marcia McClintock Folsom (New York: MLA, 2004), 41.

6. It is perhaps all the more telling that, as Linda Troost and Sayre Greenfield observe, *Emma* is the only major Austen novel set in only one community and location. See Linda Troost and Sayre Greenfield, "Filming Highbury: Reducing the Community in *Emma* to the Screen," *Persuasions On-Line Occasional Papers* 3 (1999), http://www.jasna.org/persuasions/on-line/opno3/troost_sayre.html.

7. Caryn McTighe Musil, "Educating for Citizenship," *Peer Review* 5, no. 3 (2003): 4, http://www.aacu.org/peerreview/documents/pr-spo3.pdf. On the emergence of service-learning initiatives at the university level, see Benjamin R. Barber and Richard Battistoni, "A Season of Service: Introducing Service Learning into the Liberal Arts Curriculum," *PS: Political Science and Politics* 26, no. 2 (June 1993): 235–240. For more recent work that attests to the continued growth of civic engagement on college campuses, see Susan A. Ostrander and Kent E. Portney, eds., *Acting Civically: From Urban Neighborhoods to Higher Education* (Medford, MA: Tufts University Press, 2007).

8. Jean Y. Yu, "Race Matters in Civic Engagement Work," in *Acting Civically: From Urban Neighborhoods to Higher Education*, ed. Susan A. Ostrander and Kent E. Portney (Medford, MA: Tufts University Press, 2007), 160.

9. Gregory Jay, "Service Learning, Multiculturalism, and the Pedagogies of Difference," *Pedagogy* 8, no. 2 (Spring 2008): 255.

10. Mary Schwartz, "Public Stakes, Public Stories: Service Learning in Literary Studies," *PMLA* 127, no. 4 (2012): 988–989.

11. Anna Sims Bartel, "Talking and Walking: Literary Work as Public Work," in *Community-Based Learning and the Work of Literature*, ed. Susan Danielson and Ann Marie Fallon (Bolton, MA: Anker, 2007), 86.

12. Laurie Grobman, "Is There a Place for Service Learning in Literary Studies?" *Profession* (2005): 129–130.

13. Ellen Cushman, "The Public Intellectual, Service Learning, and Activist Research," *College English* 61, no. 3 (January 1999): 332.

14. Linda Flower, "Intercultural Inquiry and the Transformation of Service," *College English* 65, no. 2 (November 2002): 186.

15. Flower, "Intercultural Inquiry," 186.

16. Christine M. Cress, Peter J. Collier, and Vicki L. Reitenauer, *Learning through Serving: A Student Guidebook for Service-Learning across the Disciplines* (Sterling, VA: Stylus, 2005), 8.

17. Jay, "Service Learning," 256–257.

18. Paula Mathieu, *Tactics of Hope: The Public Turn in English Composition* (Portsmouth, NH: Boynton/Cook Publishers, 2005), xii.

19. Mathieu, *Tactics of Hope*, xii.

20. Cushman, "The Public Intellectual," 335.

21. Since I first published this article in spring 2014, only a handful of significant projects have explored Austen's work in a service-learning context, although the practice is certainly more prevalent than this publication record suggests. See Maureen Jacrois, "Jane Austen in the 21st-Century Classroom" (Undergraduate Honors Thesis Project, Bridgewater State University, 2014); contributor Elizabeth K. Goodhue's work also speaks to the excellent pedagogical methods surrounding these perhaps unexpected topics. In nineteenth-century studies, a recent partnership between USC's Neighborhood Academic Initiative and the Dickens Universe has supported the participation of students from underserved high schools. See Sara Hayden, "Winning Essays Take 2 South LA Students to Dickens Conference," *Los Angeles Times*, August 16, 2014, http://www.latimes.com/local/la-me-dickens-contest-20140817-story.html.

22. Matthew C. Hansen, "'O Brave New World': Service-Learning and Shakespeare," *Pedagogy* 11, no. 1 (2011): 177.

23. A number of studies have cited the influence in particular of gender and race on civic engagement. Ostrander and Portney, eds., *Acting Civically*, note that people of color and low-income community members, along with many women, are often structurally unable to participate in civic work. See, for instance, Sarah Sobieraj and Deborah White, "Could Civic Engagement Reproduce Political Inequality," in *Acting Civically*, 92–112; Amy Caizza, "Don't Bowl at Night: Gender, Safety, and Civic Participation," in *Signs: Journal of Women in Culture and Society* 30, no. 2 (2005); and Nancy Burns, Kay Lehman Schlozman, and Sidney Verba, *The Private Roots of Public Action: Gender, Equality, and Political Participation* (Cambridge: Harvard University Press, 2001).

24. For information about service learning as a high-impact practice, see the Association of American Colleges and Universities, "High-Impact Educational Practices: A Brief Overview," https://www.aacu.org/leap/hips, last accessed May 25, 2018.

25. Mission statements are posted on the websites of these organizations. For 826LA, see http://826la.org/about/mission-statement/; for MEND, see http://mendpoverty.org/about-us/who-we-are/; for 18thConnect, see Laura Mandell and Liz Grumbach's essay in this collection, along with http://www.18thconnect.org/about/what-is-18thconnect/.

26. Schwartz, "Public Stakes," 990.

27. To learn more about the CSU S4 Database, see https://www.csun.edu/undergraduate-studies/community-engagement/s4-database.

28. According to Peter J. Collier and Dilafruz R. Williams, there are four main components to successful reflective activities: they must be continuous (taking place before, during, and after service); they must be challenging (involving work that pushes students to connect concepts in new ways); they must be connected (acting as "a bridge between the service experience and our discipline-based academic knowledge"); and they must be contextualized (framing content and concepts appropriately). See Collier and Williams, "Reflection in Action: The Learning-Doing Relationship," in *Learning*

through Serving: A Student Guidebook for Service-Learning across the Disciplines, ed. Christine M. Cress et al. (Sterling, VA: Stylus, 2005), 83.

29. Marilyn Butler, *Jane Austen and the War of Ideas* (New York: Oxford University Press, 1988), xliv.

30. Susan Celia Greenfield, "Of Jane Austen, the Bennet Sisters, . . . and VAWA?" *Ms.blog, Ms. Magazine*, March 6, 2013, http://msmagazine.com/blog/2013/03/06/of -jane-austen-the-bennet-sisters-and-vawa/, and "Jane Austen Weekly: Child Poverty in *Mansfield Park*," *Huffington Post*, October 26, 2012, http://www.huffingtonpost.com /susan-celia-greenfield/jane-austen-mansfield-Park_b_2024487.htm.

31. Jane Austen, *Emma*, ed. Richard Cronin and Dorothy McMillin (New York: Cambridge University Press, 2005), 3. Hereafter cited in the text.

32. Marcia McClintock Folsom, introduction to *Approaches to Teaching Austen's Emma* (New York: MLA, 2004), xvii–xxiv.

33. White, "The Experience of Class," 39.

34. In this prompt, I asked students to consider one of the following: the cottager scene from *Emma*; the scene in *Sense and Sensibility* in which John Dashwood and Elinor discuss Colonel Brandon's giving Edward Ferrars the living at Delaford (vol. III, chap. 5); the scene in *Mansfield Park* in which the Bertrams and Mrs. Norris discuss adopting Fanny (vol. I, chap. 1); or the passage where Fanny seeks to improve Susan through education (vol. III, chap. 9). Musil, "Educating for Citizenship," identifies "six expressions of citizenship: exclusionary, oblivious, naive, charitable, reciprocal, and generative" (5). These categories begin with the most intellectually disconnected and exclusionary; on the other end of the spectrum, Musil defines reciprocal service as involving a rejection of the idea that the street is deprived. Instead, students see it as a resource "to empower and be empowered by"; generative service reflects the reciprocal mentality but also "has a more all-encompassing scope with an eye to the future public good" (7).

35. All student responses have been anonymized in accordance with IRB standards; the one exception is work from Hannah Jorgenson, who is a contributor to this chapter.

36. See Austen, *Emma*, ed. Cronin and McMillin, 579, n. 2, for more on this misunderstanding.

37. Michael Kramp, "The Woman, the Gypsies, and England: Harriet Smith's National Role," *College Literature* 31, no. 1 (Winter 2004): 148.

38. Kramp, "The Woman, the Gypsies," 157.

39. Ruth Perry, "Jane Austen, Slavery, and British Imperialism," in *Approaches to Teaching Austen's Emma*, ed. Marcia McClintock Folsom (New York: MLA, 2004), 33.

40. For more information on *Emma* and the enclosure acts, see E. P. Thompson, "Eighteenth-Century English Society: Class Struggle without Class?" *Social History* 3, no. 2 (1978), and Beth Fowkes Tobin, "The Moral and Political Economy of Property in Austen's *Emma*," *Eighteenth-Century Fiction* 2, no. 3 (1990).

41. Musil, "Educating for Citizenship," 5.

42. Musil, "Educating for Citizenship," 6.

43. See Andrew McConnell Stott, "Why Clowns Keep Scaring Us," *CNN*, November 17, 2014, http://www.cnn.com/2014/10/31/opinion/stott-clowns-france/index.html.

44. For these reviews and others, see the press kit for *The Making of Jane Austen*, https://jhupbooks.press.jhu.edu/press-kit-making-jane-austen.

45. See, for instance, Devoney Looser, "Jane Austen Wasn't Shy," *New York Times*, July 15, 2017, https://www.nytimes.com/2017/07/15/opinion/sunday/jane-austen-wasnt -shy.html; "Queering the Work of Jane Austen Is Nothing New," *Atlantic*, July 21, 2017, https://www.theatlantic.com/entertainment/archive/2017/07/queering-the-work -of-jane-austen-is-nothing-new/533418/; "Whatever Her Persuasion," *Times Literary Supplement*, January 18, 2017, https://www.the-tls.co.uk/articles/public/jane-austen -in-2017/; and "Fifty Shades of Mr. Darcy: A Brief History of X-Rated Jane Austen Adaptations," *Salon*, July 16, 2017, https://www.salon.com/2017/07/16/fifty-shades-of -mr-darcy-a-brief-history-of-x-rated-jane-austen-adaptations/.

46. For this interview, see http://www.makingjaneausten.com/janeausten200-tv -radio-print.html.

47. For more information, see http://makingjaneausten.com.

48. The OpEd Project, accessed February 5, 2018, https://www.theopedproject.org.

49. Susan Celia Greenfield, "Consent and Conception," *Need to Know on PBS*, August 23, 2012, http://www.pbs.org/wnet/need-to-know/opinion/consent-and-concep tion/14573/.

50. Susan Celia Greenfield, "The Jane Austen Weekly: *Northanger Abbey* and the Presidential Campaign," *Huffington Post*, September 13, 2012, https://www.huffington post.com/entry/the-jane-austen-weekly-no_b_1880489.html.

51. Jane Austen, *Northanger Abbey*, ed. Claire Grogan (Guelph and Peterborough, ON: Broadview Press, 2004), 86.

52. For a comprehensive list of articles in the blog, see https://www.huffingtonpost .com/author/susan-celia-greenfield.

53. For a list of these articles, see https://lareviewofbooks.org/contributor/susan -celia-greenfield% and http://msmagazine.com/blog/author/susanceliagreenfield/.

54. For more information on these organizations and this work, see "The Antidote that Works," *Ms. Special K for the Homeless* (blog), September 21, 2016, https://catholic charitiesny.org/blog/ms-special-k-homeless, and "Life Skills Empowerment Program," *Interfaith Assembly on Homelessness and Housing*, http://www.iahh.org/empowerment /program-description%20.

55. Susan Celia Greenfield, "Postmortem: Jane Austen and Repealing the Affordable Care Act," *Blarb* (blog), *LA Review of Books*, August 9, 2017, https://blog.lareview ofbooks.org/literature/postmortem-jane-austen-repealing-affordable-care-act/.

56. Greenfield, "Postmortem."

57. See "Full text of John McCain's Senate floor speech: 'Let's return to regular

order,'" *USA Today*, accessed February 5, 2018, https://www.usatoday.com/story/news/politics/2017/07/25/full-text-john-mccains-senate-floor-speech/509799001/.

58. Jane Austen, *Pride and Prejudice*, 3rd ed., ed. Donald Gray and Mary A. Favret (New York: Norton, 2000), 95.

59. See, for example, the essays collected in Tyrone Howard and Nancy Parachini, eds., *Culturally Relevant Teaching* (Los Angeles: UCLA Center X, 2013), https://centerx.gseis.ucla.edu/xchange/culturally-relevant-teaching.

60. Sarah Fielding, *The Governess; Or, The Little Female Academy*, ed. Candace Ward (Guelph and Peterborough, ON: Broadview Press, 2005), 46.

61. Fielding, *The Governess*, 84.

62. See the "Frequently Challenged Books" page on the American Library Association's website, http://www.ala.org/bbooks/frequentlychallengedbooks.

63. In this course, I regularly partner with 826LA (826la.org) as well as other educational nonprofits, such as the Bresee Foundation (http://www.bresee.org/) and Mar Vista Family Center (http://marvistafc.org/), as well as schools in the Los Angeles Unified School District, especially Beethoven Elementary (http://www.beethovenschool.org/).

CHAPTER 2

1. James Edward Austen-Leigh, *A Memoir of Jane Austen* (London: R. Bentley, 1870; New York: Oxford University Press, 2002), 9. Page references are to the 2002 edition.

2. See Devoney Looser, *The Making of Jane Austen* (Baltimore: Johns Hopkins University Press, 2017), 7.

3. The full quotation, cited in Austen-Leigh's memoir, offers, according to her nephew "a playful defence of herself from a mock charge of having pilfered the manuscripts of a young relation. 'What should I do, my dearest E., with your manly, vigorous sketches, so full of life and spirit? How could I possibly join them on to a little bit of ivory, two inches wide, on which I work with a brush so fine, as to produce little effect after much labour?'" Austen-Leigh, *A Memoir of Jane Austen*, 123.

4. I attended a facilitation training workshop in Chicago at Columbia College, January 19-20, 2012. Learn more at http://civicreflection.org/.

5. I first published an article on the Jane Austen in Community project in "Teaching Jane Austen in Bits and Bytes: Digitizing Undergraduate Archival Research," *Persuasions On-Line* 34, no. 2 (Spring 2014). This article focused on the individual student research projects rather than community engagement.

6. Maria Edgeworth to Joanna Baillie, August 14, 1848, Hunter-Baillie Papers, 1704–1923, vol. 9, Royal College of Surgeons of England, London.

7. Now there are much more sophisticated technologies that can manage content and create digital timelines, such as Timeline JS from Knight Lab (www.timeline.knightlab.com).

8. Joanna Baillie, "Sunset Meditation, Under the Apprehension of Approaching

Blindness," in *A Collection of Poems, Chiefly Manuscript, and from Living Authors*, ed. Joanna Baillie (London: Longman, Hurst, Rees, Orme, and Brown, 1823). Hereafter cited in the text.

9. Maybe inspired by the friendship between Baillie and Edgeworth, during my time at Chawton House I cultivated a number of professional relationships with other women who have inspired and supported me ever since, including my coauthor Danielle. In an age when so much archival material is now available online, part of the sustaining value of physical archives is tied up in the relationships and mentoring that can happen in spaces like Chawton House. See Gillian Dow's essay on Chawton House in this volume.

10. Jane Austen in Community, http://janeaustenincommunity.wordpress.com/.

11. Edward Said, *Culture and Imperialism* (New York: Vintage, 1993); Ruth Perry, "Jane Austen, Slavery, and British Imperialism," in *Approaches to Teaching Austen's Emma*, ed. Marcia McClintock Folsom (New York: MLA, 2004).

12. Jane Austen, *Emma*, 4th ed., ed. George Justice (New York: Norton, 2012). Hereafter cited in the text.

13. Hannah More, *Betty Brown, the St. Giles's Orange Girl* (London: J. Marshall, and R. White; Bath: S. Hazard, 1795).

14. Richard De Ritter, *Imagining Women Readers, 1789–1820* (Manchester: Manchester University Press, 2014), 170.

15. Jane Austen, *Northanger Abbey*, ed. Susan Fraiman (New York: Norton, 2004), 11. Hereafter cited in the text.

16. Jane Austen in Community, 2nd ed., http://pages.stolaf.edu/janeaustenin community/.

17. Sarah Eason, "Henry Tilney: Queer Hero of *Northanger Abbey*," *Persuasions On-Line* 34, no. 1 (Winter 2013), http://www.jasna.org/persuasions/on-line/vol34no1 /eason.html.

18. See Robert Hopkins, "General Tilney and Affairs of the State: The Political Gothic of *Northanger Abbey*," *Philological Quarterly* 57, no. 2 (Spring 1978). On the meaning of the general's hobbies, see Susan Fraiman's footnotes on pages 129, 119–120, and 122 in her edition of *Northanger Abbey* (New York: Norton, 2004).

CHAPTER 3

1. For a detailed list of manuscripts in the collection, see the historical catalogue collected by the museum clerk: Samuel Ayscough, *Catalogue of the Manuscripts Preserved in the British Museum Hitherto Undescribed: Consisting of Five Thousand Volumes; including the Collections of Sir Hans Sloane, Bart., the Rev. Thomas Birch, D. D., and about Five Hundred Volumes bequeathed, presented, or purchased at various times* (London: John Rivington, 1782).

2. *Authentic Copies of the Codicils Belonging to the Last Will and Testament of Sir Hans Sloane, Bart. deceased, Which relate to his Collection of Books and Curiosities*

(London: Printed, by Order of the Executors, by Daniel Crowne, near Temple-Bar, 1753), 12.

3. *Last Will and Testament*, 20–24.

4. Of course, not all the items were British, but these objects from the empire buttressed the nation's identity as a world power.

5. For more on Sloane's storied collections, see James Delbourgo, *Collecting the World: Hans Sloane and the Origins of the British Museum* (Cambridge: Harvard University Press, 2017).

6. Barbara M. Benedict, "Collecting Trouble: Sir Hans Sloane's Literary Reputation in Eighteenth-Century Britain," *Eighteenth-Century Life* 36, no. 2 (Spring 2012): 119.

7. One anecdotal example of the odd juxtapositions found in the exhibit is captured by John and Andrew Van Rymsdyk's 1791 *Museum Britannicum*, in which they transition from a catalogue of valuable stones to national poets with remarkable dexterity: "The Egyptian pebbles are a remarkable kind of stones, from their being variegated with curious characters, those which have a variety of colours are valuable, and now we will give a slight description of another kind of Diamond, meaning *Chaucer*." This graceful transition is bolstered by a Rorschach-blot-like discussion of an Egyptian diamond on which can be found "a striking likeness of the head of *Chaucer*," in which, the author claims, "one may see his very temper," followed by a poetic ditty that compares True Wit to diamonds, as they "Cut as well as Shine!" John Van Rymsdyk and Andrew Van Rymsdyk, *Museum Britannicum; or, a Display in Thirty Two Plates, of Antiquities and Natural Curiosities, That Noble and Magnificent Cabinet, the British Museum, After the Original Designs from Nature*, 2nd ed., rev. by P. Boyle (London: J. Moore, 1791), 75–76.

8. *Last Will and Testament*, 19.

9. *Fundamental Principles from which the Trustees do not think they can in Honor or Conscience Depart* (n.p., 1753), quoted in Edward Miller, *That Noble Cabinet: A History of the British Museum* (Athens: Ohio University Press, 1974), 44.

10. British Museum, *Statutes and Rules Relating to the Inspection and Use of the British Museum* (London: Dryden Leach, 1759), 5–6.

11. British Museum, *Statutes and Rules*, 9–15.

12. J. W. L. G., *A Letter to Sir Humphrey Davy, Bart. &c. &c. &c. On His Being Elected the President of the Royal Society: With Some Observations on the Management of the British Museum, By A Fellow of the Royal Society* (London: James Ridgway, Piccadilly, 1821), 12–13, and 17.

13. Anne Goldgar, "The British Museum and the Virtual Representation of Culture in the Eighteenth Century," *Albion: A Quarterly Journal Concerned with British Studies* 32, no. 2 (Summer 2000): 202.

14. Goldgar, "The British Museum," 211.

15. Goldgar, "The British Museum," 204.

16. Christopher Wright, "Don't Call It the British Museum Library," *American Libraries* 7, no. 1 (January 1976): 50.

17. "Museums for All," Institute of Museum and Library Services, accessed January 31, 2018, https://www.imls.gov/issues/national-initiatives/museums-all.

18. See Alison Booth, *Homes and Haunts: Touring Writers' Shrines and Countries* (New York: Oxford University Press, 2016), 1; on the snooping and the séance, see 55, 56.

19. Booth, *Homes and Haunts*, 1.

20. Booth, *Homes and Haunts*, 19.

21. This desire is not a new one: Judith Pascoe notes that "Byron sneered at collectors such as Elgin, but he cherished his own modest gathering of literary souvenirs," while Godwin fantasized about visiting the tomb of fictional character Clarissa Harlowe. Judith Pascoe, *The Hummingbird Cabinet: A Rare and Curious History of Romantic Collectors* (Ithaca, NY: Cornell University Press, 2006), 97.

22. This intimacy is a double-edged sword for women writers; as Alison Booth notes, an emphasis on domesticity in author house museums can give a "prominent role [to] women as writers" while simultaneously relegating them to positions as homemakers. Booth, *Homes and Haunts*, 6.

23. See Claudia Johnson's *Jane Austen's Cults and Cultures* (Chicago: Chicago University Press, 2012), 153–179.

24. Robert Cowtan, *Memories of the British Museum* (London: Richard Bentley and Son, 1872), 7.

25. As a public museum but also a former state capitol building, the space is deeply connected to its public identity.

26. Goldgar, "The British Museum," 197.

27. Patricia Limerick, "Dancing with Professors: The Trouble with Academic Prose," *New York Times Book Review*, October 31, 1993; Susan J. Leonardi, "Recipes for Reading: Summer Pasta, Lobster a la Riseholme, and Key Lime Pie," *PMLA* 104 (May 1989).

28. Benedict, "Collecting Trouble," 112.

29. Benedict, "Collecting Trouble," 120. In stark contrast to Sloane, the author of *The General Contents of the British Museum* brags that "the judicious Reader will observe, that I have endeavoured to be as intelligible as possible; making use of very few Words but what are generally understood: I therefore flatter myself, that my Readers among the Ladies will be very numerous." This dumbing-down fallacy was as offensive to the Ladies, I suspect, then as it is now — as is his assumption that the "univalves and bivalves" will "particularly attract the Attention of the Ladies," as if they too were headless mollusks. *The General Contents of the British Museum: With Remarks. Serving as a Directory In viewing that Noble Cabinet*, 2nd ed. (London: R. and J. Dodsley, 1762), xii, 129.

30. Pascoe, *The Hummingbird Cabinet*, 99.

31. Ian R. Willison, "The National Library in Historical Perspective," *Libraries & Culture* 24, no. 1 (Winter 1989): 79. Robert Anderson's introduction to the edited collection *Enlightening the British* goes so far as to suggest that the British Museum "acted as though it were an encyclopaedia, or a dictionary based on historical principles, with sequences of rooms, their layout, and the juxtaposition of object within them providing a means of understanding relationships within the three-dimensional world of objects and specimens." *Enlightening the British: Knowledge, Discovery and the Museum in the Eighteenth Century*, ed. R. G. W. Anderson, M. L. Caygill, A. G. MacGregor, and L. Syson (London: British Museum Press, 2003), 3. Richard Yeo's chapter in the same volume explores this analogy in more depth, identifying ways that Sloane's museum, like Chambers' encyclopedia, "came to be regarded as public property; . . . were conceived as worthy of royal notice and presented as national achievements; . . . [and] raised questions about how large collections that overwhelmed the capacities of a single mind, or memory, could be put to good public use." Yeo, "Encyclopaedic Collectors: Ephraim Chambers and Sir Hans Sloane," 31.

32. Pascoe, *The Hummingbird Cabinet*, 106.

33. A Woman's Wit: Jane Austen's Life and Legacy, the Morgan Library and Museum, http://www.themorgan.org/collection/a-womans-wit-jane-austen; The Jane Austen Reading Room, Minneapolis Institute of Art, https://new.artsmia.org/living-rooms/jane-austen-reading-room/; Fame and Friendship: Pope, Roubiliac, and the Portrait Bust in Eighteenth-Century Britain, Yale Center for British Art, http://britishart.yale.edu/exhibitions/fame-and-friendship-pope-roubiliac-and-portrait-bust-eighteenth-century-britain; King's Library, the British Museum, http://www.britishmuseum.org/about_us/the_museums_story/kings_library.aspx.

34. What Jane Saw, http://www.whatjanesaw.org/.

35. For more on the complexities of access and privilege in museum spaces, see G. Wayne Clough, "Best of Both Worlds: Museums, Libraries, and Archives in a Digital Age," Smithsonian Institution (website), accessed February 4, 2018, http://www.si.edu/content/gwc/BestofBothWorldsSmithsonian.pdf; and Suse Cairns, "Do New Technologies Democratise Museum Collections, or Reinforce Conservative Values?" *Museum Geek: Exploring Museums, Technology, and Ideas* (blog), January 21, 2014, https://museumgeek.xyz/2014/01/21/do-new-technologies-democratise-museum-collections-or-reinforce-conservative-values/.

36. Though I should confess, despite my best efforts to make my writing more accessible, that the brilliant editor to this book has politely noted, "your immersion in eighteenth-century literature has definitely influenced your style of punctuation."

37. Helen Small, *The Value of the Humanities* (New York: Oxford University Press, 2013), 67.

38. Small, *The Value of the Humanities*, 65.

39. Small, *The Value of the Humanities*, 66.

40. For more information on the Gothic adaptations written and performed by

undergraduate students at the Creepy Classics event, see Bridget Draxler, "Adaptation as Interpretation: Eighteenth-Century Methods in the Twenty-First-Century Classroom," *The Eighteenth-Century Novel* 8 (September 2011).

41. Diana Nollen, "Area arts scene about to get Icky," *The Gazette* (Cedar Rapids, IA), December 16, 2009, http://thegazette.com/2009/12/16/area-arts-scene-about-to -get-icky.

CHAPTER 4

1. Grand Tourist Roger Pratt echoes these ideals, noting that nothing could be "in the Intellect, which was never in the Senses," quoted in Gillian Darley, "Wonderful Things: The Experience of the Grand Tour," *Perspecta* 41 (2008): 20; John Locke, *An Essay Concerning Human Understanding* (London: Printed by Elizabeth Holt, for Thomas Basset, at the George in Fleet Street, near St. Dunstan's Church, 1690), http:// www.gutenberg.org/files/10615/10615-h/10615-h.htm; Jean-Jacques Rousseau, *Emile*, trans. Barbara Foxley (Project Gutenberg, 2011; orig. 1762), http://www.gutenberg.org /cache/epub/5427/pg5427-images.html.

2. Gregory A. Smith, for instance, writes that in the troubled American school system, "learning becomes something gained through reading texts . . . rather than through experiencing full-bodied encounters with the world"; see his "Place-Based Education: Learning to Be Where We Are," *The Phi Delta Kappan* 83, no. 8 (April 2002): 586.

3. See, for instance, Elizabeth Zold, "Virtual Travel in *Second Life*: Understanding Eighteenth-Century Travelogues through Experiential Learning," *Pedagogy: Critical Approaches to Teaching, Literature, Language, Composition, and Culture* 14, no. 2 (Spring 2014).

4. Shankar Vedantam, "A Lively Mind: Your Brain On Jane Austen," NPR, October 9, 2012, http://www.npr.org/sections/health-shots/2012/10/09/162401053/a-lively -mind-your-brain-on-jane-austen.

5. Eric Calderwood, "Study Abroad," *Harvard Review* 40 (2011): 213.

6. Raquel Sallaberry, "Where Exactly Did Louisa Musgrove Fall?" *Jane Austen Today* (blog), May 11, 2010, http://janitesonthejames.blogspot.com/2010/05/where -exactly-did-louisa-musgrove-fall.html.

7. Mary Wollstonecraft, "Maria; or, The Wrongs of Woman," in *The Wrongs of Woman; or, Maria by Mary Wollstonecraft and Memoirs of the Author of* A Vindication of the Rights of Woman *by William Godwin*, ed. Cynthia Richards (Glen Allen, Virginia: College Publishing, 2004), 111.

8. Mary Wollstonecraft, *The Vindications: The Rights of Men, The Rights of Woman*, ed. D. L. Macdonald and Kathleen Scherf (Guelph and Peterborough, ON: Broadview Press, 1997), 198.

9. George Eliot, *Middlemarch* (London: Penguin Classics, 1994), 197.

10. Quoted in Alta Macadam and Annabel Barber, *Blue Guide: Rome*, 11th ed. (Somerset: Blue Guides Limited, 2016), 109.

11. Wollstonecraft, *The Vindications*, 241.

12. Keats to John Hamilton Reynolds, May 3, 1818, in *Letters of John Keats: A Selection*, ed. Robert Gittings (Oxford: Oxford University Press, 1970), 93.

13. See Alison Booth, *Homes and Haunts: Touring Writers' Shrines and Countries* (New York: Oxford University Press, 2016), which, in addition to exploring author house museums, also talks about other literary pilgrimages and tourism.

14. George G. Dekker, *The Fictions of Romantic Tourism: Radcliffe, Scott, and Mary Shelley* (Stanford, CA: Stanford University Press, 2005), 19.

15. *Possession*, directed by Neil LaBute (2002; Universal City, CA: Universal Pictures Home Entertainment, 2003), DVD.

16. Barbara Rockenbach posits that "undergraduates, even freshmen and sophomores, are capable of engaging with primary source materials in an attempt to build their internal authority"; see her "Archives, Undergraduates, and Inquiry-Based Learning: Case Studies from Yale University Library," *The American Archivist* 74, no. 1 (Spring/Summer 2011): 307.

17. Silvia Vong, "A Constructivist Approach for Introducing Undergraduate Students to Special Collections and Archival Research," *RBM: A Journal of Rare Books, Manuscripts, and Cultural Heritage* 17, no. 2 (Fall 2016).

18. Anne Bahde, " 'Oh, Wow!': Assessment and Affective Learning in Special Collections and Archives," in *New Directions for Special Collections: An Anthology of Practice*, ed. Lynne M. Thomas and Beth M. Whittaker (Santa Barbara, CA: Libraries Unlimited, 2017), 32.

19. David Mazella and Julie Grob, "Collaborations between Faculty and Special Collections Librarians in Inquiry-Driven Classes," *Libraries and the Academy* 11, no. 1 (January 2011): 473.

20. Cory L. Nimer and J. Gordon Daines III, "Teaching Undergraduates to Think Archivally," *Journal of Archival Organization* 10, no. 1 (May 2012): 7. For frank advice about challenges and potential for miscommunication between faculty and archives staff when mentoring undergraduate research in the archives, see Peter J. Wosh, Janet Bunde, Karen Murphy, and Chelsea Blacker, "University Archives and Educational Partnerships: Three Perspectives," *Archival Issues* 31, no. 1 (2007).

21. Jen Rajchel and Theresa R. Snyder, "The Thing Was Done in the Library: Animating an Early Eighteenth-Century Murder Mystery," *College & Undergraduate Libraries* 23, no. 2 (July 2016).

22. David Mazella and Julie Grob, "Collaborations."

23. Sarah Arkebauer et al., "Crazy for Pamela in the Rare Books Library: Undergraduates Reflect on Doing Original Research in Special Collections," in *Past or Portal: Enhancing Undergraduate Learning through Special Collections and Archives*, ed. Eleanor Mitchell, Peggy Seiden, and Suzy Taraba (Chicago: Association of College and Research Libraries, 2012), 53.

24. The Newberry Library describes itself as committed to democratic principles

through both preservation and public programming. "About," Newberry Library (website), accessed February 4, 2018, https://www.newberry.org/about.

25. Christopher J. Prom defends the value of an archive in a digital age to "preserve democratic institutions, sustain civil society, or ensure social justice"; see his "Reimagining Academic Archives," in *Hacking the Academy: New Approaches to Scholarship and Teaching from Digital Humanities*, ed. Daniel J. Cohen and Tom Scheinfeldt (Ann Arbor: University of Michigan Press, 2013), 146.

26. Generally speaking, the distinctive quality of public scholarship (as opposed to, for instance, engaged learning) is that it is academic research with a public purpose, value, or audience. The terminology here is fluid; Kathleen Woodward notes of researchers in this field, "What different terms do they deploy to describe themselves? Public scholar. Activist scholar. Scholar-activist. Scholarly producer. Scholar-citizen. Scholar-advocate. Academic-activist. Public activist-scholar. Public intellectual. The term 'applied humanities' also appears"; see her "The Future of the Humanities—in the Present and in Public," *Daedalus* 138, no. 1 (Winter 2009): 115. In short, the term describes scholars (and in this case, students) who engage with a broader community not through service or teaching, but directly through research and scholarship.

27. See Michelle Caswell, "Teaching to Dismantle White Supremacy in the Archives," *Library Quarterly* 87, no. 3 (2017).

28. "Bughouse Square Debates," the Newberry Library (website), accessed January 31, 2018, https://www.newberry.org/bughouse-square-debates.

29. We also included more traditional ways of building a scaffold for student research in the archives, such as orientations with various specialists on staff (including a favorite session on the map collections), along with informal, exploratory assignments that we called Getting into the Stacks. These short, low-stakes writing assignments were intended to help students have structured serendipity in the library, stumbling upon resources that they might not otherwise have found. For example, we told them to find an item with duplicate versions, compare them, and explain the value of having multiple versions; to choose a term related to our seminar or their individual research, find entries for it in multiple dictionaries or encyclopedias, and prepare a bibliography with five or more other resources on it; or to describe the publishing and accession history of one item in the Newberry's collection.

30. David Cooper defines the liberal arts and defends the humanities in his book *Learning in the Plural: Essays on the Humanities and Public Life* (East Lansing: Michigan State University Press, 2014), 65–66 and 86–87. On the digital liberal arts, see William Pannapacker, "No More Digitally Challenged Liberal Arts Majors," *Chronicle of Higher Education*, November 18, 2013, https://www.chronicle.com/article/No-More -Digitally-Challenged/143079?cid=wc&utm_medium=en&utm_source=wc.

31. Gardner Campbell, "A Personal Cyberinfrastructure," in *Hacking the Academy: New Approaches to Scholarship and Teaching from Digital Humanities*, ed. Daniel J. Cohen and Tom Scheinfeldt (Ann Arbor: University of Michigan Press, 2013), 100.

32. Kathleen Fitzpatrick, "Open-Access Publishing," in *Hacking the Academy: New Approaches to Scholarship and Teaching from Digital Humanities*, ed. Daniel J. Cohen and Tom Scheinfeldt (Ann Arbor: University of Michigan Press, 2013), 36.

33. "The problem, of course," Fitzpatrick continues, "is that the more we close our work away from the public, and the more we refuse to engage in dialogue with them, the more we undermine that public's willingness to fund our research and our institutions. Closing our work away from the public . . . might protect us from public criticism, but it can't protect us from public apathy." Fitzpatrick, "Open-Access Publishing," 36.

34. Teresa Mangum, "Going Public: From the Perspective of the Classroom," *Pedagogy: Critical Approaches to Teaching Literature, Language, Composition, and Culture* 12, no. 1 (Winter 2012): 5. Echoing Mangum's critique of viewing the humanities as merely "problematizing," Helen Small similarly rejects framing the humanities as mere "critique": "Both criticism and 'critique,' whatever their particular valency, omit a great deal. The work of the humanities is frequently descriptive, or appreciative, or imaginative, or provocative, or speculative, more than it is critical. It includes ways of attending to objects of study that are, variously, technical, aesthetically evaluative, curatorial. Its public purposes can include maintaining and reanimating knowledge of the cultural heritage, explication of the products and processes of culture, the stimulation of public curiosity in new subjects—again, not primarily critical activities." Small, *The Value of the Humanities*, 26.

35. Woodward, "The Future of the Humanities," 123.

36. John Unsworth, "The Crisis of Audience and the Open-Access Solution," in *Hacking the Academy: New Approaches to Scholarship and Teaching from Digital Humanities*, ed. Daniel J. Cohen and Tom Scheinfeldt (Ann Arbor: University of Michigan Press, 2013), 30–34.

37. Robert Darnton, *The Case for Books: Past, Present, and Future* (New York: PublicAffairs, 2010), 13.

38. Alison Byerly, "Digital Humanities, Digitizing Humanity," *EduCause Review*, May 19, 2014, https://er.educause.edu/articles/2014/5/digital-humanities-digitizing -humanity.

39. The Shelley-Godwin Archive, http://shelleygodwinarchive.org; Mapping the Republic of Letters, http://republicofletters.stanford.edu; Commonplace Cultures, http:// commonplacecultures.org; Locating London's Past, https://www.locatinglondon.org /index.html; The Eighteenth-Century Common, http://www.18thcenturycommon .org/; The Electronic Enlightenment, http://www.e-enlightenment.com; What Jane Saw, http://www.whatjanesaw.org/; A Sentimental Journey, http://enec3120.neatline -uva.org/neatline/show/a-sentimental-journey; the Grinnell *Beowulf*, https://digital .grinnell.edu/islandora/object/grinnell:3615#page/1/mode/2up; Through Time, http:// acadblogs.wheatoncollege.edu/wmst-101-f13; Crytek Off the Map, https://www.you tube.com/watch?v=SPY-hr-8-Mo&feature=youtu.be; The Great Chicago Fire, https://

www.greatchicagofire.org; Realizing the Newberry Idea, http://publications.newberry
.org/digitalexhibitions/exhibits/show/realizingthenewberryidea/welcome.

40. Tess Henthorne, "Uncovering the Unpublished: Construction, Publication, and Exploration of Gladys Fornell's *Montel*" (unpublished manuscript, December 5, 2014).

41. Lindsay Hansard, "The Faulkner-Cowley Dynamic (webpage)," last modified 2014, http://hansard.wix.com/faulkner-cowley.

42. Lindsay Hansard, "'Maybe Happen Is Never Once': How Malcolm Cowley's Approach to the Benjy Section of *The Sound and the Fury* Undermines Faulkner's Message about Time" (unpublished paper, December 5, 2014).

43. Hansard, "'Maybe Happen Is Never Once.'"

44. Meredith Carroll, "Punch's Apes and Darwin's Bulldog: Making Natural Knowledge at the Dawn of Darwinism" (unpublished paper, December 5, 2014).

45. Meredith Carroll, "Origins" (blog post, last modified 2014, http://origins1859
.weebly.com).

46. For an example of this uneasy relationship between academia and activism, especially when that activism critiques the academy itself, see Kelly J. Baker, "Am I an Activist?" *ChronicleVitae*, March 26, 2015, https://chroniclevitae.com/news/952-am-i
-an-activist?cid=at&utm_source=at&utm_medium=en.

47. See Dill Pickle Club Records, 1906–1941. The Newberry Library, Chicago.

48. Gregory A. Sprague, "Chicago Gay and Lesbian History Project," Gregory Sprague Papers, 1972–1987, Chicago History Museum, Chicago.

49. John D'Emilio, "Rethinking Queer History: Or, Richard Nixon, Gay Liberationist?" in *Out in Chicago: LGBT History at the Crossroads*, ed. Jill Austin and Jennifer Brier (Chicago: Chicago History Museum, 2011), 96–97.

50. John D'Emilio, "Rethinking Queer History: Or, Richard Nixon, Gay Liberationist?," in *Out in Chicago: LGBT History at the Crossroads*, ed. Jill Austin and Jennifer Brier (Chicago: Chicago History Museum, 2011), 96–97.

51. Ai Miller, "Sometimes You Have to Shoot the Storyteller in the Neck: Reexamining the Role of the Dill Pickle Club in the Queer Community of the Near North Side, 1920–1935" (unpublished paper, December 5, 2014).

CHAPTER 5

1. Elisa Shearer and Jeffrey Gottfried, "News Use across Social Media Platforms," Pew Research Center (website), September 7, 2017, http://www.journalism.org/2017
/09/07/news-use-across-social-media-platforms-2017/.

2. Jonathan Swift, "Battel of the Books," *The Essential Writings of Jonathan Swift*, ed. Claude Rawson and Ian Higgins (New York: Norton, 2010), 102.

3. L'Estrange was officially appointed Surveyor of the Imprimury in 1663 and subsequently as Licenser of the Press until the lapsing of the Print Act in 1679. For more on L'Estrange, see Harold Love, "L'Estrange, Sir Roger," in the *Oxford Dictionary of*

National Biography (Oxford: Oxford University Press, 2004), https://doi.org/10.1093/ref:odnb/16514, and Adrian Johns, *The Nature of the Book: Print and Knowledge in the Making* (Chicago: University of Chicago Press, 1998), 234-235.

4. Peter Stallybrass, "'Little Jobs': Broadsides and the Printing Revolution," in *Agent of Change: Print Culture Studies after Elizabeth L. Eisenstein*, ed. Sabrina Alcorn Baron, Eric N. Lindquist, and Eleanor F. Shevlin (Amherst: University of Massachusetts Press, 2007), 315.

5. Jonathan Swift, "A Tale of a Tub," in *The Essential Writings of Jonathan Swift*, ed. Claude Rawson and Ian Higgins (New York: Norton, 2010), 16-17. Hereafter cited in the text.

6. For background on Swift's contribution to the ancient/modern debate, see, among others, Carole Fabricant, "The Battle of the Ancients and (Post)Moderns: Rethinking Swift through Contemporary Perspectives," *The Eighteenth Century: Theory and Interpretation* 32, no. 3 (Autumn 1991); Frank T. Boyle, *Swift as Nemesis: Modernity and Its Satirist* (Stanford: Stanford University Press, 2000); and Ashley Marshall, "Swift and the Historians, Ancient and Modern," in *Swift and History: Politics and the English Past* (Cambridge: Cambridge University Press, 2015).

7. Johns, *The Nature of the Book*, 230.

8. Johns, *The Nature of the Book*, 234.

9. For more on the lapsing of the Licensing Act, see Raymond Astbury, "The Renewal of the Licensing Act in 1693 and Its Lapse in 1695," *Library* 33, no. 4 (December 1978). For Swift's early satires in the context of the lapsing of the act and its connection to the potential for civil war, see Randy Robertson, "Swift's 'Leviathan' and the End of Licensing," *Pacific Coast Philology* 40, no. 2 (2005): 42-43. For more on the state of print culture during Swift's composition of the "Tale," see Katie Lanning, "'Fitted to the Humour of the Age': Alteration and Print in Swift's *A Tale of a Tub*," *Eighteenth-Century Fiction* 26, no. 4 (Summer 2014).

10. Although most students can speak to their experiences with such contemporary media practices without secondary sources, a useful overview of this phenomenon is offered by Jeffrey P. Jones, "The 'New' News as No 'News': US Cable News Channels as Branded Political Entertainment Television," *Media International Australia* 144, no. 1 (August 1, 2012), http://mediaandsocialidentity.com/wp-content/uploads/2013/12/No-news-as-news-Jones.pdf.

11. To the extent that this term has been used by scholars of reading, it has referred either to online reading in general or to reading online as part of social networks. I revise this term to consider analog and digital reading practices together and use the term "network" to encourage discussions of multiple agents of production and meaning-making, aligned with Darnton's concept of the communications circuit. See, for instance, Roger Osborne and Cherie Allan, "Networked Reading: Using Austlit to Assist Reading and Understanding of Texts from the Past," *English in Australia* 47, no. 2 (2012), https://eprints.qut.edu.au/54220/1/Networked_Reading_EnglishinAustralia%5B1%5D.pdf.

12. Gérard Genette, *Palimpsests: Literature in the Second Degree*, trans. Channa Newman and Claude Doubinsky (Lincoln: University of Nebraska Press, 1997), 5. Here I refer to Robert Darnton's influential concept of the communications circuit in book history. See Darnton, "What Is the History of Books?" *Daedalus* 111, no. 3 (Summer 1982): 68.

13. Elizabeth L. Eisenstein, *The Printing Press as an Agent of Change* (Cambridge: Cambridge University Press, 1980), 137.

14. See, for instance, Matthew Kirschenbaum, "What Is Digital Humanities and What's It Doing in English Departments?" *ADE Bulletin* 150 (2010): 55, https://www.ade.mla.org/content/download/7914/225677. See also William Pannapacker, "Stop Calling it Digital Humanities," *Chronicle of Higher Education*, February 18, 2013, https://www.chronicle.com/article/Stop-Calling-It-Digital/137325.

15. Alan Liu, "The Meaning of the Digital Humanities," *PMLA* 128, no. 2 (March 2013): 409.

16. William Pannapacker, "Cultivating Partnerships in the Digital Humanities," *Chronicle of Higher Education*, May 13, 2013, https://www.chronicle.com/article/Cultivating-Partnerships-in/139161.

17. Kirschenbaum, "What Is . . . English Departments?" 58, 59.

18. Kirschenbaum, "What Is . . . English Departments?" 59.

19. Laurie Grobman and Roberta Rosenberg, *Service Learning and Literary Studies in English* (New York: MLA, 2015), 26.

20. Amanda Phillips, "#transformDH — A Call to Action Following ASA 2011 (blog post)," HASTAC (website), October 26, 2011, https://www.hastac.org/blogs/amanda-phillips/2011/10/26/transformdh-call-action-following-asa-2011. For more on digital humanities and social justice, see Angela David Nieves, "Digital Humanities + Social Justice = 'Does Not Compute?' " (blog post), Victoria2011.thatcamp.org, June 9, 2011, http://victoria2011.thatcamp.org/06/09/digital-humanities-social-justice-does-not-compute/.

21. Jessie Daniels and Polly Thiselthwaite, *Being a Scholar in the Digital Era: Transforming Scholarly Practice for the Public Good* (Chicago: Policy Press for the University of Bristol Press, 2016), loc. 272 of 3230, Kindle.

22. Liu, "The Meaning of the Digital," 409.

23. See, for instance, Franco Moretti, *Distant Reading* (New York: Verso, 2013), 48, in which he represents the limits of the canon.

24. Katherine Bode, "The Equivalence of 'Close' and 'Distant' Reading; or, Toward a New Object for Data-Rich Literary History," *Modern Language Quarterly* 78, no. 1 (March 2017): 91. Matthew L. Jockers uses a data-mining metaphor to explain how these bifurcated reading practices are complementary, not antagonistic: "Close reading, traditional searching, will continue to reveal nuggets, while the deeper veins lie buried beneath the mass of gravel layered above. What are required are methods for aggregating and making sense out of both the nuggets and the tailings . . . to unearth, for

the first time, what these corpora really contain." Matthew L. Jockers, *Macroanalysis: Digital Methods and Literary History* (Urbana: University of Illinois Press, 2013), 9–10.

25. For more on clustering, see "keyphrase_clustering," Github (website), accessed February 18, 2018, https://github.com/dhfbk/keyphrase_clustering.

26. "What Is 18thConnect?" 18thconnect.org, accessed February 18, 2018, http://www.18thconnect.org/about/what-is-18thconnect/.

27. "Welcome to TypeWright," 18thConnect.org, accessed February 18, 2018, http://www.18thconnect.org/typewright/documents ref.

28. English Short Title Catalogue, http://estc.bl.uk.

29. Some excellent references for eighteenth-century bibliographic and typographic terms can be found in John Carter and Nicolas Barker, *ABC for Book Collectors* (New Castle, DE: Oak Knoll Press, 2004), and D. C. Greetham, *Textual Scholarship: An Introduction* (New York: Routledge, 1994).

30. Jürgen Habermas, *The Structural Transformation of the Public Sphere: An Inquiry into a Category of Bourgeois Society*, trans. Thomas Burger (Cambridge, MA: MIT Press, 1991); Michael McKeon, *The Secret History of Domesticity* (Baltimore: Johns Hopkins University Press, 2005); Simon Varey, *Space and the Eighteenth-Century English Novel* (New York: Cambridge University Press, 1990); Cynthia Wall, *The Literary and Cultural Spaces of Restoration London* (New York: Cambridge University Press, 1998).

31. Edward Soja, *Seeking Spatial Justice* (Minneapolis: University of Minnesota Press, 2010).

32. Laetitia Montague, *The Housewife. Being a Most Useful Assistant in All Domestic Concerns, Whether in a Town or Country Situation* (London, 1785), 34–35.

33. Jonathan Swift, *Gulliver's Travels*, ed. Allan Ingram (Guelph and Peterborough, ON: Broadview Press, 2012), 333.

34. Swift, *Gulliver's Travels*, 289.

35. Swift, *Gulliver's Travels*, 309.

36. For more on the concept of the thinkable, see David Scott Kastan, *Shakespeare after Theory* (New York: Routledge, 1999), 50.

37. Mary Shelley, *Frankenstein*, ed. D. L. MacDonald and Kathleen Scherf (Guelph and Peterborough, ON: Broadview Press, 1999), 88.

38. "Blindness Solutions: JAWS," Freedom Scientific (website), accessed February 5, 2018, http://www.freedomscientific.com/Products/Blindness/JAWS.

39. Daniels and Thiselthwaite, *Being a Scholar*, loc. 307 of 3230, Kindle.

40. Gregory Jay, "The Engaged Humanities: Principles and Practices for Public Scholarship and Teaching," *Journal of Community Engagement and Scholarship* 3, no.1 (2010).

41. Networked Infrastructure for Nineteenth-Century Electronic Scholarship (NINES), www.nines.org.

42. See, for instance, Medieval Electronic Scholarly Alliance, www.mesa-medieval

.org; Modernist Networks, www.modnets.org; and Studies in Radicalism Online, www .studiesinradicalism.org.

43. For the Early Modern OCR Project (EMOP), see http://emop.tamu.edu. For more information on TypeWright, see www.18thConnect.org/typewright/documents.

44. Videos on how to use TypeWright are available on YouTube: http://bit.ly/2E 4i6wO.

45. The Advanced Research Consortium (www.ar-c.org), the overarching organization supporting NINES, 18thConnect, MESA, and Studies in Radicalism Online, is located at Texas A&M University, which has been awarded an NHPRC-Mellon Digital Publishing Cooperatives Grant to develop the ARCScholar Publishing Cooperative. Users of TypeWright have asked for help publishing their digital editions, and this organization will make that possible.

46. EMOP's OCR is better and worse than Gale's, in various instances, but a particular method developed by eMOP founder Mandell helps.

CHAPTER 6

1. "Project Gutenberg Mission Statement," Project Gutenberg (website), last modified December 25, 2007, https://www.gutenberg.org/wiki/Gutenberg:Project_Guten berg_Mission_Statement_by_Michael_Hart.

2. Katherine Bode, "The Equivalence of 'Close' and 'Distant' Reading; or, Toward a New Object for Data-Rich Literary History," *Modern Language Quarterly* 78, no. 1 (March 2017): 79.

3. Yin Liu, "Ways of Reading, Models for Text, and the Usefulness of Dead People," *Scholarly and Research Communication* 5, no. 2 (2014), http://src-online.ca/index.php /src/article/view/148/293.

4. See, for instance, Andreas van Cranenberg, "Rich Statistical Parsing and Literary Language" (PhD diss., University of Amsterdam, 2016), https://pure.uva.nl/ws /files/2717528/177511_Cranenburgh_phdthesis_complete.pdf.

5. Jessie Daniels and Polly Thiselthwaite, *Being a Scholar in the Digital Era: Transforming Scholarly Practice for the Public Good* (Chicago: Policy Press for the University of Bristol, 2016), loc. 163 of 3230, Kindle.

6. Daniels and Thiselthwaite, *Being a Scholar*, loc. 163, 170 of 3230, Kindle.

7. The digital edition is accessible at http://thecountessofdellwyn.weebly.com/.

8. Quoted in Daniels and Thiselthwaite, *Being a Scholar*, loc. 272 of 3230, Kindle.

9. Gérard Genette, *Palimpsests: Literature in the Second Degree*, trans. Channa Newman and Claude Dobinsky (Lincoln: University of Nebraska Press, 1997); Julia Kristeva, *Desire in Language: A Semiotic Approach to Literature and Art*, ed. Leon S. Roudiez, trans. Thomas Gora and Alice A. Jardine (New York: Columbia University Press, 1982).

10. Daniels and Thiselthwaite, *Being a Scholar*, loc. 2113 of 3230, Kindle.

11. Susan Carlile, *Masters of the Marketplace: British Women Novelists of the 1750s*

(Bethlehem, PA: Lehigh University Press, 2010); Sara Gadaken, "Managing and Marketing Virtue in Sarah Fielding's *History of the Countess of Dellwyn*," *Eighteenth-Century Fiction* 15, no. 1 (October 2002); Kate Rumbold, "Shakespeare's 'Propriety' and the Mid-Eighteenth-Century Novel: Sarah Fielding's *The History of the Countess of Dellwyn*," in *Reading 1759: Literary Culture in Mid-Eighteenth-Century Britain and France*, ed. Shaun Regan (Lewisburg: Bucknell, 2013); Betty A. Schellenberg, "Bluestockings and the Genealogy of the Modern Novel," *University of Toronto Quarterly* 79, no. 4 (Fall 2013).

12. Henry Thomas Kitchener, *Letters on Marriage, on the Causes of Matrimonial Infidelity, and on the Reciprocal Relations of the Sexes* (London, 1812).

13. ENGL 630DW assignment prompt, last updated 13 February 2014, http://scalar .usc.edu/works/engl-630dw/assignment.

14. Ellen E. Jarosz and Stephen Kutay, "Guided Resource Inquiries: Integrating Archives into Course Learning and Information Literacy Objectives," *Communications in Information Literacy* 11, no. 1 (2017).

15. Jarosz and Kutay, "Guided Resource Inquiries," 217.

16. Public humanities are defined by Wikipedia contributors as the work of cultural organizations interested in engaging publics in conversations. Because of the expansive definition of the discipline, national agencies and professionals host events solely to showcase the many methods and practices of public humanities. The Academic Council of Learned Societies (ACLS) hosts a fellowship program dedicated to placing scholars in a multitude of venues as public fellows, while Brown University's Center for Public Humanities hosted an entire Day of Public Humanities to showcase the different methods of public humanities practitioners across the nation. See "Public Humanities," Wikipedia, accessed November 18, 2017, https://en.wikipedia.org/wiki/Public _humanities; for ACLS's Public Fellows Program, see https://www.acls.org/programs /publicfellows/; and for Day of Public Humanities, see the National Council on Public History (NCPH) blog, http://ncph.org/history-at-work/day-of-public-humanities/.

17. Educational studies from multiple disciplines show the importance of student attitudes in the classroom. See, for example, Matthew Lovelace and Peggy Brickman, "Best Practices for Measuring Students' Attitudes toward Learning Science," *CBE Life Sciences Education* 12, no. 4 (2013), https://www.ncbi.nlm.nih.gov/pmc/articles /PMC3846512/. See also Mandy L. Sedden and Kevin R. Clark, "Motivating Students in the 21st Century," *Radiologic Technology* 87, no. 6 (2016); Bryan J. Hains and Brittany Smith, "Student-Centered Course Design: Empowering Students to Become Self-Directed Learners," *Journal of Experiential Education* 35, no. 2 (2012); and Lonnie Rowell and Eunsook Hong, "Academic Motivation: Concepts, Strategies, and Counseling Approaches," *Professional School Counseling* 16, no. 3 (2013).

18. Patricia Bizzell and Bruce Herzberg argue for the importance of teaching research as a social act; see their "Research as a Social Act," *The Clearing House* 60, no. 7 (1987).

19. For information on the statistics of Wikipedia consumption, see Mostafa Mesgari et al., " 'The Sum of All Human Knowledge': A Systematic Review of Scholarly Research on the Content of Wikipedia," *Journal of the Association for Information Science and Technology* 66, no. 2 (2015).

20. https://en.wikipedia.org/wiki/Wikipedia:Meetup/Art_and_Social_Justice.

21. Recommended readings include Jeff Loveland and Joseph Reagle, "Wikipedia and Encyclopedic Production," *New Media and Society* 15, no. 8 (2013); Claudia Wagner et al., "It's a Man's Wikipedia? Assessing Gender Inequality in an Online Encyclopedia," *International AAAI Conference on Web and Social Media* (preprint, submitted March 23, 2015), https://arxiv.org/pdf/1501.06307.pdf.

22. For more on the unequal representation of women and minorities in Wikipedia, see Ewa S. Callahan and Susan C. Herring, "Cultural Bias in Wikipedia Content on Famous Persons," *Journal of the Association for Information Science and Technology* 62, no. 10 (2011).

23. The late Adrianne Wadewitz, a digital humanist and scholar of eighteenth-century literature, was one of the first to recognize Wikipedia as a significant medium for scholarly work in our field. To honor her legacy, colleagues in eighteenth-century studies routinely host an edit-a-thon featuring eighteenth-century media at our annual conference, the American Society for Eighteenth-Century Studies. See, for instance, https://en.wikipedia.org/wiki/Wikipedia:Wadewitz_Tribute_Edit-a-thons.

24. Classroom Salon (website), accessed February 5, 2018, https://www.corporate salon.com.

25. Claire Lamont, "Annotating a Text: Literary Theory and Electronic Hypertext," *Electronic Text: Investigations in Method and Theory*, ed. Katheryn Sutherland (New York: Oxford University Press, 1998), 54.

26. Alice Walker, "Principles of Annotation: Some Suggestions for Editors of Shakespeare," *Studies in Bibliography* 9 (1957): 105.

27. Martin Battestin, "A Rationale of Literary Annotations: The Example of Fielding's Novels," *Studies in Bibliography* 34 (1981): 20.

28. For information on TEI Guidelines, see http://www.tei-c.org/index.xml.

29. For information on Lexos, see https://wheatoncollege.edu/academics/special -projects-initiatives/lexomics/lexos-installers/; for stylometric analyses, see https://sites .google.com/site/computationalstylistics/ and http://mallet.cs.umass.edu.

30. "The Countess of Dellwyn," Wikipedia, accessed February 5, 2018, https:// en.wikipedia.org/wiki/The_History_of_the_Countess_of_Dellwyn.

CONCLUSION

1. Whitney Mannies, "Yes, in the U.S., the People Can Reject a President—If They Are Sure He's a Tyrant," *Washington Post*, November 22, 2016, https://www .washingtonpost.com/news/monkey-cage/wp/2016/11/22/yes-in-the-u-s-the-people -can-reject-a-president-if-theyre-convinced-hes-a-tyrant/?utm_term=.371128de0ad2.

2. Jess Zimmerman, "The Myth of the Well-Behaved Women's March," *The New Republic*, January 24, 2017, https://newrepublic.com/article/140065/myth-well-behaved-womens-march.

3. Cassie da Costa, " 'Make Art, and Fight the Power': A Historically Black National Book Awards," *The New Yorker*, 17 November 2016, www.newyorker.com/books/page-turner/joy-is-an-act-of-resistance-a-historically-black-national-book-awards.

4. da Costa, " 'Make Art, and Fight the Power.' "

5. Wayne Au, Bill Bigelow, and Stan Karp, "Introduction: Creating Classrooms for Equity and Social Justice," in *Rethinking Our Classrooms: Teaching for Equity and Justice*, ed. Wayne Au, Bill Bigelow, and Stan Karp (Milwaukee, WI: Rethinking Schools, Ltd., 2007).

6. Claudia Rankine, *Citizen: An American Lyric* (Minneapolis: Graywolf Press, 2015).

7. György Lukács, *The Theory of the Novel*, trans. Anna Bostock (Cambridge, MA: MIT Press, 1971), 88.

8. For more information about the Bringing Theory to Practice grant, see https://www.bttop.org/.

BIBLIOGRAPHY
熱 深

Alighieri, Dante. *Inferno*. Translated by John Ciardi. New York: Signet Classics, 2001.

Anderson, Robert. Introduction to *Enlightening the British: Knowledge, Discovery and the Museum in the Eighteenth Century*, edited by R. G. W. Anderson, M. L. Caygill, A. G. Macgregor, and L. Syson, 1–4. London: British Museum Press, 2003.

Aphra Behn Online Public. http://www.aphrabehn.org/ABO/.

Arkebauer, Sarah, Toni Bowers, Lauren Corallo, Eoin Ennis, Rivka Fogel, Jessica Kim, Michael Masciandaro, John Pollack, Tatum Regan, Tyler Russell, Sandra Sohn, Marykate Stopa, Jessica Sutro, and Valeria Tsygankova. "Crazy for Pamela in the Rare Books Library: Undergraduates Reflect on Doing Original Research in Special Collections." In *Past or Portal: Enhancing Undergraduate Learning through Special Collections and Archives*, edited by Eleanor Mitchell, Peggy Seiden, and Suzy Taraba, 53–70. Chicago: Association of College and Research Libraries, 2012.

Astbury, Raymond. "The Renewal of the Licensing Act in 1693 and Its Lapse in 1695." *Library* 33, no. 4 (December 1978): 296–322.

Au, Wayne, Bill Bigelow, and Stan Karp. "Introduction: Creating Classrooms for Equity and Social Justice." In *Rethinking Our Classrooms: Teaching for Equity and Justice*, edited by Wayne Au, Bill Bigelow, and Stan Karp, x–xi. Milwaukee, WI: Rethinking Schools, Ltd., 2007.

Austen, Jane. *Emma*. Edited by Richard Cronin and Dorothy McMillin. New York: Cambridge University Press, 2005.

———. *Emma*. 4th ed. Edited by George Justice. New York: Norton, 2012.

———. *Mansfield Park*. Edited by Claudia L. Johnson. New York: Norton, 1998.

———. *Northanger Abbey*. Edited by Claire Grogan. Guelph and Peterborough, ON: Broadview Press, 2004.

———. *Northanger Abbey*. Edited by Susan Fraiman. New York: Norton, 2004.

———. *Pride and Prejudice*. 3rd ed. Edited by Donald Gray and Mary A. Favret. New York: Norton, 2000.

Austen-Leigh, James Edward. *A Memoir of Jane Austen*. London: R. Bentley, 1870. New York: Oxford University Press, 2002. Page references are to the 2002 edition.

Authentic Copies of the Codicils Belonging to the Last Will and Testament of Sir Hans Sloane, Bart. deceased, Which relate to his Collection of Books and Curiosities.

London: Printed, by Order of the Executors, by Daniel Crowne, near Temple-Bar, 1753, https://catalog.hathitrust.org/Record/101823623.

Ayscough, Samuel. *Catalogue of the Manuscripts Preserved in the British Museum Hitherto Undescribed: Consisting of Five Thousand Volumes; Including the Collections of Sir Hans Sloane, Bart., the Rev. Thomas Birch, D. D., and about Five Hundred Volumes Bequeathed, Presented, or Purchased at Various Times.* London: John Rivington, 1782.

Bahde, Anne. "'Oh, Wow!': Assessment and Affective Learning in Special Collections and Archives." In *New Directions for Special Collections: An Anthology of Practice*, edited by Lynne M. Thomas and Beth M. Whittaker, 31–38. Santa Barbara, CA: Libraries Unlimited, 2017.

Baillie, Joanna. "Sunset Meditation, Under the Apprehension of Approaching Blindness." In *A Collection of Poems, Chiefly Manuscript, and from Living Authors*, edited by Joanna Baillie, 227–229. London: Longman, Hurst, Rees, Orme, and Brown, 1823.

Baker, Kelly J. "Am I an Activist?" *Chronicle Vitae*, March 26, 2015, https://chronicle vitae.com/news/952-am-i-an-activist?cid=at&utm_source=at&utm_medium=en.

Barber, Benjamin R., and Richard Battistoni. "A Season of Service: Introducing Service Learning into the Liberal Arts Curriculum." *PS: Political Science and Politics* 26, no. 2 (June 1993): 235–240.

Bartel, Anna Sims. "Talking and Walking: Literary Work as Public Work." In *Community-Based Learning and the Work of Literature*, edited by Susan Danielson and Ann Marie Fallon, 81–102. Bolton, MA: Anker, 2007.

Battestin, Martin. "A Rationale of Literary Annotations: The Example of Fielding's Novels." *Studies in Bibliography* 34 (1981): 1–22.

Benedict, Barbara M. "Collecting Trouble: Sir Hans Sloane's Literary Reputation in Eighteenth-Century Britain." *Eighteenth-Century Life* 36, no. 2 (Spring 2012): 111–142.

Beowulf. Grinnell, IA: Grinnell College. https://digital.grinnell.edu/islandora/object /grinnell:3615#page/1/mode/2up.

Bernstein, Susan David. *Roomscape: Women Writers in the British Museum from George Eliot to Virginia Woolf*. Edinburgh: Edinburgh University Press, 2013.

Bizzell, Patricia, and Bruce Herzberg. "Research as a Social Act." *The Clearing House* 60, no. 7 (1987): 303–306.

Bode, Katherine. "The Equivalence of 'Close' and 'Distant' Reading; or, Toward a New Object for Data-Rich Literary History." *Modern Language Quarterly* 78, no. 1 (March 2017): 77–106.

Booth, Alison. *Homes and Haunts: Touring Writers' Shrines and Countries*. New York: Oxford University Press, 2016.

Boyle, Frank T. *Swift as Nemesis: Modernity and Its Satirist*. Stanford: Stanford University Press, 2000.

British Museum. *Statutes and Rules Relating to the Inspection and Use of the British Museum*. London: Dryden Leach, 1759. https://archive.org/details/statutesrules reloobrit.

Brooks, Peter, and Hilary Jewett, eds. *The Humanities and Public Life*. New York: Fordham University Press, 2014.

"Bughouse Square Debates." Newberry Library (website). Accessed January 31, 2018. https://www.newberry.org/bughouse-square-debates.

Burgett, Bruce, and Glenn Hendler, eds. *Keywords for American Cultural Studies*. New York: NYU Press, 2007.

Burns, Nancy, Kay Lehman Schlozman, and Sidney Verba. *The Private Roots of Public Action: Gender, Equality, and Political Participation*. Cambridge: Harvard University Press, 2001.

Burstein, Andrew, and Catherine Mowbray. "Jefferson and Sterne." *Early American Literature* 29, no. 1 (1994): 19-34. http://www.jstor.org/stable/25056954.

Butler, Marilyn. *Jane Austen and the War of Ideas*. New York: Oxford University Press, 1988.

Byerly, Alison. "Digital Humanities, Digitizing Humanity." *EduCause Review*. May 19, 2014. https://er.educause.edu/articles/2014/5/digital-humanities-digitizing -humanity.

Byron, George Gordon. *Childe Harold's Pilgrimage: Canto IV* (stanzas 140-41). *The Oxford Authors: Byron*, ed. Jerome J. McGann, 188-189. Oxford: Oxford University Press, 1986.

Cairns, Suse. "Do New Technologies Democratise Museum Collections, or Reinforce Conservative Values?" *Museum Geek: Exploring Museums, Technology, and Ideas* (blog). January 21, 2014. https://museumgeek.xyz/2014/01/21/do-new-technologies -democratise-museum-collections-or-reinforce-conservative-values/.

Caizza, Amy. "Don't Bowl at Night: Gender, Safety, and Civic Participation." *Signs: Journal of Women in Culture and Society* 30, no. 2 (2005): 1607-1631.

Calderwood, Eric. "Study Abroad." *Harvard Review* 40 (2011): 210-218.

Callahan, Ewa S., and Susan C. Herring. "Cultural Bias in Wikipedia Content on Famous Persons." *Journal of the Association for Information Science and Technology* 62, no. 10 (2011): 1899-1915.

Campbell, Gardner. "A Personal Cyberinfrastructure." In *Hacking the Academy: New Approaches to Scholarship and Teaching from Digital Humanities*, edited by Daniel J. Cohen and Tom Scheinfeldt, 100-104. Ann Arbor: University of Michigan Press, 2013.

Carlile, Susan, ed. *Masters of the Marketplace: British Women Novelists of the 1750s*. Bethlehem, PA: Lehigh University Press, 2010.

Carroll, Meredith. "Punch's Apes and Darwin's Bulldog: Making Natural Knowledge at the Dawn of Darwinism." Unpublished paper, December 5, 2014.

Carter, John, and Nicolas Barker. *ABC for Book Collectors*. New Castle, DE: Oak Knoll Press, 2004.

Caswell, Michelle. "Teaching to Dismantle White Supremacy in the Archives." *Library Quarterly* 87, no. 3 (2017): 222–235.

Cavendish, Margaret. *The Description of a New World, Called the Blazing World and Other Writings*. N.p., 1666.

Clark, Roger, ed. *Jane Austen's Geographies*. New York: Routledge, 2018.

Clough, Wayne. "Best of Both Worlds: Museums, Libraries, and Archives in a Digital Age." Smithsonian Institution (website). Accessed February 4, 2018. http://www .si.edu/content/gwc/BestofBothWorldsSmithsonian.pdf.

Cohen, Daniel J., and Tom Scheinfeldt, eds. *Hacking the Academy: New Approaches to Scholarship and Teaching from Digital Humanities*. Ann Arbor: University of Michigan Press, 2013.

Collier, Peter J., and Dilafruz R. Williams. "Reflection in Action: The Learning-Doing Relationship." In *Learning through Serving: A Student Guidebook for Service-Learning across the Disciplines*, edited by Christine M. Cress, Peter Collier, and Vicki Reintenauer, 83–97. Sterling, VA: Stylus, 2005.

Commonplace Cultures. http://commonplacecultures.org.

Cooper, David D. *Learning in the Plural: Essays on the Humanities and Public Life*. East Lansing: Michigan State University Press, 2014.

Countess of Dellwyn Digitization Project. http://thecountessofdellwyn.weebly.com/.

Cowtan, Robert. *Memories of The British Museum*. London: Richard Bentley and Son, 1872.

Cress, Christine M., Peter Collier, and Vicki Reintenauer, eds. *Learning through Serving: A Student Guidebook for Service-Learning across the Disciplines*. Sterling, VA: Stylus, 2005.

Crytek Off the Map, https://www.youtube.com/watch?v=SPY-hr-8-M0&feature =youtu.be.

Cushman, Ellen. "The Public Intellectual, Service Learning, and Activist Research." *College English* 61, no. 3 (January 1999): 328–336.

da Costa, Cassie. "'Make Art, and Fight the Power': A Historically Black National Book Awards." *The New Yorker*, November 17, 2016. www.newyorker.com/books /page-turner/joy-is-an-act-of-resistance-a-historically-black-national-book-awards.

Daniels, Jessie, and Polly Thiselthwaite. *Being a Scholar in the Digital Era: Transforming Scholarly Practice for the Public Good*. Chicago: Policy Press for the University of Bristol, 2016.

Darley, Gillian. "Wonderful Things: The Experience of the Grand Tour." *Perspecta* 41 (2008): 17–29.

Darnton, Robert. *The Case for Books: Past, Present, and Future*. New York: PublicAffairs, 2010.

———. "What Is the History of Books?" *Daedalus* 111, no. 3 (Summer 1982): 65–83.

Davidson, Cathy. "What Would Thomas Jefferson Say about the Internet?" *HASTAC* (blog). August 8, 2014. https://www.hastac.org/blogs/cathy-davidson/2014/08/08/what-would-thomas-jefferson-say-about-internet.

Dekker, George G. *The Fictions of Romantic Tourism: Radcliffe, Scott, and Mary Shelley*. Stanford, CA: Stanford University Press, 2005.

Delbourgo, James. *Collecting the World: Hans Sloane and the Origins of the British Museum*. Cambridge: Harvard University Press, 2017.

D'Emilio, John. "Rethinking Queer History: Or, Richard Nixon, Gay Liberationist?" In *Out in Chicago: LGBT History at the Crossroads*, edited by Jill Austin and Jennifer Brier, 95–107. Chicago: Chicago History Museum, 2011.

De Ritter, Richard. *Imagining Women Readers, 1789–1820*. Manchester: Manchester University Press, 2014.

Dill Pickle Club Records, 1906–1941. The Newberry Library, Chicago.

Draxler, Bridget. "Adaptation as Interpretation: Eighteenth-Century Methods in the Twenty-First-Century Classroom." *The Eighteenth-Century Novel* 8 (September 2011): 319–338.

———. "Teaching Jane Austen in Bits and Bytes: Digitizing Undergraduate Archival Research." *Persuasions On-Line* 34, no. 2 (2014). http://www.jasna.org/persuasions/on-line/vol34no2/draxler.html?

Early Modern OCR Project. http://emop.tamu.edu.

Eason, Sarah. "Henry Tilney: Queer Hero of *Northanger Abbey*." *Persuasions On-Line* 34, no. 1 (Winter 2013). http://www.jasna.org/persuasions/on-line/vol34no1/eason.html?

18th-Century Common. www.18thcenturycommon.org.

18thConnect. "Welcome to TypeWright." Last accessed February 18, 2018. http://www.18thconnect.org/typewright/documents.

———. "What Is 18thConnect?" Last accessed February 18, 2018. http://www.18thconnect.org/about/what-is-18thconnect/.

Eisenstein, Elizabeth L. *The Printing Press as an Agent of Change*. Cambridge: Cambridge University Press, 1980.

Electronic Enlightenment. http://www.e-enlightenment.com.

Eliot, George. *Middlemarch*. New York: Penguin Classics, 1994.

Elkin, Lauren. *Flaneuse: Women Walk the City in Paris, New York, Tokyo, Venice, and London*. New York: Farrar, Straus, and Giroux, 2017.

English Short Title Catalogue. http://estc.bl.uk.

Fabricant, Carole. "The Battle of the Ancients and (Post)Moderns: Rethinking Swift through Contemporary Perspectives." *The Eighteenth Century: Theory and Interpretation* 32, no. 3 (Autumn 1991): 256–273.

———. "Swift in His Own Time and Ours." In *The Profession of Eighteenth-Century Literature: Reflections on an Institution*, edited by Leo Damrosch, 113–134. Madison: University of Wisconsin Press, 1992.

Fame and Friendship: Pope, Roubiliac, and the Portrait Bust in Eighteenth-Century
Britain (exhibit). Yale Center for British Art. http://britishart.yale.edu/exhibitions
/fame-and-friendship-pope-roubiliac-and-portrait-bust-eighteenth-century-britain.

Faulkner, William. *The Portable Faulkner*. Edited by Malcolm Cowley. New York:
Viking Press, 1954.

Fielding, Henry. *Tom Jones*. Edited by John Bender and Simon Sterne. New York:
Oxford University Press, 2008.

Fielding, Sarah. *The Adventures of David Simple*. London: Andrew Millar, 1744.

———. *The Governess; Or, The Little Female Academy*. Edited by Candace Ward.
Guelph and Peterborough, ON: Broadview Press, 2005.

———. *The History of the Countess of Dellwyn*. London: Andrew Millar, 1759.

Fitzpatrick, Kathleen. "Open-Access Publishing." In *Hacking the Academy: New
Approaches to Scholarship and Teaching from Digital Humanities*, edited by
Daniel J. Cohen and Tom Scheinfeldt, 35–39. Ann Arbor: University of Michigan
Press, 2013.

Flower, Linda. "Intercultural Inquiry and the Transformation of Service." *College
English* 65, no. 2 (November 2002): 181–201.

Folsom, Marcia McClintock. Introduction to *Approaches to Teaching Austen's* Emma,
edited by Marcia McClintock Folsom, xvii–xliii. New York: MLA, 2004.

———. "The Privilege of My Own Profession: The Living Legacy of Austen."
Persuasions On-Line 29, no. 1 (Winter 2008). http://jasna.org/persuasions/on-line
/vol29no1/folsom.html.

Frank, Joseph. *The Beginnings of the English Newspaper, 1620–1660*. Cambridge:
Harvard University Press, 1961.

Freedom Scientific. "Blindness Solutions: JAWS." Last accessed February 18, 2018.
http://www.freedomscientific.com/Products/Blindness/JAWS.

Freud, Sigmund. *Civilization and Its Discontents*. In *The Freud Reader*, ed. Peter Gay.
New York: W. W. Norton, 1989.

Gadaken, Sara. "Managing and Marketing Virtue in Sarah Fielding's *History of the
Countess of Dellwyn*." *Eighteenth-Century Fiction* 15, no. 1 (October 2002): 19–34.

Gardner, Victoria. "Reading All About It: Eighteenth-Century News Culture."
History Workshop Journal 77, no. 1 (April 1, 2014): 291–298. https://doi.org
/10.1093/hwj/dbu004.

*General Contents of the British Museum: With Remarks. Serving as a Directory In
Viewing that Noble Cabinet*, 2nd ed. London: R. and J. Dodsley, 1762.

Genette, Gérard. *Palimpsests: Literature in the Second Degree*. Translated by Channa
Newman and Claude Doubinsky. Lincoln: University of Nebraska Press, 1997.

Github, s.v. "keyphrase_clustering." Accessed February 5, 2018. https://github.com
/dhfbk/keyphrase_clustering.

Goldgar, Anne. "The British Museum and the Virtual Representation of Culture in the Eighteenth Century." *Albion: A Quarterly Journal Concerned with British Studies* 32, no. 2 (Summer 2000): 195–231.

Great Chicago Fire. https://www.greatchicagofire.org.

Greenblatt, Stephen, and M. H. Abrams. *The Norton Anthology of English Literature.* 7th ed. New York: W. W. Norton & Company, 1999.

Greenfield, Susan Celia. "Child Poverty in *Mansfield Park*." "Jane Austen Weekly" (blog series). *Huffington Post*, October 26, 2012. http://www.huffingtonpost.com/susan-celia-greenfield/jane-austen-mansfield-Park_b_2024487.htm.

———. "Consent and Conception." *Need to Know on PBS*, August 23, 2012. http://www.pbs.org/wnet/need-to-know/opinion/consent-and-conception/14573/.

———. "*Northanger Abbey* and the Presidential Campaign." "Jane Austen Weekly" (blog series). *Huffington Post*, September 13, 2012. https://www.huffingtonpost.com/entry/the-jane-austen-weekly-no_b_1880489.html.

———. "Of Jane Austen, the Bennet Sisters, . . . and VAWA?" *Ms.blog. Ms. Magazine*, March 6, 2013. http://msmagazine.com/blog/2013/03/06/of-jane-austen-the-bennet-sisters-and-vawa/.

———. "Postmortem: Jane Austen and Repealing the Affordable Care Act." *Blarb* (blog). *LA Review of Books*, August 9, 2017. https://blog.lareviewofbooks.org/literature/postmortem-jane-austen-repealing-affordable-care-act/.

Greetham, D. C. *Textual Scholarship: An Introduction.* New York: Routledge, 1994.

Grobman, Laurie. "Is There a Place for Service Learning in Literary Studies?" *Profession* (2005): 129–140. http://www.jstor.org/stable/25595806.

Grobman, Laurie, and Roberta Rosenberg. *Service Learning and Literary Studies in English.* New York: MLA, 2015.

Habermas, Jürgen. *The Structural Transformation of the Public Sphere: An Inquiry into a Category of Bourgeois Society.* Translated by Thomas Burger. Cambridge, MA: MIT Press, 1991.

Hains, Bryan J., and Brittany Smith. "Student-Centered Course Design: Empowering Students to Become Self-Directed Learners." *Journal of Experiential Education* 35, no. 2 (2012): 357–374.

Hansard, Lindsay. "The Faulkner-Cowley Dynamic (webpage)." Last modified December 5, 2014. http://hansard.wix.com/faulkner-cowley.

———. "'Maybe Happen Is Never Once': How Malcolm Cowley's Approach to the Benjy Section of *The Sound and the Fury* Undermines Faulkner's Message about Time." Unpublished paper, last modified December 5, 2014.

Hansen, Matthew C. "'O Brave New World': Service-Learning and Shakespeare." *Pedagogy* 11, no. 1 (2011): 177–197.

Hay, Daisy. *Young Romantics: The Shelleys, Byron, and Other Tangled Lives.* New York: Farrar, Straus, and Giroux, 2011.

Hayden, Sara. "Winning essays take 2 South LA students to Dickens conference."

Los Angeles Times, August 16, 2014. http://www.latimes.com/local/la-me-dickens
-contest-20140817-story.html.

"High-Impact Educational Practices: A Brief Overview." *Association of American
Colleges & Universities*. https://www.aacu.org/leap/hips.

Hirsch, E. D., Joseph F. Kett, and James S. Trefil. *The New Dictionary of Cultural
Literacy: What Every American Needs to Know*. 3rd ed. Boston: Houghton Mifflin,
2002.

Hopkins, Robert. "General Tilney and Affairs of the State: The Political Gothic of
Northanger Abbey." *Philological Quarterly* 57, no. 2 (Spring 1978): 213–224.

Howard, Tyrone, and Nancy Parachini, eds. *Culturally Relevant Teaching*. Los
Angeles: UCLA Center X, 2013. https://cxarchive.gseis.ucla.edu/xchange
/culturally-relevant-teaching.

Hunt, Lynn. *Inventing Human Rights: A History*. New York: Norton, 2007.

Hunter-Baillie Papers, 1704–1923. Royal College of Surgeons of England, London.

Jacrois, Maureen. "Jane Austen in the 21st-Century Classroom." Undergraduate
Honors Thesis Project, Bridgewater State University, 2014.

Jane Austen in Community, 1st ed. http://janeausteninincommunity.wordpress.com/.

Jane Austen in Community, 2nd ed. https://pages.stolaf.edu/janeaustenin
community/.

Jane Austen Reading Room, Minneapolis Institute of Art. https://new.artsmia.org
/living-rooms/jane-austen-reading-room/.

Jarosz, Ellen E., and Stephen Kutay. "Guided Resource Inquiries: Integrating
Archives into Course Learning and Information Literacy Objectives."
Communications in Information Literacy 11, no. 1 (2017): 204–220.

Jay, Gregory. "The Engaged Humanities: Principles and Practices for Public
Scholarship and Teaching." *Journal of Community Engagement and Scholarship*
3, no.1 (2010): 51–63.

———. "Service Learning, Multiculturalism, and the Pedagogies of Difference."
Pedagogy 8, no. 2 (Spring 2008): 255–281.

Jockers, Matthew L. *Macroanalysis: Digital Methods and Literary History*. Urbana:
University of Illinois Press, 2013.

Johns, Adrian. *The Nature of the Book: Print and Knowledge in the Making*. Chicago:
University of Chicago Press, 1998.

Johnson, Claudia. *Jane Austen's Cults and Cultures*. Chicago: University of Chicago
Press, 2012.

Johnson, Samuel. *A Dictionary of the English Language*. London: W. Strahan, 1755.

Jokic, Olivera. "Teaching to the Resistance: What to Do When Students Dislike
Austen." *Persuasions On-Line* 34, no. 2 (Spring 2014). http://www.jasna.org
/persuasions/on-line/vol34no2/jokic.html.

Jones, Jeffrey P. "The 'New' News as No 'News': US Cable News Channels as
Branded Political Entertainment Television." *Media International Australia* 144,

no. 1 (August 1, 2012): 146-155. http://mediaandsocialidentity.com/wp-content/uploads/2013/12/No-news-as-news-Jones.pdf.

J. W. L. G. *A Letter to Sir Humphrey Davy, Bart. &c. &c. &c. On His Being Elected the President of the Royal Society: With Some Observations on the Management of the British Museum, By A Fellow of the Royal Society.* London: James Ridgway, Piccadilly, 1821. General Collection, Newberry Library, Chicago.

Kastan, David Scott. *Shakespeare after Theory.* New York: Routledge, 1999.

Kaufmann, Walter. *Nietzsche: Philosopher, Psychologist, Antichrist.* Princeton, NJ: Princeton University Press, 1950.

Keats, John. John Keats to John Hamilton Reynolds, 3 May 1818. In *Letters of John Keats: A Selection*, edited by Robert Gittings, 90-97. Oxford: Oxford University Press, 1970.

King's Library, the British Museum. http://www.britishmuseum.org/about_us/the_museums_story/kings_library.aspx.

Kirschenbaum, Matthew. "What Is Digital Humanities and What's It Doing in English Departments?" *ADE Bulletin* 150 (2010): 55-61. https://www.ade.mla.org/content/download/7914/225677.

Kitchener, Henry Thomas. *Letters on Marriage, on the Causes of Matrimonial Infidelity, and on the Reciprocal Relations of the Sexes.* London, 1812.

Kramp, Michael. "The Woman, the Gypsies, and England: Harriet Smith's National Role." *College Literature* 31, no. 1 (Winter 2004): 146-168.

Kristeva, Julia. *Desire in Language: A Semiotic Approach to Literature and Art.* Edited by Leon S. Roudiez, translated by Thomas Gora and Alice A. Jardine. New York: Columbia University Press, 1982.

LaBute, Neil, dir. *Possession.* 2002; Universal City, CA: Universal Pictures Home Entertainment, 2003. DVD.

Lagemann, Ellen Condliffe, and Harry Lewis. "Renewing the Civic Mission of American Higher Education." In *What Is College For? The Public Purpose of Higher Education*, edited by Ellen Condliffe Lagemann and Harry Lewis, 9-45. New York: Teachers College Press, 2011.

Lamont, Claire. "Annotating a Text: Literary Theory and Electronic Hypertext." In *Electronic Text: Investigations in Method and Theory*, edited by Katheryn Sutherland, 47-66. New York: Oxford University Press, 1998.

Lanning, Katie. " 'Fitted to the Humour of the Age': Alteration and Print in Swift's *A Tale of a Tub.*" *Eighteenth-Century Fiction* 26, no. 4 (Summer 2014): 515-536.

Leffel, John C. " 'Where Woman, Lovely Woman, for Wealth and Grandeur Comes from Far': Representations of the Colonial Marriage Market in Gillray, Topham, Starke, and Austen." In *Transnational England: Home and Abroad, 1780–1860*, edited by Monika Class and Terry F. Robinson, 208-232. Newcastle upon Tyne: Cambridge Scholars Publishing, 2009.

Leonardi, Susan J. "Recipes for Reading: Summer Pasta, Lobster a la Riseholme, and Key Lime Pie." *PMLA* 104 (May 1989): 340-347.

Limerick, Patricia. "Dancing with Professors: The Trouble with Academic Prose." *New York Times Book Review*, October 31, 1993.

Liu, Alan. "The Meaning of the Digital Humanities." *PMLA* 128, no. 2 (March 2013): 409-423.

Liu, Yin. "Ways of Reading, Models for Text, and the Usefulness of Dead People." *Scholarly and Research Communication* 5, no. 2 (2014). Accessed February 5, 2018. http://src-online.ca/index.php/src/article/view/148/293.

Locating London's Past. https://www.locatinglondon.org/index.html.

Locke, John. *An Essay Concerning Human Understanding*. London: Printed by Elizabeth Holt, for Thomas Basset, at the George in Fleet Street, near St. Dunstan's Church, 1690. http://www.gutenberg.org/files/10615/10615-h/10615-h.htm.

———. *The Second Treatise on Civil Government*. Amherst, NY: Prometheus Books, 1986.

Looser, Devoney. "Fifty Shades of Mr. Darcy: A Brief History of X-Rated Jane Austen Adaptations." *Salon*, July 16, 2017. https://www.salon.com/2017/07/16 /fifty-shades-of-mr-darcy-a-brief-history-of-x-rated-jane-austen-adaptations/.

———. "Jane Austen Wasn't Shy." *New York Times*, July 15, 2017. https://www .nytimes.com/2017/07/15/opinion/sunday/jane-austen-wasnt-shy.html.

———. *The Making of Jane Austen*. Baltimore: The Johns Hopkins University Press, 2017.

———. "Queering the Work of Jane Austen is Nothing New." *Atlantic*, July 21, 2017. https://www.theatlantic.com/entertainment/archive/2017/07/queering-the-work-of -jane-austen-is-nothing-new/533418/.

———. "'A Very Kind Undertaking': *Emma* and Eighteenth-Century Feminism." *Approaches to Teaching Austen's* Emma, edited by Marcia McClintock Folsom, 100-109. New York: MLA, 2004.

———. "Whatever Her Persuasion." *Times Literary Supplement*, January 18, 2017. https://www.the-tls.co.uk/articles/public/jane-austen-in-2017/.

Love, Harold. "L'Estrange, Sir Roger (1616-1704)." In *Oxford Dictionary of National Biography*. Oxford University Press, 2004; online ed., October 2007, accessed September 12, 2015. http://www.oxforddnb.com/view/article/16514.

Lovelace, Matthew, and Peggy Brickman. "Best Practices for Measuring Students' Attitudes toward Learning Science." *CBE Life Sciences Education* 12, no. 4 (2013): 606-617. https://www.ncbi.nlm.nih.gov/pmc/articles/PMC3846512/.

Loveland, Jeff, and Joseph Reagle. "Wikipedia and Encyclopedic Production." *New Media and Society* 15, no. 8 (2013): 1294-1311.

Lukács, György. *The Theory of the Novel*. Translated by Anna Bostock. Cambridge: MIT Press, 1971.

Lynch, Deidre. *Loving Literature: A Cultural History.* Chicago: University of Chicago Press, 2016.

Lyons, Martyn. *Books: A Living History.* London: Thames and Hudson, 2013.

Macadam, Alta, and Annabel Barber. *Blue Guide: Rome.* 11th ed. Taunton, Somerset, UK: Blue Guides Limited, 2016.

Macartney, George. *An Account of Ireland in 1773 by a Late Chief Secretary of that Kingdom.* London, 1773.

Machiavelli, Niccolò. *The Prince.* Trans. and ed. by Peter Bondanella. Oxford: Oxford World's Classics, 2005.

Mangum, Teresa. "Going Public: From the Perspective of the Classroom." *Pedagogy: Critical Approaches to Teaching Literature, Language, Composition, and Culture* 12, no. 1 (Winter 2012): 5–18.

Mannies, Whitney. "Yes, in the U.S., the People Can Reject a President — If They Are Sure He's a Tyrant." *Washington Post*, November 22, 2016. https://www .washingtonpost.com/news/monkey-cage/wp/2016/11/22/yes-in-the-u-s-the -people-can-reject-a-president-if-theyre-convinced-hes-a-tyrant/?utm_term =.371128de0ad2.

Mapping the Republic of Letters. http://republicofletters.stanford.edu.

Marshall, Ashley. *Swift and History: Politics and the English Past.* Cambridge: Cambridge University Press, 2015.

Mariani, Mike. "The Tragic, Forgotten History of Zombies." *The Atlantic*, October 28, 2015. https://www.theatlantic.com/entertainment/archive/2015/10/how -america-erased-the-tragic-history-of-the-zombie/412264/.

Mathieu, Paula. *Tactics of Hope: The Public Turn in English Composition.* Portsmouth, NH: Boynton/Cook Publishers, 2005.

Mazella, David, and Julie Grob. "Collaborations between Faculty and Special Collections Librarians in Inquiry-Driven Classes." *Libraries and the Academy* 11, no. 1 (January 2011): 467–487.

McKeon, Michael. *The Secret History of Domesticity.* Baltimore: Johns Hopkins University Press, 2005.

Medieval Electronic Scholarly Alliance. www.mesa-medieval.org.

Menand, Louis. *The Marketplace of Ideas: Reform and Resistance in the American University.* New York and London: W. W. Norton & Company, 2010.

Mesgari, Mostafa, Chitu Okoli, Mohamad Mehdi, Finn Årup Nielsen, and Arto Lanamäki. "'The Sum of All Human Knowledge': A Systematic Review of Scholarly Research on the Content of Wikipedia." *Journal of the Association for Information Science and Technology* 66, no. 2 (2015): 219–245.

Miller, Ai. "Sometimes You Have to Shoot the Storyteller in the Neck: Reexamining the Role of the Dill Pickle Club in the Queer Community of the Near North Side, 1920–1935." Unpublished paper, last modified December 5, 2014.

Miller, Edward. *That Noble Cabinet: A History of the British Museum*. Athens, OH: Ohio University Press, 1974.

Modernist Networks. www.modnets.org.

Montague, Laetitia. *The Housewife. Being a Most Useful Assistant in All Domestic Concerns, Whether in a Town or Country Situation*. London: Printed for J. Dixwell, 1785.

More, Hannah. *Betty Brown, the St. Giles's Orange Girl*. London: J. Marshall, and R. White; Bath: S. Hazard, 1795.

Moretti, Franco. *Distant Reading*. New York: Verso, 2013.

Museum Britannicum, or, A Display in Thirty Two Plates, of Antiquities and Natural Curiosities, in That Noble and Magnificent Cabinet, the British Museum, After the Original Designs, from Nature. 2nd ed. Revised by P. Boyle. London: J. Moore, 1791.

Musil, Caryn McTighe. "Educating for Citizenship." *Peer Review* 5, no. 3 (April 2003): 4–8. https://www.aacu.org/publications-research/periodicals/educating -citizenship.

Networked Infrastructure for Nineteenth-Century Electronic Scholarship (NINES). www.nines.org.

Nieves, Angela David. "Digital Humanities + Social Justice = 'Does Not Compute?' " Victoria2011.thatcamp.org (blog), June 9, 2011. http://victoria2011.thatcamp.org /06/09/digital-humanities-social-justice-does-not-compute/.

Nimer, Cory L., and J. Gordon Daines III. "Teaching Undergraduates to Think Archivally." *Journal of Archival Organization* 10, no. 1 (May 2012): 4–44.

OpEd Project. https://www.theopedproject.org/.

Osborne, Roger, and Cherie Allan. "Networked Reading: Using Austlit to Assist Reading and Understanding of Texts from the Past." *English in Australia* 47, no. 2 (2012): 18–26. https://eprints.qut.edu.au/54220/1/Networked_Reading_Englishin Australia%5B1%5D.pdf.

Ostrander, Susan A., and Kent E. Portney, eds. *Acting Civically: From Urban Neighborhoods to Higher Education*. Medford, MA: Tufts University Press, 2007.

Oxford Dictionaries, s.v. "First-World problem." Oxford University Press, 2014. Accessed January 16, 2018. http://www.oxforddictionaries.com/us/definition /american_english/First-World-problem.

Pannapacker, William. "Cultivating Partnerships in the Digital Humanities." *Chronicle of Higher Education*, May 13, 2013. https://www.chronicle.com/article /Cultivating-Partnerships-in/139161.

———. "No More Digitally Challenged Liberal Arts Majors." *Chronicle of Higher Education*, November 18, 2013. https://www.chronicle.com/article/No-More -Digitally-Challenged/143079?cid=wc&utm_medium=en&utm_source=wc.

———. "Stop Calling it Digital Humanities." *Chronicle of Higher Education*,

February 18, 2013. https://www.chronicle.com/article/Stop-Calling-It-Digital /137325.

Pascoe, Judith. *The Hummingbird Cabinet: A Rare and Curious History of Romantic Collectors*. Ithaca, NY: Cornell University Press, 2006.

Perry, Ruth. "Jane Austen, Slavery, and British Imperialism." In *Approaches to Teaching Austen's* Emma, edited by Marcia McClintock Folsom, 26–33. New York: MLA, 2004.

Phillips, Amanda. "#transformDH — A Call to Action Following ASA 2011." *HASTAC* (blog). October 26, 2011. https://www.hastac.org/blogs/amanda-phillips/2011/10 /26/transformdh-call-action-following-asa-2011.

Postman, Neil. *Building a Bridge to the 18th Century: How the Past Can Improve Our Future*. New York: Vintage Books, 1999.

Project Gutenberg. www.gutenberg.org.

Prom, Christopher J. "Reimagining Academic Archives." In *Hacking the Academy: New Approaches to Scholarship and Teaching from Digital Humanities*, edited by Daniel J. Cohen and Tom Scheinfeldt, 146–149. Ann Arbor: University of Michigan Press, 2013.

Rajchel, Jen, and Theresa R. Snyder. "The Thing Was Done in the Library: Animating an Early Eighteenth-Century Murder Mystery." *College & Undergraduate Libraries* 23, no. 2 (July 2016): 193–203.

Rankine, Claudia. *Citizen: An American Lyric*. Minneapolis: Graywolf Press, 2015.

Raymond, Joad. *The Invention of the Newspaper: English Newsbooks 1641–1660*. Oxford: Oxford University Press, 1996.

"Realizing the Newberry Idea" (exhibit). The Newberry Library. http://publications .newberry.org/digitalexhibitions/exhibits/show/realizingthenewberryidea /welcome.

Robertson, Randy. "Swift's 'Leviathan' and the End of Licensing." *Pacific Coast Philology* 40, no. 2 (2005): 38–55.

Rockenbach, Barbara. "Archives, Undergraduates, and Inquiry-Based Learning: Case Studies from Yale University Library." *The American Archivist* 74, no. 1 (Spring/ Summer 2011): 297–311.

Rousseau, Jean-Jacques. *Emile*. Translated by Barbara Foxley. Project Gutenberg, 2011. http://www.gutenberg.org/cache/epub/5427/pg5427-images.html.

Rowell, Lonnie, and Eunsook Hong. "Academic Motivation: Concepts, Strategies, and Counseling Approaches." *Professional School Counseling* 16, no. 3 (2013): 158–171.

Rumbold, Kate. "Shakespeare's 'Propriety' and the Mid-Eighteenth-Century Novel: Sarah Fielding's *The History of the Countess of Dellwyn*." In *Reading 1759: Literary Culture in Mid-Eighteenth-Century Britain and France*, edited by Shaun Regan, 187–205. Lewisburg: Bucknell University Press, 2013.

Said, Edward. *Culture and Imperialism*. New York: Vintage, 1993.

Sallaberry, Raquel. "Where Exactly Did Louisa Musgrove Fall?" *Jane Austen Today* (blog), May 11, 2010. http://janitesonthejames.blogspot.com/2010/05/where -exactly-did-louisa-musgrove-fall.html.

Schellenberg, Betty A. "Bluestockings and the Genealogy of the Modern Novel." *University of Toronto Quarterly* 79, no. 4 (Fall 2013): 1023–1034.

Schwartz, Mary. "Public Stakes, Public Stories: Service Learning in Literary Studies." *PMLA* 127, no. 4 (2012): 987–993.

Scott, Walter. *Waverley*. Edinburgh, 1814.

Sedden, Mandy L., and Kevin R. Clark. "Motivating Students in the 21st Century." *Radiologic Technology* 87, no. 6 (2016): 609–616.

Sentimental Journey. http://enec3120.neatline-uva.org/neatline/show/a-sentimental -journey.

Shearer, Elisa, and Jeffrey Gottfried. "News Use Across Social Media Platforms 2017." Pew Research Center (website), September 7, 2017. http://www.journalism .org/2017/09/07/news-use-across-social-media-platforms-2017/.

Shelley, Mary Wollstonecraft. *Frankenstein*. Edited by D. L. McDonald and Kathleen Scherf. Guelph and Peterborough, ON: Broadview Press, 2012.

Shelley-Godwin Archive. http://shelleygodwinarchive.org.

Small, Helen. *The Value of the Humanities*. Oxford: Oxford University Press, 2013.

Smith, Gregory A. "Place-Based Education: Learning to Be Where We Are." *The Phi Delta Kappan* 83, no. 8 (April 2002): 584–594.

Sobieraj, Sarah, and Deborah White. "Could Civic Engagement Reproduce Political Inequality?" In *Acting Civically: From Urban Neighborhoods to Higher Education*, edited by Susan A. Ostrander and Kent E. Portney, 92–112. Medford, MA: Tufts University Press, 2007.

Soja, Edward. *Seeking Spatial Justice*. Minneapolis: University of Minnesota Press, 2010.

Sprague, Gregory A. "Chicago Gay and Lesbian History Project," unpublished paper. Gregory Sprague Papers, 1972–1987, Chicago History Museum, Chicago.

Spratt, Danielle. "Taking *Emma* to the Street: Toward a Civic Engagement Model of Austen Pedagogy." *Persuasions On-Line* 34, no. 2 (Spring 2014). http://www.jasna .org/persuasions/on-line/vol34no2/spratt.html.

Stallybrass, Peter. "'Little Jobs': Broadsides and the Printing Revolution." In *Agent of Change: Print Culture Studies after Elizabeth L. Eisenstein*. Edited by Sabrina Alcorn Baron, Eric N. Lindquist, and Eleanor F. Shevlin, 315–341. Amherst: University of Massachusetts Press, 2007.

Stott, Andrew McConnell. "Why Clowns Keep Scaring Us." CNN (website), November 17, 2014. http://www.cnn.com/2014/10/31/opinion/stott-clowns-france /index.html.

Studies in Radicalism Online. www.studiesinradicalism.org.

Swift, Jonathan. "Battel of the Books." In *The Essential Works of Jonathan Swift*, edited by Claude Rawson and Ian Higgins, 94-111. New York: Norton, 2010.

———. *Gulliver's Travels*. Edited by Allan Ingram. Guelph and Peterborough, ON: Broadview Press, 2012.

———. "A Tale of a Tub." In *The Essential Works of Jonathan Swift*, edited by Claude Rawson and Ian Higgins, 1-92. New York: Norton, 2010.

Thompson, E. P. "Eighteenth-Century English Society: Class Struggle without Class?" *Social History* 3, no. 2 (1978): 133-165.

Through Time. http://acadblogs.wheatoncollege.edu/wmst-101-f13.

Tobin, Beth Fowkes. "The Moral and Political Economy of Property in Austen's *Emma*." *Eighteenth-Century Fiction* 2, no. 3 (1990): 229-254.

Tripp, C. A. *The Intimate World of Abraham Lincoln*. New York: Free Press, 2005.

Troost, Linda, and Sayre Greenfield. "Filming Highbury: Reducing the Community in *Emma* to the Screen." *Persuasions On-Line Occasional Papers* 3 (1999). http://www.jasna.org/persuasions/on-line/opno3/troost_sayre.html.

Under the Banner of Waverley. http://waverly.lib.uiowa.edu/.

Unsworth, John. "The Crisis of Audience and the Open-Access Solution." In *Hacking the Academy: New Approaches to Scholarship and Teaching from Digital Humanities*, edited by Daniel J. Cohen and Tom Scheinfeldt, 30-34. Ann Arbor: University of Michigan Press, 2013.

van Cranenberg, Andreas. "Rich Statistical Parsing and Literary Language." PhD diss., University of Amsterdam, 2016. https://pure.uva.nl/ws/files/2717528/177511_Cranenburgh_phdthesis_complete.pdf.

Van Rymsdyk, John, and Andrew Van Rymsdyk. *Museum Britannicum; or, a Display in Thirty Two Plates, of Antiquities and Natural Curiosities, That Noble and Magnificent Cabinet, the British Museum, After the Original Designs from Nature*, 2nd ed. Revised by P. Boyle. London: J. Moore, 1791.

Varey, Simon. *Space and the Eighteenth-Century English Novel*. New York: Cambridge University Press, 1990.

Vedantam, Shankar. "A Lively Mind: Your Brain on Jane Austen." NPR, October 9, 2012. http://www.npr.org/sections/health-shots/2012/10/09/162401053/a-lively-mind-your-brain-on-jane-austen.

Vong, Silvia. "A Constructivist Approach for Introducing Undergraduate Students to Special Collections and Archival Research." *RBM: A Journal of Rare Books, Manuscripts, and Cultural Heritage* 17, no. 2 (Fall 2016): 148-171.

Wagner, Claudia, David Garcia, Mohsen Jadidi, and Markus Strohmaier. "It's a Man's Wikipedia? Assessing Gender Inequality in an Online Encyclopedia." Preprint, submitted March 23, 2015. *International AAAI Conference on Web and Social Media*. https://arxiv.org/pdf/1501.06307.pdf.

Walker, Alice. "Principles of Annotation: Some Suggestions for Editors of Shakespeare." *Studies in Bibliography* 9 (1957): 95-105.

Wall, Cynthia. *The Literary and Cultural Spaces of Restoration London*. New York: Cambridge University Press, 1998.

Weldon, Amy. *The Hands-On Life: How to Wake Yourself Up and Save the World*. Eugene, OR: Cascade Books, 2018.

———. *The Writer's Eye: Observation and Inspiration for Creative Writers*. London: Bloomsbury, 2018.

What Jane Saw. http://www.whatjanesaw.org/.

White, Laura Mooneyham. "The Experience of Class, *Emma*, and the American College Student." *Approaches to Teaching Austen's* Emma, edited by Marcia McClintock Folsom, 34-46. New York: MLA, 2004.

Williams, Raymond. *Keywords: A Vocabulary of Culture and Society*. New York: Oxford University Press, 1985.

Willison, Ian R. "The National Library in Historical Perspective." *Libraries & Culture* 24, no. 1 (Winter 1989): 75-95.

Wollstonecraft, Mary. "Maria; or, The Wrongs of Woman." In *The Wrongs of Woman; or, Maria by Mary Wollstonecraft and Memoirs of the Author of* A Vindication of the Rights of Woman *by William Godwin*. Edited by Cynthia Richards, 37-197. Glen Allen, VA: College Publishing, 2004.

———. *The Vindications: The Rights of Men, The Rights of Woman*. Edited by D. L. Macdonald and Kathleen Scherf. Guelph and Peterborough, ON: Broadview Press, 1997.

Woman's Wit, A: Jane Austen's Life and Legacy (exhibit). The Morgan Library and Museum. http://www.themorgan.org/collection/a-womans-wit-jane-austen.

Woodward, Kathleen. "The Future of the Humanities—in the Present and in Public." *Daedalus* 138, no. 1 (Winter 2009): 110-123.

Wosh, Peter J., Janet Bunde, Karen Murphy, and Chelsea Blacker. "University Archives and Educational Partnerships: Three Perspectives." *Archival Issues* 31, no. 1 (2007): 83-103.

Wright, Christopher. "Don't Call It the British Museum Library." *American Libraries* 7, no. 1 (January 1976): 48-50.

Yeo, Richard. "Encyclopaedic Collectors: Ephraim Chambers and Sir Hans Sloane." In *Enlightening the British: Knowledge, Discovery and the Museum in the Eighteenth Century*, edited by R. G. W. Anderson, M. L. Caygill, A. G. Macgregor, and L. Syson, 29-36. London: British Museum Press, 2003.

Yu, Jean Y. "Race Matters in Civic Engagement Work." In *Acting Civically: From Urban Neighborhoods to Higher Education*, edited by Susan A. Ostrander and Kent E. Portney, 158-182. Medford, MA: Tufts University Press, 2007.

Zimmerman, Jess. "The Myth of the Well-Behaved Women's March." *The New*

Republic, January 24, 2017. https://newrepublic.com/article/140065/myth-well
-behaved-womens-march.

Zold, Elizabeth. "Virtual Travel in *Second Life*: Understanding Eighteenth-Century
Travelogues through Experiential Learning." *Pedagogy: Critical Approaches to
Teaching, Literature, Language, Composition, and Culture* 14, no. 2 (Spring 2014):
225–250.

INDEX

❧❧

18thConnect, 5, 12-13, 16, 32, 48-49, 168, 184, 222; about, 188, 189; and *Countess of Dellwyn* project, 206, 207; Early Modern OCR Project by, 190, 191; and *Gulliver's Travels*, 181-82, 183; and networked reading, 174-79; partnerships by, 189-90

826LA, 15, 22, 29, 32, 49; service-learning project at, 35-37

Academic Council of Learned Societies (ACLS), 254n16

Academy of American Poets, 185

active reflection activities, 38, 237n28

activist research, 155, 157-58

Advanced Research Consortium, 253n45

Affordable Care Act (ACA), 59, 212

Akin, Todd, 56

Almendarez, Gabriela, 211-12, 218-21

Alter, Peter, 149-50

American Library Association (ALA), 63

archives and archival work: digital, 71-72, 147-48, 168, 247n25; and libraries, 149, 247n29; at Newberry, 142-43, 144-47, 148-49, 155; and public scholarship, 155; significance of, 140-42; and Waverley project, 131-33

Associated Colleges of the Midwest (ACM), 143-44, 145, 146

Astell, Mary, 745

Au, Wayne, 219-20

audio recordings, 184, 186, 188

Austen, Jane: and British Empire, 4, 87, 91-92; at Chawton House, 73; on class and race, 42-44, 69, 87-88; and gender issues, 22-23, 38-39, 43, 69-70; literary devices used by, 40-41, 71, 87; myth of politeness about, 68, 70; OpEd Project on, 55-60; and popular culture, 67; and present-day issues, 39; public outreach efforts around, 21-22, 52-54; reading groups on, 15-16, 69, 76, 77, 80, 85, 86-87, 92-93, 219; as revolutionary, 54, 69-70, 216; as satirist, 59, 69, 76, 89; service-learning study of, 23-24, 31-32, 38; on slavery, 42-43, 44, 69, 71, 82, 87; social commentary by, 38-39, 44-45, 50, 69, 82, 84, 86-87, 89, 91-92, 216; stereotypes about, 18, 19; in Western cultural imagination, 31; works: *Emma*, 15, 22-24, 27, 38-40, 41, 42-45, 47-48, 59-60, 87-88, 236n6; letters, 72; *Mansfield Park*, 4, 38, 69, 86-87, 130; *Northanger Abbey*, 18, 57, 76, 89, 90-93, 216; *Persuasion*, 18, 38; *Pride and Prejudice*, 2-3, 18, 69, 76, 77, 80, 81, 82, 85; *Sanditon*, 31, 50; *Sense and Sensibility*, 18, 38, 69

Austen-Leigh, James Edward, 70, 73

Australian Newspaper Project, 189

authentic materials, 143

author house museums, 100-101

Bahde, Anne, 141

Baillie, Joanna, 72; "Sunset Meditation," 75-76

community partnerships, 61, 63–64, 78–81, 123, 188–89, 224; and civic engagement projects, 26, 86, 107–8, 127; with libraries, 78, 86, 87–89; and reciprocity, 27, 101, 123, 127. *See also* civic and community engagement

contact zones, 29, 30

copyright, 1, 12; in archives, 169; and deregulation, 13; and expiration, 193; and paywalls, 192, 235n27; restrictions, 141

Countess of Dellwyn project. See *The History of the Countess of Dellwyn*

Cowley, Malcolm, 156–57

Cowtan, Robert, 101

crowd-sourcing, 188–91, 204

Cushman, Ellen, 27

Daniels, Jessie, 194

Dante Alighieri: *Inferno*, 137

Darnton, Robert, 148, 153–54, 168

Darwin, Charles, 157

Davidson, Cathy, 234–35n26

Defoe, Daniel: *A Journal of the Plague Year*, 219; *Robinson Crusoe*, 13

Dekker, George, 139–40

D'Emilio, John, 159, 161

democratization of knowledge, 12, 111, 153–54, 164, 244n31

Dickens, Charles, 135–36

digital editions, 192–210; annotating, 204–7; of *Countess of Dellwyn*, 16, 155, 194, 195–97, 198, 200–201, 204, 206, 207–9; crowd-sourced, 193–94, 204; genius.com, 204; and Guided Resource Inquiry (GRI) tool, 199–200; guidelines for editing, 204–6; and printed source texts, 209–10; value of, 193, 195

digital humanities: activist potential of, 194; collaborative nature of, 107, 170–

72, 173, 176, 202, 203, 204; and digital archives, 16, 71–72, 147–48, 168; and digital reading, 192–93, 200, 250n11; and digital timelines, 72, 76; and digitization of culture, 149; and digitized texts, 194, 205, 222; as engaged pedagogical practice, 170–73; and networked reading, 168–69, 173–79, 192–93, 197, 200–201, 209; and open-access projects, 12–13; and preservation/access of materials, 169–70, 172, 176, 195; and public humanities, 5, 10–11, 154–55; as service, 168, 172; techniques of, 173–74, 178–79, 194; and Wikipedia entries, 201–3, 209, 255n23

Digital Public Library of America, 12, 148

Dill Pickle Club, 158–59, 161

distant reading, 168, 173, 175, 178, 251–52n24

Dominguez, Alyssa, 182–83

Dow, Gillian, 72, 73–75

Early English Books Online (EEBO), 189–90, 222

Early Modern OCR Project, 190, 191

Eason, Sarah, 91

Edgeworth, Maria, 72, 75–76; *Castle Rackrent*, 179, 219

Eggers, Dave, 15

Eighteenth-Century Collections Online (ECCO), 176, 189–90, 208, 222

eighteenth-century studies, 7, 47, 51, 222; and audio recordings, 184–87; Austen's depictions as valuable for, 50–51; and experiential learning practices, 170; and media technologies, 11–12, 165–67; and public humanities, 13–14; relevance of, 11–15, 169–70

Eisenstein, Elizabeth, 169–70

Eliot, George: *Middlemarch*, 135

Percy, Walker, 134
Perry, Ruth, 77
Persuasion (Austen), 18, 38, 58
Peterson, Gracie, 117
Phillips, Amanda, 171
Phillips, Natalie, 130
Poetry Foundation, 185
political freedom, 11, 26, 54, 59, 98, 212, 214, 215
Pope, Alexander, 13
Portable Faulkner (Cowley), 156-57
Portney, Kent E., 31, 237n23
Possession, 141
presentism, 68-69, 214
Pride and Prejudice (Austen), 18, 69, 76, 81, 82; characters in, 2-3, 19, 39, 50, 58, 59-60, 84, 90, 122; reading groups on, 76-77, 80, 82, 84-85, 87, 193
Pride and Prejudice and Zombies (Grahame-Smith), 1-3, 4-5
Project Gutenberg, 185, 192, 193
Project on Civic Reflection, 70
Prom, Christopher J., 247n25
ProQuest, 189, 190
public: no single, 150-51; vs. private, 9-10; writing for general, 213-16
public good: concept of, 10; and digital humanities, 157, 188, 189, 190, 195; and higher education, 127; humanities as, 128-29, 149; and literature, 10; museums serving, 96, 97-98, 99, 110, 120; and private interests, 153-54
public humanities: and breaking down barriers, 9, 223; and civic participation, 5-6, 15, 223-24; and collaborative efforts, 5-6, 15, 127, 188-89; defining characteristics of, 6, 9, 10, 254n16; and digital humanities, 5, 10-11, 154-55; and graduate educa-
tion, 124-26; and historical literature, 9, 10, 11, 13-15, 16-17; and literary history, 13, 14-15, 61, 64; as moral imperative, 153, 248n33; museums as face of, 99; pedagogy of, 61-62, 63-64, 201; and public intellectuals, 7-8; value and purpose of, 13-14, 54, 97, 101-2, 109-10, 128-29, 149, 153. *See also* archives and archival work; civic and community engagement; community partnerships; digital editions; digital humanities; libraries; museums; service learning
public intellectual, 7-11, 213
public scholars and scholarship, 203; and activist research, 157-58; and archives, 155; and digital humanities, 153; distinctive quality of, 247n26; and elitism, 214-15; genealogy of, 128; and historical literature, 68, 153; and liberal arts education, 151-52; and libraries, 65-67, 148, 150, 155, 157; and museums, 99-100, 120, 127, 128; and writing for general public, 213-16
public spaces, 9; archives as, 147; libraries as, 15, 217, 223-24; museums as, 11, 16, 99
Punch, 157

queer history, 158, 159-62

Rankine, Claudia: *Citizen*, 220
reading, 6, 13; and bodily experience, 130-31; and book groups, 15-16, 69, 76, 77, 80, 85, 86-87, 92-93, 219; by children, 62-63; close, 70-71, 168, 173, 175, 179, 251n24; and community, 8; digital, 192-93, 200-201; distant, 168, 173, 175, 178, 251-52n24; intertextual and hypertextual, 195; and

of, 196–97; Mary Shelley treatment of, 182–83; and rape, 56; Richardson on, 27; Swift on, 186; Wollstonecraft on, 134

Woodward, Kathleen, 153, 247n26

Wordsworth, William, 140

Wright, Christopher, 99

Wright Art Museum, 118–19

Writing as Civic Engagement symposium, 113, 224

XML (Extensible Markup Language), 169, 178, 206–7, 208

Yale Center for British Art, 120

Yearsley, Ann, 13

Yu, Jean Y., 24–25

Zimmerman, Jess, 216

zombies, 3–5

The Penelope Project: An Arts-Based Odyssey to Change Elder Care
edited by Anne Basting, Maureen Towey, and Ellen Rose

*Contested City: Art and Public History as Mediation at
New York's Seward Park Urban Renewal Area*
by Gabrielle Bendiner-Viani

Engaging the Age of Jane Austen: Public Humanities in Practice
by Bridget Draxler and Danielle Spratt

*See You in the Streets: Art, Action, and Remembering the
Triangle Shirtwaist Factory Fire*
by Ruth Sergel